Forensic Mental Health Evaluations in the Digital Age

Ashley B. Batastini • Michael J. Vitacco
Editors

Forensic Mental Health Evaluations in the Digital Age

A Practitioner's Guide to Using Internet-Based Data

Springer

Editors
Ashley B. Batastini
University of Southern Mississippi
Hattiesburg, MS, USA

Michael J. Vitacco
Augusta University
Augusta, GA, USA

ISBN 978-3-030-33907-4 ISBN 978-3-030-33908-1 (eBook)
https://doi.org/10.1007/978-3-030-33908-1

This Springer imprint is published by the registered company Springer Nature Switzerland AG
The registered company address is: Gewerbestrasse 11, 6330 Cham, Switzerland

Contents

About the Editors

Ashley B. Batastini, Ph.D. is an Assistant Professor at the University of Southern Mississippi, where she directs the Correctional and Forensic Psychology Research Laboratory. She also maintains a private practice conducting pretrial evaluations as a Licensed Psychologist in the state of Mississippi. She earned her doctorate in Counseling Psychology at Texas Tech University after completing a predoctoral internship at Western State Hospital in Tacoma, Washington. She has authored or coauthored several peer-reviewed publications and book chapters related to the psychological effects of administrative segregation, community reentry barriers, violence risk communication, and applications of telepsychology in corrections. Additionally, she is the Lead Developer of an evidence-based program for inmates with mental health concerns who are detained in or prone to restrictive housing environments (*Stepping Up, Stepping Out*).

Michael J. Vitacco, Ph.D., ABPP is an Associate Professor of Psychiatry and Health Behavior in the Institute of Public and Preventive Health at Augusta University in Augusta, Georgia, where he serves as the Director of the Postdoctoral Fellowship Program in Forensic Psychology. He also maintains a private practice conducting pretrial, preemployment, and risk evaluations as a licensed psychologist in the states of Georgia and Wisconsin. He completed his Ph.D. in Clinical Psychology at the University of North Texas, his internship at the University of North Carolina School of Medicine in conjunction with the US Department of Justice, and his Postdoctoral Fellowship in Forensic Psychology at the University of Massachusetts Medical School. He has 15 years of clinical expertise in conducting forensic mental health assessments and has been board certified in forensic psychology since 2016. In addition, he is highly published on topics related to forensic mental health treatment and assessment, including violence risk, detection of malingering, and the civil commitment of NRGI patients.

About the Editors

Chapter 1
An Introduction to Internet-Based Data and Its Relevance to Forensic Mental Health Assessments

Ashley B. Batastini, Ashley C. T. Jones, Olivia K. Miller, and Michael J. Vitacco

Use of the Internet, and social networking sites (SNS) in particular, has steadily increased in the United States and throughout the world. In fact, a 2018 poll from the Pew Research Center showed that 68% of American adults are using SNS such as Facebook, Twitter, YouTube, and Snapchat (Smith and Anderson 2018), with only a slight increase by 2019 to 69% (Perrin and Anderson 2019). Never before have people been so readily able to communicate their immediate thoughts, feelings, and behaviors, or access those of other people. Often SNS users share personal information on these sites several times a day across multiple outlets, creating an in-the-moment electronic footprint on an almost daily (or even hourly) basis. Furthermore, it is becoming commonplace to maintain and make available other types of records and reports via online databases and websites, some of which can be uncovered with a simple Google search (i.e., so-called "Internet stalking"). Information that is merely a few clicks away has clear implications, both direct and indirect, for the practice of forensic mental health. In particular, this information is relevant to forensic practitioners who conduct evaluations of psycho-legal issues for the courts. Currently, there is minimal guidance on how to appropriately use and incorporate Internet-based data into such evaluations.

Forensic Mental Health Evaluations in the Digital Age: A Practitioner's Guide to Using Internet-Based Data is the first compilation to directly address the manner in which forensic practitioners can rely on social media and other Internet-based information as important collateral data to inform their psycho-legal opinions. Although there are several practitioner-focused books available that address various

A. B. Batastini (✉) · A. C. T. Jones · O. K. Miller
University of Southern Mississippi, Hattiesburg, MS, USA
e-mail: ashley.batastini@usm.edu; ac.jones@usm.edu; olivia.k.miller@usm.edu

M. J. Vitacco (✉)
Augusta University, Augusta, GA, USA
e-mail: mvitacco@augusta.edu

A. B. Batastini, M. J. Vitacco (eds.), *Forensic Mental Health Evaluations in the Digital Age*, https://doi.org/10.1007/978-3-030-33908-1_1

aspects of forensic mental health evaluations, ranging from how to conduct them to legal implications of forensic evaluations, there are no resources tailored to the unique aspects—both challenges and benefits—regarding the use of SNS and other personal online information as data sources. Given the increasing popularity of these sites, their availability to forensic evaluators, and potential clinical relevance to both criminal and civil psycho-legal questions, this book provides clinicians with best practice guidelines about the practical and ethical uses of data obtained from the Internet, with particular focus on the information posted to SNS of legally involved parties.

1.1 The Proliferation of Social Media and Online-Accessible Information

The invention of the World Wide Web in the 1990s is credited to computer scientist Tim Berners-Lee (Andrews 2013). No one, perhaps except music icon David Bowie, could predict the vast and swift change in how our culture would get and share information. In a 1999 BBC News Night interview, well before the introduction of social media, Bowie eerily and with great prescience disagreed with host Jeremy Paxman's skepticism about the future of the Internet, saying "The potential of what the Internet is going to do to society, both good and bad, is unimaginable. We're actually on the cusp of something exhilarating and terrifying… The actual context and the state of content is going to be so different to anything we can envisage at the moment, where the interplay between the user and the provider will be so in simpatico it's going to crush our ideas of what mediums are all about…." Few would now argue that Bowie was wrong.

1.1.1 Who Is Represented on SNS?

The proliferation of the use of social media sites or SNS within the last decade in particular has been a revolutionary event in the world of information and communication technology (ICT). With sites like Facebook, Twitter, Instagram, and Snapchat, users have the opportunity to share extensive amounts of information about their lives in real-time. According to a 2019 global summary report, more than 4.3 billion people access the Internet worldwide and 3.4 billion of those people are active social media users (Kemp 2019). According to this 2019 report, the average time per day users spend on social media is two hours and sixteen minutes. Worldwide, users manage an average of 8.9 social media accounts; the average American has 7.1 accounts (Kemp 2019). Of the eight most popular social media platforms (i.e., Twitter, Instagram, Facebook, Snapchat, YouTube, WhatsApp, Pinterest, and LinkedIn) surveyed in the 2018 Pew poll, the typical American adult uses at least three of these daily (Smith and Anderson 2018). While most people use these sites to socialize recreationally, social media is increasingly being used more intentionally for marketing, event promotion, and career development (e.g., through LinkedIn, ResearchGate). Many companies now hire employees specifically to manage social media accounts. In the 2019 global survey, 24% of respondents (and 14% of Americans) had used SNS for work purposes (Kemp 2019).

Unsurprisingly, young adults (ages 18–24) consume social media at the highest rate, with Snapchat and Instagram being particularly popular (Perrin and Anderson 2019). However, even among older adults, there has been a significant rise in usage. Compared to just 2% of elderly (65+) SNS users in 2005, about 35% were using SNS by 2015 (Perrin 2015). Facebook appears to have the widest age range of users compared to other common SNS. Approximately 70% of adults reported having a Facebook profile, with roughly three quarters of these users reporting daily use (Perrin and Anderson 2019). The frequency of SNS use does not differ by gender, though some differences have been observed based on the site (e.g., women accessing Pinterest more frequently than men; Perrin and Anderson 2019). Likely due to easier access to technology, higher-income households use social media more frequently than low-income households (Perrin 2015). College-educated individuals are also more likely to use SNS on a consistent basis than those with a high school education or less (Perrin 2015). By region, suburban and urban neighborhoods use SNS more often than rural communities, though more than 50% of residents in rural communities use some type of social media platform regularly (Perrin 2015).

Clearly, social media and Internet use in general is increasing for everyone, irrespective of individual factors, making the likelihood of encountering these data in forensic mental health assessments (FMHA) all the more likely. And, current trends in who is more likely to have access to Internet-based data creates another potential source of bias. For example, if forensic evaluators inform evaluees about their intent to conduct an Internet search, those who use Internet data less frequently may be less skilled at protecting or changing their online information. This may create a disparity in the demographic of examinees who are unaffected or even harmed by Internet searches in FMHA. Understanding the unique demographic of social media and Internet users may help forensic evaluators conceptualize where biases may exist and the types of examinees for whom social media data is more likely to be available. Having greater knowledge of social medial issues and including such information in forensic evaluations may decrease biases.

1.1.2 The Good, the Bad, and the Unimaginable: Motives, Antecedents, and Consequences of SNS Use

Having a general awareness about the specific motivations and antecedents that drive SNS use may further assist evaluators in developing hypotheses about a person's thought processes, emotional stability, interpersonal functioning, or personality pattern. Across adults and young people, a primary motivation for remaining active on social media is to connect with others. For adults, this appears to be related more so to a desire to maintain contact with current friends and family members or to re-connect with people from the past (Smith 2011). For youth, many also report a desire to form new connections (Barbovschi et al. 2015) in addition to having regular contact with friends (Gray 2018). A smaller percentage of adults (about 14%) primarily use SNS to connect with groups of people who share mutual interests and hobbies (Smith 2011).

A growing research base has begun to explore the connections between individual characteristics or personality traits and less adaptive forms of social media activity. Many studies (see Gil de Zúñiga et al. 2017), for example, have focused on the Big 5 personality traits and their relation to problematic online use. Much of this work targets teens, emerging adults, and Millennials and is largely based on correlational designs. In one study, low levels of agreeableness, conscientiousness, openness to experience, self-esteem, and emotional stability predicted addictive Internet and social media behaviors (Hawi and Samaha 2019). Other studies have shown that emotional instability, extroversion, and decreased agreeableness are associated with proactively (i.e., cold or planned) aggressive Internet behaviors such as "trolling" or posting inflammatory comments on an online platform to incite an emotionally reactive response (McCreery and Kathleen Krach 2018; Miller and Lynam 2006). Users with lower levels of conscientiousness are also about three times more likely to experience real-life social isolation (Whaite et al. 2018).

Not surprisingly, disordered personality traits are more commonly associated with antisocial cyber behaviors. A recent meta-analysis of 26 studies showed that traits consistent with the Dark Tetrad (i.e., sadism, psychopathy, narcissism, and Machiavellianism) are related to trolling, online aggression, sending unsolicited explicit images and 'sexts,' problematic online gaming, social media addiction, intimate partner cyberstalking, technology-facilitated sexual violence (e.g., online child pornography), and technology-facilitated infidelity. Psychopathic traits were found to have the largest effects (Moor and Anderson 2019). Childhood maltreatment and an anxious attachment style have also been found to share a positive relationship with maladaptive online behaviors (Worsley et al. 2018). Of course, these ingrained characterological and historical antecedents are not intended to forgive or excuse abhorrent online activity; instead, they may prompt the forensic examiner to consider variables beyond a post's content that may help explain online behavior or make predictions about a person's thoughts, behaviors, and experiences leading up to online behavior.

Other studies have attempted to explain the causes or effects of SNS use on well-being. Greater texting and use of social media have been linked to a decrease in reflective thought and placing less importance on moral life goals (Annisette and Lafreniere 2017), lower emotional intelligence (Süral et al. 2018), and higher levels of psychological impairment including depression (Yoon et al. 2019), body dissatisfaction (Hogue and Mills 2019), and symptoms of acute stress disorder (Goodwin et al. 2015). The development of these issues seems to be explained by primarily upward social comparison (Hogue and Mills 2019; Yoon et al. 2019), which is the tendency to make direct comparisons between our social status and others perceived to be of a higher social status, when browsing SNS.

However, it has been suggested that the quality of SNS use is more important than the frequency of use in understanding problematic online behaviors and their consequences (Marino 2018). For example, those who post about their feelings or use SNS as a tool to vent tend to experience lower moods and self-esteem and more paranoid-type beliefs than those who post about their general daily activities (Berry et al. 2005). And, users who are less likely to know their online friends and followers outside SNS are more likely to report feeling distressed by content on SNS (Gray 2018). Of note, much of the research on social media use and its consequences is correlational in nature and does not necessarily mean social media is the cause of reported psychological or emotional issues.

Especially for youth, the Internet has become a common space to communicate signs of mental distress, including suicidal ideation (Laffier 2016). While the Internet has the power to share information and connect people to needed support systems, a number of disturbing trends have been popularized on the Internet and SNS, often through the use of hashtags (i.e., a way of labeling personal images online so they can be pooled and searched) such as #thinspo (a pro-Anorexia tag) or #cutting, #sue, or #secretsociety123 to form covert communities devoted to self-harm. (Moreno et al. 2016). The Blue Whale Challenge is a terrifying example of the influence of the Internet and social media pressures on at-risk users. The game, which gives players a series of 50 dark and dangerous tasks to perform over 50 days, began in 2013 and gained media attention in 2016. To "win" the challenge, game "curators" demand participants end their lives on the 50th and final challenge. Though SNS are designed for individuals older than thirteen, there is an alarming rate of children with profiles on these sites (Barbovschi et al. 2015). Barbovschi and colleagues examined factors associated with underage (ages 9–12) Facebook use and found that kids report similar motives for using SNS as adolescents and adults. Notably, this includes seeking new friends as well as online disinhibition (e.g., cyberbullying behavior; Barbovschi et al. 2015; Lowry et al. 2016). Children whose parents provide less restrictive access or oversight were more likely to have personal profiles. Though less likely to have their own profiles, children as young as preschool age are using mobile apps like YouTube on their parents' phones (Sapsaglam 2018).

Recognizing the extent of child and teen SNS use is relevant to forensic practitioners. As part of a child custody evaluation, for example, an evaluator may inquire as to whether children are accessing harmful or uncensored information without parental supervision. When the youth is the perpetrator of a crime, a search of their online behavior may help clarify legal capacities or culpability when considered alongside other data such as the child's age, developmental level, and mental functioning. Taken together, research suggests that young people are perhaps the most impressionable of SNS users and that their decisions, therefore, may represent a decreased agency or autonomy secondary to cyber provocation or peer influence. The legal system has long recognized the diminished intent of young people (*Miller v. Alabama* 2012; *Roper v. Simmons* 2005), as well as vulnerable adults (*Atkins v. Virginia* 2002), due to their cognitive and emotional immaturity. In the current state of ICT, the use of SNS simply allows for a larger-scale and more accessible display of these preexisting vulnerabilities.

To best understand the virtual content posted by examinees, forensic evaluators are advised to keep current with, or consult about, the meaning of and trends in online vernacular or "text speak." Acronyms, for example, can be as innocuous as LOL (laugh out loud) or something substantially more provocative and suggestive like IWSN (I want sex now) or GNOC (get naked on camera). This may seem like a difficult task given the fast pace with which the language of the Internet evolves. In fact, by the time this edition hits the market, or shortly thereafter, today's verbiage may already be replaced. However, a quick Internet search will generate a number of useful and up-to-date Internet slang dictionaries.

1.1.3 The Normalization of a Virtual Global Community: Beyond Individual Use

While SNS began as a way to casually communicate and share details of one's thoughts and feelings amongst friends, loved ones, and even strangers (e.g., "followers" or "friends"), social media and web-based platforms are increasingly being used as a tool with far-reaching implications. As Coffey et al. (2018) highlighted, statements or actions posted on the Internet can quickly become newsworthy events. In the current political climate, for example, SNS posts, especially "tweets," are a hub for political talk and are often used as major political dissemination tools for leverage in elections by increasing a candidate's social capital (Kim et al. 2016). Around the time of this publication, this was perhaps best exemplified by the 2016 presidential election and the subsequent rise politicians who gained popularity by speaking directly (albeit virtually) to both their constituents and the entire world. While studying the influence of SNS on political behavior among the general population, Kim et al. (2016) showed a positive link between SNS use for political purposes and strength of political ideology as well as self-reported political involvement, suggesting that SNS can also unite people on a political front. For better or worse, political activism in the age of social media has the potential to rapidly spread ideas and calls to action. It seems that the tweets of politicians, celebrities, and other Internet-made personalities or "influencers" are reviewed and dissected on a near daily basis by newscasters and online commentators (e.g., Buzzfeed News, Huffington Post), making it difficult to ignore the normalization of communicating and connecting through SNS. SNS have allowed previously unreachable people feel familiar and part of our daily lives, while also opening the door for nearly anyone to have their 15-min—and sometimes much longer—of fame. It is time for the field of forensic mental health assessment to catch up with the view that social media interactions are commonplace and, as such, regularly consider it along with any other information that may be available and relevant to understanding an evaluee's thoughts, behaviors, insights, and/or motives in relation to a given psycho-legal issue. With caution and objectivity, we, too, may find ourselves needing to review and dissect the words and actions posted for the world to see.

1.1.4 *Fact or Fiction, Person or Persona: Acknowledging the Internet's Falsehoods*

While SNS and Internet-based data need to be considered on the same playing field as other collateral sources, it can nonetheless be a breeding ground for disseminating misleading or false information. Online inaccuracies can range from a harmless Snapchat filter that blurs blemishes by adding make-up and freckles (or cat ears and funky glasses) to a more sinister breakout of dangerous conspiracy theories. While a broader and more complete set of recommendations for assessing the veracity and credibility of social media and Internet data has been saved for the concluding chapter of this volume, we thought it relevant to acknowledge the prevalence of online distortion upfront—to emphasize that we recognize the flaws in online representations and personas and, as such, do not advocate for blind trust in what is posted in the depths of the web. Like all collateral data, information contained in SNS posts has significant potential to be taken out of context, may be limited in scope and therefore easily misinterpreted, or could come from a source other than the person to whom the account or profile belongs. However, evaluators should not approach Internet-based data with the assumption that information is inherently colored by impression management or mischaracterizations of reality. In many cases, and just like other types of collateral data, online data also has the potential to shine a brighter light on the truth. For example, consider a defendant who presents with cognitive deficits during a forensic interview, showing signs of poor language comprehension, reading and writing difficulties, tangential and disjointed speech, and impaired recall. Yet, in reviewing this evaluee's Facebook and Twitter accounts, he is found to be actively and quite frequently posting coherent comments related to current events. Using his posts as one data point, the evaluator finds other evidence consistent with feigned impairment. Thus, while impression management and falsehoods are rampant on the web, we must remain open to the idea that social media and other Internet sources may be a helpful (and perhaps necessary) component in formulating stronger, more defensible opinions. For instance, consider if data were only present in SNS and the forensic examiner failed to consider such data in their clinical opinion. Such an oversight would be ripe for cross examination. As an illustrative example, in a recent case one of the authors recently completed, an opposing expert used the defendant's reported inability to use social media as further evidence for concluding the individual had an intellectual disorder. Yet, this evaluator never checked the veracity of that claim. By conducting a basic Internet search, the author found several videos apparently uploaded by the defendant where he clearly spoke about future plans using relatively advanced vocabulary. Ultimately, the defendant acknowledged that he did in fact upload the videos and that many statements provided to the other examiner were wholly false.

1.2 The Emergence of SNS and Internet-Based Data in Legal, Clinical, and Forensic Practice Contexts

The thoughts, opinions, and activities that people willingly offer to the public saturate the Internet, but what many users fail to consider when posting the details of their daily lives is that this information can easily be accessed by unintended parties, some of whom may use such information against them. Take the example of a Texas woman who was fired from a daycare facility before she even started working there after she posted about her disdain for being around children. Other users have gone so far as to post the commission of crimes, or behaviors in close proximity to them, online. Steve Stephens received notoriety in 2017 for uploading a video to Facebook of himself fatally shooting an elderly man, Robert Godwin, Sr. Stephens later killed himself. In this next section, we highlight the emerging uses—both acceptable and questionable—of Internet, and in particular SNS, content in legal, clinical, and forensic mental health practice.

1.2.1 Use in Legal Contexts

A 2014 survey of legal professionals, law enforcement, and members of the news media revealed numerous examples of reliance on information obtained from social media including identifying and locating suspects, obtaining probable cause for search warrants, and alerting the public about criminal activity (LexisNexis Risk Solutions 2014). Law enforcement and news outlets often turn to the Internet to help corroborate witness accounts of criminal activity, piece together circumstantial evidence, determine motive, or establish culpability. Following a number of high-profile events including the mass shootings at Mother Emanuel Church in Charleston, South Carolina and the Stoneman Douglas High School in Parkland, Florida, disturbing images posted to the perpetrators' social media profiles became national headline news. Attorneys are also incorporating SNS data into their practices more frequently. Though some have expressed doubts about using such information, others routinely examine their client's social networking websites prior to developing a case (Gilliland 2013).

Beyond law enforcement, media, and attorneys using SNS information to apprehend suspects or build a legal argument, the information obtained from these sites can influence the actual outcomes of court cases. A survey of state and federal courts found that over a 2-year period, social media evidence was discussed in the written decisions of 674 cases, most of which dealt with criminal allegations, insurance and personal injury claims, and employment related litigation (Patzakis 2014). As exemplified in Coffey et al. (2018), SNS evidence factors into legal decisions in a variety of ways. In *Herrera v. State* (2012), the defendant's MySpace posts were used to prove his involvement in a criminal street gang. In *Hoffman v. State* (2012), photographs found on the defendant's Facebook page led to his conviction of vehicular manslaughter.

Harassing Facebook comments have been used to support a plaintiffs' request for a restraining order (e.g., *Martinelli v. Mitchell* 2012). In *Harris v. Harris* (2014), a father's threatening posts and online evidence showing he violated custody terms (e.g., leaving the child in the care of his girlfriend) were used to support awarding the mother sole physical custody. *Elonis v. United States* (2015) was the first time the Supreme Court agreed to hear a case involving the prosecution of threats made explicitly on social media. Anthony Elonis was convicted of making threats to his ex-wife and children, co-workers, a kindergarten class, the local police, and an FBI agent. Elonis used a pseudonym on Facebook to post self-composed, violently graphic rap lyrics that included a plan to "initiate the most heinous school shooting ever imagined" and wanting to see his estranged wife's body "soaked in blood and dying from all the little cuts." Elonis' case has implications for how first amendment rights apply (or do not apply) to social media. In an 8–1 ruling, the court overturned Elonis' conviction. Internet search histories are another tool commonly used in deciding legal outcomes. In 2010, a California court of appeals upheld a 53-year sentence for Manuel Mares (*The People vs. Manuel Mares*), who was convicted of the murder of a mother and her child in part based on Internet searches that included the phrases "homemade silencers," "Faces of Death," and "anarchist cookbook."

1.2.2 Use in General Clinical Practice

Professional clinicians, as well as psychology graduate trainees, have not been exempt from the growing population of SNS users (Johnstone 2011; Kolmes 2009). In addition to having their own profiles, placing them at risk for unintentional boundary crossings (e.g., "friending" clients) and breaches of confidentiality, many professional mental health clinicians also purposefully consult social media in the context of their practice. This might include examining information to glean insight into their client's relationships and behaviors (Kolmes 2012) and identifying treatment-related factors clients may find challenging to disclose in session (Pirelli et al. 2016). In non-forensic situations there are obvious potential problems with perusing client profiles without their knowledge or consent. Namely, clients are likely to feel violated when their trusted clinicians take it upon themselves to discover personal information before they are comfortable disclosing it themselves (Pirelli et al. 2016; Kaslow et al. 2011).

On the other hand, there may be instances in which SNS access is useful for treatment purposes or even necessary to prevent harm. For example, Lehavot et al. (2009) describe the case of a client diagnosed with bipolar disorder who indicated suicidal intent and possession of a firearm on social media, even though the client had denied ideation when in sessions. During the course of therapy, the clinician received a warning concerning the client's troubling online behavior from a social worker who had worked with this individual in the past. The clinician located the client's profile, which included a profile picture showing the client with a gun pressed up against his head, as well as other explicit photos and statements indicating suicidal ideation and access to weapons. In cases involving a threat of self-harm, it may be justified to check a clients' social media (Lehavot et al. 2012).

In cases of domestic violence, perpetrators may use SNS to manipulate or threaten their partner through messenger features. More sophisticated abusers may employ spyware and key logs to track their partner's communication patterns on both social media and texting applications (Chatterjee et al. 2018). Information like this can prove useful when clinicians are assessing for possible emotional abuse, physical abuse or manipulative tendencies within a couple's therapy context. As an illustrative example, the case of *N.B. v. J.A.B* (2017) a social worker had disclosed to authorities that a male client explicitly made violent threats against his former girlfriend while in a group therapy session. The social worker and authorities consulted the client's social media and had found evidence of previous domestic violence.

Although access to client information on social media may prevent harm in some cases, it is imperative that clinicians keep the client's best interest in mind and avoid seeking information simply out of curiosity. To ensure clients are informed in their decision to engage in therapy where access to their online activity may be monitored for therapeutic purposes, clinicians should include their potential consultation of SNS data within their informed consent procedures.

1.2.3 Use in Forensic Mental Health Practice

While cautioned against it for general clinical purposes, the utility of social media and Internet-based data may prove essential in forensic mental health assessments (FMHA) given the in-depth information it can provide about the individual(s) in question (Recupero 2010). The 'digital footprint' a person leaves on SNS can contribute extensive collateral information about their behavior and cognition that may not be evident in during a clinical interview alone (Metzner and Ash 2010). Social media is perhaps especially useful in cases involving a determination of behavior at some point in the past. In criminal responsibility evaluations, for example, timestamped social media content may help evaluators piece together a defendant's thoughts and emotional state closer to the time of the act than would otherwise be afforded (Vitacco et al. 2018).

A handful of surveys have begun to identify the extent of SNS and Internet data use in FMHA, the types of psycho-legal issues they are most often used, the benefits of its use, and perceived concerns as expressed by evaluators. Coffey et al. (2018) investigated the proportion of forensic mental health evaluators who consult SNS, what types of evaluations they typically use it for, and what legal and ethical concerns (regardless of their own use) they felt SNS posed to FMHA. Sixty-five (63.7%) of the 102 survey respondents, primarily consisting of private practitioners (64.3%) and state hospital employees (57.6%), disclosed using SNS as collateral sources in constructing FMHA at least one time in either civil or criminal contexts. Examples of the referral questions addressed using SNS data included[1]: mental state at the time of the offense (MSO; $n = 38$ out of 46), adjudicative competency (CST; $n = 34$ out of 49), violence risk-threat assessment ($n = 36$ out of 50), child custody-parental fitness ($n = 19$), disability ($n = 12$), and personal injury ($n = 8$). Respondent's main reasoning for using SNS were qualitatively categorized into the following six themes, ordered from the most to least frequently mentioned: to (1) assess for signs of mental illness and mental state, (2) corroborate information provided by the examinee regrading symptoms, (3) examine posts directly related to legal offense, (4) obtain behavioral observations, (5) determine examinee capabilities-skills, and (6) help score psychological instruments (Coffey et al. 2018).

Although the addition of reviewing collateral information has more benefits over using traditional interviewing techniques alone in formulating forensic opinions, there still seems to be some skepticism amongst evaluators concerning the true authenticity and reliability of data retrieved from SNS. As a sample, participants largely believe SNS could be useful in FMHA (M = 60.31 on a scale of 0–100), but rated SNS data much lower in terms of overall validity (M = 39.51). In ranking SNS alongside 11 other common collateral sources, SNS was rated only slightly more helpful than another inmate's report. Respondents also reported a moderate level of concern about ethical and legal issues that could arise when incorporating SNS data into their opinions. In comparing those who used SNS before to those who had not, the authors found medium to large effect sizes such that those without experience had greater concerns about the ethicality and validity of SNS data. Reported barriers to using SNS fell into four general categories: (1) the authenticity of the data, (2) the truthfulness or reliability of the content, (3) privacy and consent to access the data, and (4) the relevance of SNS data in answering psycho-legal questions (Coffey et al. 2018).

Among other concerns for forensic mental health evaluators are the lack of available resources to guide consultation of SNS, including insufficient ethics codes in the Specialty Guidelines for Forensic Psychology and other academic literature (Pirelli et al. 2018). In Pirelli et al. (2018), professional and graduate student respondents indicated the importance of being cautious when interpreting and evaluating collateral sources collected from SNS, given insufficient guidelines in place for determining what practices are required, permitted, or prohibited (Pirelli et al. 2018).

Separate from perceived barriers to using Internet data in FMHA, there is emerging evidence that Internet data, like other sources of data in assessment, is subject to biased decision-making on the part of the evaluator. Batastini et al. (2019) found support for source credibility bias against social media data, with forensic professionals and lay people alike judging the same content posted as a Twitter comment as significantly less credible (professionals $M = 38.29$, lay people $M = 38.24$) than when it was included as part of a medical note (professionals $M = 53.03$, lay people $M = 59.19$) or in a forensic psychological report (professionals $M = 50.80$, lay peo-

[1] Clinicians were asked to mark N/A if they did not perform the type of evaluation listed; therefore, responses are out of the total number of respondents who indicated the evaluation type is within the scope of their practice.

ple $M = 65.70$). This study also found that that evaluators gave significantly less weight to the same content when posted as a Twitter comment than when it was in a medical note or a forensic psychological report. These findings suggest that examiners and triers of fact may give less weight to SNS than other data sources when making decisions that have implications for an individual's liberties or public safety. Although these new findings are informative and expand our understanding of the fields' opinions on using Internet data for psychology-law purposes, there is a need for continued research on the use of Internet data; for example, exploring elements of a case or an evaluation that may prevent or alter the use of Internet data and surveying the opinions of legal professionals. Beyond its use in FMHA, some have also made the case that trial consultants should browse online profile content to identify favorable jury characteristics and eliminate those with less favorable views or whose online behaviors are associated with undesirable personality traits (Nance 2015).

1.3 What Do Existing Professional Guidelines Say about Consulting SNS and Internet-Based Data?

Social media information and other Internet data are increasingly relevant to legal and applied mental health contexts—two overlapping disciplines that cover a range of professions, from lawyers and trial consultants to social workers, psychologists, and psychiatrists. But, to what extent has Internet data made its way into existing professional guidelines? Mental health practitioners and legal scholars are held to stringent ethical and professional guidelines on how they should perform their duties, maintain privacy, and act in the best interest of their clients. Most commonly, these guidelines are set forth by respective governing bodies of the field (e.g., the American Psychological Association [APA], National Association of Social Workers [NASW], American Psychiatric Association [APA], American Bar Association [ABA], American Counseling Association [ACA]). Within these fields, additional professional guidelines are frequently developed to address a unique skillset or practice area. Perhaps most relevant to FMHA is APA's revised *Specialty Guidelines for Forensic Psychology* (SGFP; 2013) and the American Academy of Psychiatry and Law's (AAPL) *Ethical Guidelines for the Practice of Forensic Psychiatry* (1995). However, other sets of forensically relevant professional practice guidelines exist, including APA's *Guidelines for Child Custody Evaluations in Family Law Proceedings* (2010) and the International Association of Chiefs of Police's (IACP) *Preemployment Psychological Evaluation Guidelines* (2014). Such guidelines address topics distinctive to these areas, including how general ethical guidelines (e.g. confidentiality) are adapted to unique relationships and how to manage relationships with evaluees who are not the client.

Typically, professional guidelines are aspirational in nature, but can result in professional sanctions when serious violations occur. Professionals are, of course, also held to legal standards, including case law. And, when working more closely within the legal system, mental health professionals must maintain a greater awareness of relevant legal standards and related case law precedents. To date, the primary concerns about using Internet data as evidence pertains to its admissibility as evidence and the way to sufficiently authenticate such data. Legal precedents involving Internet evidence have addressed some issues of admissibility and authentication for Internet data, specifically whether it is admissible in court and its standards of authentication.

1.3.1 Guidelines Relevant to Legal Professionals

Despite the absence of specific guidelines for using Internet evidence in the ABA's *Model Rules of Professional Conduct* (2016), the ethical code for attorneys and judges, the Federal Rules of Evidence (2017) guide attorneys and triers of fact in determining what general types of evidence are admissible in court. As the rules read, to be permitted in a trial, evidence in any content or modality must be relevant to facts of the case and can reasonably help in trying fact or making decisions (Article IV, Rule 401). After a judge has determined evidence as admissible in court, it must then be authenticated to ensure it represents what it intends to (Article IX, Rule 901). There are several ways in which evidence can be authenticated depending on the type of evidence in question (Federal Rules of Evidence 2017). For example, handwriting evidence can be authenticated by a witness testifying to the similarity of the handwriting in evidence to the handwriting of the defendant.

1.3.1.1 Admission of Internet Data

Over time, judges have become more comfortable allowing Internet data to be used as evidence in cases. At one point, however, courts denied the admission of Internet data. In *St. Clair v. Johnny's Oyster & Shrimp, Inc.* (1999), the court rejected the use of a printed copy of a webpage documenting the ownership of an ocean vessel as belonging to the defendant on the premise that the Internet is "one large catalyst for rumor, innuendo, and misinformation" (p. 775). As the use of the Internet has proliferated and normalized, more recent courts have agreed that Internet data is admissible and subject to the same Federal Rules of Evidence (2017) as non-Internet data (*Lorraine v. Markel American Insurance Co.,* 2007). Specifically, the courts determined that admissible electronically stored information (ESI) must be relevant to the case, authenticated, not meet criteria for hearsay, and have significant probative value that would outweigh any potential prejudice. This decision was echoed in other cases where Internet evidence was admitted into court, despite later being excluded on the basis of insufficient authentication (*Commonwealth v. Williams,* 2010).

1.3.1.2 Authentication of Internet Data

Regarding Internet evidence, authentication of the source (e.g., ensuring an account was not hacked or its content doctored) appears to be the most salient concern, as it can prevent Internet evidence from being used—or even overturn convictions—if requirements for authentication are not met (for an example, see *Griffin v. State of Maryland,* 2011). The Federal Rules of Evidence (2017) require that, for evidence to be considered authentic, the representation of what it intends to represent must be demonstrated (Article IX, Rule 901). The ABA asserted that a traditional interpretation of the Rules of Evidence (2017) provides a uniform guide in determining both the admission and authentication of Internet evidence (ABA 2017). In 2017, the Federal Rules of Evidence (2017) were amended to include "records generated by an electronic process or system" and "data copied from an electronic device, storage medium, or file" in the list of evidence that is inherently self-authenticating (Article IX, Rule 902 (11,12)). These rules indicate that computerized data, such as web pages or information stored on a USB drive, can be authenticated with a certification from an expert that meets requirements as outlined in the Federal Rules of Evidence (FRE 2017; Toft 2018). Although the language in this rule is vague, it nonetheless acknowledges the increasing use of technological and Internet data as evidence in court cases. Like many legal guidelines, this is open to interpretation and may permit different types of experts (e.g., a technical support specialist or a web page designer) to provide specific certification of authenticity depending on the Internet data in question.

However, more concrete guidance is needed. Internet data is not yet explicitly included in the list of common evidence used in Rule 901: Authenticating or Identifying Evidence (FRE 2017), making the process of authenticating Internet data that does not obviously qualify as self-authenticating ambiguous for attorneys and other legal professionals. This ambiguity leaves Internet data at the mercy of a traditional reading of the FRE (2017)—a rather conservative reading that may be less forgiving for Internet data. That is, interpretation of the rules may result in a threshold for authentication that is too high for Internet data to meet, given the ease with which SNS posts, online news articles, and websites can be falsified or created under false pretenses (Murphy and Fontecilla 2013). For example, it is difficult to demonstrate who actually sent Internet e-mails and messages, or what the factual basis is for Internet webpages or public posts—all of which are details that evidence authentication sets out to prove. These authentication challenges, coupled with general concerns about Internet data (e.g., the difficulty in interpreting meaning or context of Internet data, its susceptibility to impression management; Metzner and Ash 2010), result in scrutinizing Internet evidence by triers of fact to a greater extent than other types of evidence, despite its probative value (see *Clair v. Johnny's Oyster & Shrimp, Inc.*, 1999 for example).

The difficulty in authenticating Internet data has been exemplified in several cases. *Griffin v. State of Maryland* (2011) determined that authentication of ESI requires a higher threshold than other types of evidence. The court noted that evidence (in this case, a public post) derived from the MySpace page of a trial witness must be authenticated and that distinguishable characteristics connecting the Internet evidence to one person are not sufficient for authentication (*Griffin v. State of Maryland* 2011). Another case determined that, to sufficiently authenticate the printed copy of private messages received over MySpace, testimony must demonstrate that the person who appeared to send the messages online was in fact the person who sent them, and address aspects of the website, including its level of security and whether passcodes are needed to access specific profiles (*Commonwealth v. Williams* 2010).

Despite the potential for heightened scrutiny with Internet-based data, a recent law review showed that attorneys have successfully authenticated or justified Internet evidence using the FRE (2017) by emphasizing the protected and personal nature of social media accounts and by offering additional evidence or testimony that corroborates the evidence found in Internet data (Gilliland 2017). The results of this law review support the idea that, although SNS evidence may be challenging to authenticate, it is not held to a substantially higher standard than other evidence, making authentication possible (Gilliland 2017). In other words, online information is likely no more susceptible to doctoring or misrepresentation than any other evidence presented in court.

1.3.2 Relevant Guidelines for Forensic Mental Health Professionals

Although many organizational guidelines have yet to address the issue of Internet data in the context of FMHA (Pirelli et al. 2016), some guidelines, like APA's *Ethical Principles for Psychologists and Code of Conduct* (EPPCC) and those set forth by AAPL either address ethical Internet use or have guidelines for general aspects of the profession, such as the client-therapist relationship and confidentiality, that can be applied to the use of Internet data in FMHA. And, specific to FMHA, the *Specialty Guidelines for Forensic Psychology* (SGFP) provide recommendations that have relevance for Internet data. More recently, APA proposed guidelines specific to social media use that would also have some applicability to FMHA (Baker et al. 2018); however, the currently unpublished nature of these guidelines limits accessibility to psychologists and other mental health professionals at large.

The most recent versions of both the EPPCC (APA 2017) and the SGFP (APA 2013) include general language that could be broadly applied to the use of such data for forensic assessment purposes. The EPPCC (2017) state that psychologists are obligated to obtain informed consent from the evaluee before conducting an evaluation unless the assessment is mandated by law or when it is being conducted to evaluate decisional capacity (Rule 9.03(a)(b)(c)). However, an assessor's obligations to clients as outlined in the EPPCC is complicated by the change of client in forensic relationships. Unlike traditional therapeutic relationships, the "client" to whom the forensic evaluator has allegiance is the court, as the evaluator's purpose is to provide objective, unbiased information to assist in legal decision-making

(Melton et al. 2018). In FMHA, the defendant is never the client. Therefore, it is unclear if evaluators have the same obligations to the evaluee (e.g. obtaining informed consent from defendant).

The SGFP (2013) also affirms that psychologists are obligated to disclose the methods used in conducting their assessments and their intended use of any data or information gathered during the assessment process (Rule 6.03). Although these Rules do not directly mention their applicability to Internet data, they broadly imply the way in which professionals may be expected to list and reference any and all Internet data used in FMHA. Nonetheless, given that the client in forensic relationships is not the defendant, it is unclear whether the evaluator has any obligation to disclose such intentions to the court (i.e., the judge), or if the evaluator should still list the fact that they conducted an Internet search, even if the search does not reveal useful information.

While not explicit in any officially adopted professional guidelines, other commentary exists offering recommendations for navigating ethical concerns specific to the Internet and social media. APA, for example, has disseminated articles addressing the ethical use of social media and provided guidance for how psychologists can prepare themselves for the inevitable ethical dilemmas that arise from social networking and the Internet, with recommendations including setting higher security levels on personal social media accounts and conducting regular online self-searches to be aware of what personal data you have on the Internet (Lannin and Scott 2014). In an unpublished draft on the optimal use of social media in professional psychological practice (noted earlier; Baker et al. 2018), APA outlines the value of SNS in health services provision, the ethical and clinical risks and implications of its use, and the need for sufficient education and training. Although these initial guidelines do not provide detailed recommendations on how to go about using Internet data or social media as evidence in FMHA, they acknowledge that, while some guidelines, such as not conducting Internet searches on clients without their informed consent (Guideline 2.3), are key in traditional counseling relationships, "additional considerations may weigh heavily" in other contexts like forensic assessments (Baker et al. 2018). AAPL, on the other hand, both recognized and acknowledged the usefulness of this emerging category of information in a more official capacity and included recommendations for forensic psychiatrists in their ethical guidelines, such as obtaining permission to use Internet data when conducting assessments and cautioning evaluators to consider impression management and misrepresentation when incorporating such data (Glancy et al. 2015).

The SGFP (2013) guidelines require evaluators to share details about the evaluation to potential third-party sources (e.g., collateral sources), as it may influence their decision to provide information about the examinee to the evaluator (Rule 6.04). This rule also has applicability for reliance on Internet data, as it would seem to imply that all third-party interviewees are entitled to know whether an evaluator intends to collect Internet data from their own accounts because access to their SNS information may likewise influence whether they consent to the evaluation. Because most Internet data, by nature, are voluntarily made public, one could argue that the use of such data should not influence a third party's consent to participate. Additionally, if an evaluee's Internet data is used in an assessment and involves another person (e.g., an exchange of comments or messages), that data could in theory be used in the assessment regardless of the collateral person's consent to be interviewed because it is already qualified assessment data through its direct association to the defendant. Based on existing SGFP recommendations, the core issue then becomes: must third parties similarly be notified that their own Internet-based data as related to the case at hand may be accessed and used in an FMHA, and does such a notification warrant inclusion in the informed consent despite the data's public nature?

Attempts to contextualize professional guidelines for Internet data in FMHA were made by Pirelli et al. (2016) when they recommended new, more specific guidelines. To summarize, the following recommendations were proposed:

1. Conceptualize Internet-based data as a type of collateral (rather than self-report) information;
2. Weigh the potential utility of the data against possible prejudicial effects on a case-by-case basis;
3. Discuss the process of data-gathering and potential use of SNS data with the examinee during the informed consent process (e.g., whether it was received as part of discovery or in independent searches for collateral information);
4. Share data obtained from the Internet with examinees and give them an opportunity to address it;
5. Be explicit and transparent about the use of and reliance on SNS data in reports and testimony.

The Pirelli et al. (2016) guidelines are conservative in many ways, as they afford defendants several courtesies not typical in the context of FMHA. Contrary to their recommendations, the SGFP (2013) state that evaluators are only expected to present and explain data to the court; the evaluee (i.e., the defendant) is *not* entitled to the data used in an evaluation without the retaining party's consent (Rule 8.02). Further, these same guidelines recommend that evaluators seek consent from the retaining attorney or party before accessing such information (Rule 8.03), suggesting evaluators may need to seek permission from the attorney or court, not the evaluee, to search for Internet data on the evaluee. And, in cases where Internet data is provided to the evaluator in discovery, the voluntary provision of the information would imply permission to use it, regardless of the defendant's wishes. Given that mandated evaluations do not require informed consent from the evaluee, and they are not entitled to knowledge of the data collected during the assessment, it could be argued that the evaluee is also not entitled to know about, let alone have a chance to dispute the content of, any Internet data used in their FMHA. To their credit, Pirelli and colleagues acknowledged the intentionality of their better-safe-than-sorry approach, given they were the first set of guidelines presented to the professional community. And, notably, other recommendations suggesting Internet-based data be treated in much the same way as collateral data not derived from online sources seem far less contentious.

All things considered, the professional debate on how Internet data should be handled by forensic mental health evaluators compared to other types of assessment data used in FMHA remains unclear. Indeed, a lack of research on the appropriate and inappropriate use of Internet and social media data in FMHA leaves more questions than answers. And, while the above guidelines offer a useful start, little is known about the extent to which forensic examiners as a group agree. Recommendations for handling Internet data within the context of FMHA, including those set forth by Pirelli et al. (2016), will be reviewed again and expanded upon in Chap. 9.

1.4 Overview of Remaining Chapters

With some background regarding the popular use of online data, as well as the current state of practice when using these types of data to inform legal and psychological opinions, the next seven chapters cover distinct psycho-legal issues that forensic mental health practitioners are commonly asked to address. These issues include mental state at the time of the offense (criminal responsibility), adjudicative competency, violence risk and threat assessment, civil commitment for sexual violence, child custody and parental fitness, fitness for duty and employment screenings, and disability and personal injury. This, of course, is not an exhaustive list of mental health issues that evaluators may encounter in civil or criminal proceedings; however, we believe the recommendations and lessons learned across these diverse contexts can provide a solid translational framework for other contexts not explicitly discussed here. Each of these chapters uniformly includes four components: (1) a brief overview of the psycho-legal issue and general best practices to quickly orient the reader, (2) clinical applications of consulting Internet-based data, (3) ethical and legal considerations, and (4) de-identified case examples. Of note, all case examples have been completely de-identified and do not necessarily contain all information obtained or used in the original evaluation; rather, these are snapshots of cases that illustrate the use of Internet material as collateral data. The final chapter then concludes by summarizing common themes and providing clearer recommendations for practice and continued research.

Although online data may prove useful to the forensic practitioner, to date, practitioners have been left to their own devices to determine if the information is relevant and how to ethically navigate the acquisition and application of such information when formulating their forensic opinions. Through the use of case studies and integrating the latest information from the scientific community as well as anecdotal evidence from practitioners, we hope this book fills a needed gap for seasoned and novice professionals alike.

References

American Academy of Psychiatry & the Law (1995). *Ethical Guidelines for the Practice of Forensic Psychiatry.* Retrieved from http://library.law.columbia.edu/urlmirror/CJAL/14CJAL1/ethics.html.

American Bar Association (2016). *Model Rules of Professional Conduct.* Retrieved from https://www.americanbar.org/groups/professional_responsibility/publications/model_rules_of_professional_conduct/model_rules_of_professional_conduct_table_of_contents/.

American Psychological Association. (2010). Guidelines for child custody evaluations in family law proceedings. *American Psychologist, 65*(9), 863–867. https://doi.org/10.1037/a0021250.

American Psychological Association. (2013). Specialty guidelines for forensic psychologists. *American Psychologist, 68*(1), 7–19. https://doi.org/10.1037/a0029889.

American Psychological Association (2017). *Ethical Principles of Psychologists and Code of Conduct.* Retrieved from https://www.apa.org/ethics/code/.

Andrews, E. (2013). Who invented the internet? The history channel. Retrieved from https://www.history.com/news/who-invented-the-internet.

Annisette, L. E., & Lafreniere, K. D. (2017). Social media, texting, and personality: A test of the shallowing hypothesis. *Personality and Individual Differences, 115*, 154–158. https://doi.org/10.1016/j.paid.2016.02.043.

Atkins v. Virginia. No. 00-8452, 536 U.S. 304 (2002).

Baker, D. C., Barnes, A., Deutsch, R. M., Hardiman, M. G., Hunter, S. J., Melchert, T. P., Tansy, M. E., & Varghese, F. P. (2018). *Proposed guidelines for the optimal use of social media in professional psychological practice*. Washington, D.C.: American Psychological Association.

Barbovschi, M., Macháčková, H., & Ólafsson, K. (2015). Underage use of social network sites: It's about friends. *CyberPsychology, Behavior & Social Networking, 18*(6), 328–332. https://doi.org/10.1089/cyber.2014.0553.

Batastini, A. B., Vitacco, M. J., Jones, A. C. T., Davis, R. M. (2019). *Perceived credibility of social media data as a collateral source in criminal responsibility evaluations*. Manuscript in prep.

Berry, J., Worthington, E., Wade, N., Van Oyen Witvliet, C., & Kiefer, R. (2005). Forgiveness, moral identity, and perceived justice in crime victims and their supporters. Humboldt Journal of Social Relations, 29(2), 136-162.

Chatterjee, R., Doerfler, P., Orgad, H., Havron, S., Palmer, J., Freed, D., et al. (2018). The spyware used in intimate partner violence. In *2018 IEEE Symposium on Security and Privacy (SP)* (pp. 441–458). Institute of Electrical and Electronics Engineers.

Coffey, A. C., Batastini, A. B., & Vitacco, M. J. (2018). Clues from the digital world: A survey of clinicians' reliance on social media as collateral data in forensic evaluations. *Professional Psychology: Research and Practice, 49*(5-6), 345–354. https://doi.org/10.1037/pro0000206

Commonwealth v. Williams. 456 Mass. 857 (2010). 926 N.E.2d 1162.

Elonis v. United States, No. 13-983, 135 S.Ct. 2001 (2015).

Federal Rules of Evidence (2017). Authenticating or identifying evidence. Article IX, Rule 901.

Gil de Zúñiga, H., Diehl, T., Huber, B., & Liu, J. (2017). Personality traits and social media use in 20 countries: How personality relates to frequency of social media use, social media news use, and social media use for social interaction. *Cyberpsychology, Behavior and Social Networking, 20*(9), 540–552.

Gilliland, J. (2013). iWitness: The admissibility of social media evidence. Litigation, 39(1). Retrieved from https://www.americanbar.org/groups/litigation/publications/litigation_journal/2012_13/winter/the_admissibility_social_media_evidence/

Gilliland, J. (2017). iWitness: The admissibility of social media evidence. Litigation. Retrieved at https://www.americanbar.org/groups/litigation/publications/litigation_journal/2012_13/winter/the_admissibility_social_media_evidence/.

Glancy, G. D., Ash, P., Bath, E. P. J., Buchanan, A., Fedoroff, P., Frierson, R. L., Harris, V. L., Friedman, S. J. H., Hauser, M. J., Knoll, J., Norko, M., Pinals, D., Price, M., Recupero, P., Scott, C. L., & Zonana, H. V. (2015). AAPL practice guideline for the forensic assessment. *The Journal of the American Academy of Psychiatry and the Law, 43*(2), S3–S53.

Gray, L. (2018). Exploring how and why young people use social networking sites. *Educational Psychology in Practice, 34*(2), 175–194. https://doi.org/10.1080/02667363.2018.1425829.

Griffin v. State of Maryland. 19 A.3d 415 (2011). 419 Md. 343.

Harris v. Harris, 446 S.W.3d (Mo. Ct. App. 2014).

Hawi, N., & Samaha, M. (2019). Identifying commonalities and differences in personality characteristics of internet and social media addiction profiles: Traits, self-esteem, and self-construal. *Behaviour & Information Technology, 38*(2), 110–119. https://doi.org/10.1080/0144929X.2018.1515984.

Herrera v. The State of Texas, No. 05-11-00240-CR (Tex. Ct. App., 5th Dist. 2012).

Hoffman v. State of Delaware, No. 540, 2011 (Del. Sup. Ct. 2012).

Hogue, J. V., & Mills, J. S. (2019). The effects of active social media engagement with peers on body image in young women. *Body Image, 28*, 1–5. https://doi.org/10.1016/j.bodyim.2018.11.002.

IACP Police Psychological Services Section (2014). *Preemployment Psychological Evaluation Guidelines.* Retrieved from https://www.theiacp.org/sites/default/files/all/p-r/Psych-PreemploymentPsychEval.pdf.

Johnstone, L. (2011). Media column. *Clinical Psychology Forum, 225*, 49–50.

Kaslow, F. W., Patterson, T., & Gottlieb, M. (2011). Ethical dilemmas in psychologists accessing Internet data: Is it justified? *Professional Psychology: Research and Practice, 42*, 105–112. https://doi.org/10.1037/a0022002.

Kemp, S. (2019, January). *Digital 2019: Essential insights into how people around the world use the internet, mobile devices, social media, and e-commerce* (Rep.). Retrieved from https://www.juancmejia.com/wp-content/uploads/2019/03/Digital-2019-WeAreSocial-y-HootSuite.pdf

Kim, T., Atkin, D. J., & Lin, C. A. (2016). The influence of social networking sites on political behavior: Modeling political involvement via online and offline activity. *Journal of Broadcasting & Electronic Media, 60*(1), 23–39. https://doi.org/10.1080/08838151.2015.1127242.

Kolmes, K. (2009). Managing Facebook as a mental health professional. Articles for Clinicians Using Social Media. Retrieved from https://drkkolmes.com/2009/06/08/managing-facebook-as-a-mental-health-professional/.

Kolmes, K. (2012). Social media in the future of professional psychology. *Professional Psychology: Research and Practice, 43*, 606–612. https://doi.org/10.1037/a0028678.

Laffier, J. L. (2016). Social relations: Exploring how youth use social media to communicate signs and symptoms of depression and suicidal ideation. In M. Walrave, K. Ponnet, E. Vanderhoven, J. Haers, & B. Segaert (Eds.), *Youth 2.0: Social media and adolescence: Connecting, sharing and empowering* (pp. 161–178). Cham: Springer International Publishing.

Lannin, D. G., & Scott, N. A. (2014). Best practices for an online world. *Monitor on Psychology, 45*(2), 56.

Lehavot, K., Ben-Zeev, D., & Neville, R. (2012). Ethical considerations and social media: A case of suicidal postings on Facebook. *Journal of Dual Diagnosis, 8*(4), 341–346. https://doi.org/10.1080/15504263.2012.718928.

Lorraine v. Markel Am. Ins. Co., 241 F.R.D. 534 (2007).

Lowry, P. B., Zhang, J., Wang, C., & Siponen, M. (2016). Why do adults engage in cyberbullying on social media? An integration of online disinhibition and deindividuation effects with the social structure and social learning model. *Information Systems Research, 27*(4), 962–986. https://doi.org/10.1287/isre.2016.0671.

Marino, C. (2018). Quality of social-media use may matter more than frequency of use for adolescents' depression. *Clinical Psychological Science, 6*(4), 455. https://doi.org/10.1177/2167702618771979.

Martinelli v. Mitchell, No. SD 31504 (Mo. Ct. App., Southern Dist., 1st Div. 2012).

McCreery, M. P., & Kathleen Krach, S. (2018). How the human is the catalyst: Personality, aggressive fantasy, and proactive-reactive aggression among users of social media. *Personality and Individual Differences, 133*, 91–95. https://doi.org/10.1016/j.paid.2017.06.037.

Melton, G. B., Petrila, J., Poythress, N. G., Slobogin, C., Otto, R. K., Mossman, D., & Condie, L. O. (2018). *Psychological evaluations for the courts* (4th ed.). New York: The Guilford Press.
Metzner, J. L., & Ash, P. (2010). Commentary: The mental status examination in the age of the internet: Challenges and opportunities. *Journal of the American Academy of Psychiatry and the Law, 38*, 27–31. Retrieved from http://www.jaapl.org/content/38/1/27.full.
Miller, J. D., & Lynam, D. R. (2006). Reactive and proactive aggression: Similarities and differences. *Personality and Individual Differences, 41*(8), 1469–1480. https://doi.org/10.1016/j.paid.2006.06.004.
Miller v. Alabama, Nos. 10-9646, 10.9647. 132 S. Ct. 2455 (2012).
Moor, L., & Anderson, J. R. (2019). A systematic literature review of the relationship between dark personality traits and antisocial online behaviours. *Personality & Individual Differences, 144*, 40–55. https://doi.org/10.1016/j.paid.2019.02.027.
Moreno, M. A., Ton, A., Selkie, E., & Evans, Y. (2016). Secret society 123: Understanding the language of self-harm on Instagram. *Journal of Adolescent Health, 58*(1), 78–84. https://doi.org/10.1016/j.jadohealth.2015.09.015.
Murphy, J. P, & Fontecilla, A. (2013). Social media evidence in government investigations and criminal proceedings: A Frontier of new legal issues, Richmond Journal of Law and Technology, 19(3). Retrieved from http://www.jolt.richmond.edu/v19i3/article11.pdf.
N.B. v. J.A.B., 2017 N.J. Super. Unpub. LEXIS 56, 2017 WL 85570 (Superior Court of New Jersey, Appellate Division January 10, 2017, Decided).
Nance, A. R. (2015). Social media selection: How jury consultants can use social media to build a more favorable jury. *Law & Psychology Review, 39*, 267–286.
Patzakis, J. (2014, January 26). Social media more relevant than ever: Hundreds of thousands of cases estimated to address social media in 2014 [Web log post]. Retrieved from http://blog.x1discovery.com/2015/01/26/social-media-more-relevant-than-ever-hundreds-of-thousands-oflegal-.cases-estimated-to-address-social-media-in-2014/.
Perrin, A. (October 2015). Social media usage: 2005–2015. *Pew Research Center.*
Perrin, A., & Anderson, M. (2019). Share of U.S. adults using social media, including Facebook, is mostly unchanged since 2018. Retrieved from https://www.pewresearch.org/fact-tank/2019/04/10/share-of-u-s-adults-using-social-media-including-facebook-is-mostly-unchanged-since-2018/.
Pirelli, G., Otto, R. K., & Estoup, A. (2016). Using internet and social media data as collateral sources of information in forensic evaluations. *Professional Psychology: Research and Practice, 47*(1), 12–17.
Pirelli, G., Hartigan, S., & Zapf, P. A. (2018). Using the internet for collateral information in forensic mental health evaluations. *Behavioral Sciences & the Law, 36*, 157–169. https://doi.org/10.1002/bsl.2334.
Recupero, P. R. (2010). The mental status examination in the age of the internet. *Journal of the American Academy of Psychiatry and the Law, 38*(1), 15–26.
Roper v. Simmons, 543 U.S. 551 (2005).
Sapsaglam, Ö. (2018). Social media awareness and usage in preschool children. *International Journal of Eurasia Social Sciences, 9*(31), 728–746.
Smith, A. (2011). Why Americans use social media Retrieved from https://www.pewinternet.org/2011/11/15/why-americans-use-social-media/
Smith, A., & Anderson, M. (2018). Social media use 2018: Demographics and statistics Retrieved from https://www.pewinternet.org/2018/03/01/social-media-use-in-2018/
LexisNexis Risk Solutions. (2014). *Survey of law enforcement personnel and their use of social media*. Retrieved from www.lexisnexis.com/investigations.
St. Clair v. Johnny's Oyster & Shrimp, *Inc.* 76 F.Supp.2d 773 (1999).
Süral, I., Griffiths, M. D., Kircaburun, K., & Emirtekin, E. (2018). Trait emotional intelligence and problematic social media use among adults: The mediating role of social media use motives. *International Journal of Mental Health and Addiction., 17*, 336–345. https://doi.org/10.1007/s11469-018-0022-6.

Toft, A. (2018). New rules for self-authenticating electronic evidence. Litigation. Retrieved from: https://www.americanbar.org/groups/litigation/committees/trial-evidence/practice/2018/new-rules-electronic-evidence/.

Vitacco, M. J., Gottfried, E. D., & Batastini, A. B. (2018). Using technology to improve The objectivity of criminal responsibility evaluations. *Journal of the American Academy of Psychiatry and the Law, 46*(1), 71–77.

Whaite, E. O., Shensa, A., Sidani, J. E., Colditz, J. B., & Primack, B. A. (2018). Social media use, personality characteristics, and social isolation among young adults in the United States. *Personality and Individual Differences, 124*, 45–50. https://doi.org/10.1016/j.paid.2017.10.030.

Worsley, J. D., McIntyre, J. C., Bentall, R. P., & Corcoran, R. (2018). Childhood maltreatment and problematic social media use: The role of attachment and depression. *Psychiatry Research, 267*, 88–93. https://doi.org/10.1016/j.psychres.2018.05.023.

Yoon, S., Kleinman, M., Mertz, J., & Brannick, M. (2019). Is social network site usage related to depression? A meta-analysis of Facebook–depression relations. *Journal of Affective Disorders, 248*, 65–72. https://doi.org/10.1016/j.jad.2019.01.026.

Chapter 2
Criminal Responsibility

Michael J. Vitacco, Diandra Sigurdsson, Alynda M. Randolph, and Ashley B. Batastini

Evaluations of criminal responsibility, also referred to as insanity evaluations or mental state at the time of the offense (MSTO), are some of the most highly contested evaluations in the psycho-legal arena. These evaluations require clinicians to retrospectively evaluate an individual's mental state at the time when the individual allegedly committed an offense. However, clinicians are often asked to evaluate an individual's MSTO weeks, months, or even years after an alleged crime occurred. Several years ago, one of the authors of this chapter received a court order to evaluate an individual's criminal responsibility over 20 years after an alleged murder. Fortunately, such an extensive amount of time between an event and the evaluation are rare, but it underscores both the inherent difficulty in conducting insanity evaluations and the need for a complete and thorough review of extant collateral information. As will be highlighted in this chapter, information valuable to determining one's MSTO includes clinical interviews with the defendant, interviews with family members and others familiar with the defendant, discovery information, records generated from previous admissions to mental health and substance treatment facilities, and information from individuals who may have witnessed the alleged criminal behavior.

An emerging area requiring reflection is how to appropriately integrate data generated from social media platforms, such as social networking sites (SNS), into criminal and civil forensic evaluations. This is especially salient in criminal responsibility evaluations because they require the clinician to conduct retrospective evaluations of a person's mental state. As such, data generated in real time, like the type of information found on someone's SNS profile, can provide information relevant to one's mental state at a specific time. Consider for example someone's Facebook posts that are increasingly bizarre with lengthy denunciations toward the government and an evalu-

M. J. Vitacco (✉) · D. Sigurdsson · A. M. Randolph
Augusta University, Augusta, GA, USA
e-mail: mvitacco@augusta.edu; Alynda.randolph@dbhdd.ga.gov

A. B. Batastini (✉)
University of Southern Mississippi, Hattiesburg, MS, USA
e-mail: ashley.batastini@usm.edu

A. B. Batastini, M. J. Vitacco (eds.), *Forensic Mental Health Evaluations in the Digital Age*, https://doi.org/10.1007/978-3-030-33908-1_2

ator receives this information as part of the discovery packet provided by the defense after the individual was charged with Terroristic Threats toward a congressperson. This chapter's goal is to summarize extant knowledge and provide an outline of how to appropriately consider data from SNS in forming opinions on criminal responsibility. Prior to discussing the specifics of using social media in criminal responsibility evaluations, we will provide some historical context to the current state of the defense. As we examine information on social media in criminal responsibility evaluations, we will also discuss unique ethical issues that are ubiquitous when relying on data from social media as part of criminal responsibility evaluations.

2.1 The Insanity Defense and Society

Data on public views of the insanity defense routinely find high levels of skepticism toward the insanity defense (Perlin 2017). This skepticism is revealed in studies showing that the public views the insanity defense as a widely used loophole employed by unscrupulous defendants, buttressed by unprincipled defense attorneys who purchase mental health testimony to support their position. These ideas about the insanity defense are also revealed in the misperceptions about individuals who use the insanity defense. These misperceptions include that individuals who malinger psychopathology are often found not guilty by reason of insanity (NGRI), individuals found NGRI do "easy time" in state institutions, and that NGRI findings can lead to a spike in violent recidivism because of the speed at which these individuals navigate through the mental health system (Perlin 2017). Such perceptions are not, however, grounded in empirical data, but instead based on popular, but unfounded opinions.

2.1.1 Nature of the Insanity Defense

The reality of criminal responsibility evaluations is that they are rarely successful, and individuals found NGRI can spend more time in a secure and often locked facility than individuals who are adjudicated guilty for similar offenses (Melton et al. 2018; Cirincione et al. 1995). Considering recidivism, individuals adjudicated NGRI have a much lower risk of both general and violent recidivism than comparative groups that have left other forms of incarceration, especially when NGRI individuals are under intense supervision, which is often a condition of their release from a secure psychiatric facility.

What is telling about such data are that, even when provided accurate information about the use and success of the insanity defense, most individuals do not deviate from their original, and often unsubstantiated ideas about the insanity defense. Some of the vitriol toward the insanity defense appears rooted in high-stakes, high-profile cases that have received a significant amount of media attention. As an illustrative example, the media widely covered John W. Hinckley, Jr.'s trial after he attempted to kill then president Ronald Reagan with a .22 caliber Rohm RG 14 revolver on March 30, 1981. Hinckley was ultimately adjudicated NGRI and committed to St. Elizabeth's Hospital in Washington, DC, and in the wake of the trial, there were over 60 bills introduced in Congress to make changes to insanity laws. In an unprecedented move, five jurors from Hinckley's trial provided testimony before Congress, with some indicating they did not understand the law and the judge's instructions regarding the insanity defense. The insanity defense remains misunderstood today, which further increases the likelihood that people will remain biased in their views.

2.2 Brief History and Case Law of the Insanity Defense

Even considering the generally strong distaste of the insanity defense, the defense itself has a long and noteworthy history with roots in historical philosophy. Both Plato and Aristotle spoke of conditions that could excuse someone from moral and criminal culpability. Plato noted the following, "Someone may perhaps commit an act when mad or afflicted with disease… let him pay simply for the damage, whatever he may have done; and let him be exempt from other punishments..." (1859, p. 372). Aristotle said, "Those acts which are done in ignorance of the circumstances are mistakes when the object, the instrument, or the effect is other than the agent supposed." The Talmud, an early text of Jewish law, also provided special dispensation for a subset of individuals who have broken the law. In language consistent with the day, the book allowed for "Idiots, lunatics, and children below a certain age ought not to be held criminally responsible because they could not distinguish good from evil, right from wrong, and were thus blameless in the eyes of God and man." These historical contexts provided some important underpinnings that were ultimately reflected in formal insanity laws.

The basis for modern-day insanity law is a trilogy of cases originating in England. The first occurred in 1724 and involved Edward Arnold shooting and wounding Lord Onslow. In *Rex*[1] *v. Arnold* the court had to determine if Mr. Arnold should be excused for the crime due to lunacy and it was ruled that "it must be a man that is totally deprived of his understanding and memory, and doth not know what he is doing; no more than an infant, than a brute, or a wild beast, such a one is never the object of punishment." Although it is an extremely high bar for even the most seriously mentally ill person to meet this requirement, this standard has generated a substantial amount of scholarship as legal scholars have sought to expound on this ruling (Robinson 1996). The second case occurred in 1800 and involved James Hadfield, who attempted to assassinate the King of England. Hadfield, who was defended by the famous barrister Thomas Erskine, was acquitted NGRI. Erskine managed to add to the law on NGRI with a new focus on delusional thoughts. The new law indicated that insanity included, "A delusive image, the inseparable

[1] Rex refers to the King. In the United States this would be similar to the United States government prosecuting a case that falls under federal authority.

companion of real insanity, thrust upon the subjugated understanding, incapable of resistance because unconscious of attack."

Finally, the most noteworthy of the three cases with long-lasting implications was the criminal case of Daniel M'Naghten who was adjudicated NGRI for murdering a leader of the Tory party. After the NGRI finding, the Queen of England demanded changes to the insanity laws, indicating her strong distaste for the M'Naghten verdict. The committee, assembled by the Queen, developed this new standard: "To establish a defense on the ground of insanity, it must be clearly proved that at the time of the committing of the act, the party accused was laboring under such a defect of reason, from disease of the mind, as not to know the nature and quality of the act he was doing, or if he did know it, that he did not know he was doing what was wrong" (8 Eng. Rep. 718, 1843).

This trilogy of cases helped established insanity laws in the United States and most jurisdictions continue to rely on the so-called M'Naghten standard and its focus on knowledge of right and wrong. Notably, Georgia, in addition to relying on M'Naghten, has a delusional compulsion prong, with a clear origin in the Hatfield case.

Other case law originating in the United States have been instrumental in the shaping of how we contextualize insanity. As an illustrative example is the "Irresistible Impulse Test." Trumpeted by Isaac Ray, the eminent American psychiatrist, in his 1838 classic textbook titled: A *Treatise on the Medical Jurisprudence of Insanity*, was the notion of persons being "irresistibly impelled" to commit criminal acts. Similarly, Dr. Forbes Winslow in his 1843 publication *The Plea of Insanity in Criminal Cases* referred to persons being driven by an "irresistible impulse" to commit wrongful acts despite being able to distinguish between right and wrong. In 1887 in *Parsons v. State*, Alabama incorporated the concept of an irresistible impulse to the state's insanity statue, adding defining language to what is now referred to as the "Irresistible Impulse Test." Specifically, the Supreme Court of Alabama stated that a mentally ill defendant who had the capacity to distinguish right from wrong may nevertheless not be legally responsible:

> If, by reason of the duress of such mental disease, he had so far lost the power to choose between the right and wrong, and to avoid doing the act in question, as that his free agency was at the time destroyed, and if at the same time, the alleged crime was so connected with such mental disease, in the relation of cause and effect, as to have been the product of it solely.

The irresistible impulse test never gained momentum as a stand-alone test of insanity, but became a prong often integrated with cognitively based prongs of right and wrong to form comprehensive statutes of insanity.

The most widely accepted and adopted insanity definition was developed by the American Law Institute (ALI) in its published Model Penal Code in 1985. This definition from the ALI integrated both the cognitive prong of knowing right from wrong prominent in M'Naghten and a second prong of irresistible impulse. Both were predicated on the presence of a serious mental disease or defect that interfered with a defendant's functional capacities. The majority of states that maintain the insanity defense continue to rely on portions of the ALI, most prominently the cognitive prong. Notably, four states (Idaho, Kansas, Montana, and Utah) no longer have insanity statues on the books as a result of concern over misuse of the defense. These states' removal of the insanity defense has generated scholarship arguing it is a violation of due process (Morse and Bonnie 2013). Historically, the United States Supreme Court has refused to grant certiorari to determine the Constitutionality of a state to eliminate the ability of a defendant to proffer an insanity defense. However, in 2019, the Supreme Court agreed to hear the case of *Kansas v. Kahler*, which focuses on Kansas' defendants not having access to the insanity defense. This case will be seminal in deciding the future of the insanity defense across the United States.

The final area to be broached in this section is burden of proof. Prior to Hinckley, the federal government had the burden of proving sanity as part of their case in chief. After Hinckley, the burden of proof for the federal government changed such that defendants were presumed sane and the burden was placed on defendants to prove their insanity. According to 18 U.S. Code § 17, the insanity defense is an "affirmative defense to a prosecution under any Federal statute that, at the time of the commission of the acts constituting the offense, the defendant, as a result of a severe mental disease or defect, was unable to appreciate the nature and quality or the wrongfulness of his acts. Mental disease or defect does not otherwise constitute a defense." The Code stipulates that the defendant must prove they were insane by clear and convincing evidence. In *Clark v. Arizona* (2006), in a 5–4 decision the Supreme Court upheld the Constitutionality of placing the burden of proof on the defendant and ruled that the state of Arizona could continue to significantly limit testimony relevant to the insanity defense.

There is an abundance of case law on the insanity defense, most of which was not covered in this brief compendium of laws relevant to conducting insanity evaluations. Clinicians looking to gain further information on case law relevant to the insanity defense are advised to read some of the comprehensive works available on the topic (see Frederick et al. 2007). From this point forward, this chapter will focus on conducting insanity evaluations and the use of collateral information in forming well-reasoned and supported opinions. As will be developed in the next section, this involves integrating collateral information with interview data from multiple sources, including social media.

2.3 Conducting Insanity Evaluations

This section of the chapter will provide information regarding the clinical assessment of insanity. However, this section is designed to be relatively brief and is by no means a comprehensive "how to" in conducting these evaluations (see Packer 2009). Instead, this section will highlight the acquisition of information pertinent to developing an informed opinion of criminal responsibility. This section also sets the table for an in-depth discussion on using collateral information, with an emphasis on social media, in the evaluations of criminal responsibility. This basic outline will provide a template for information that is beneficial to collect when developing opinions on criminal responsibility.

As evaluators initiate insanity evaluations, their first duty is to have knowledge of the statute in their state and what they are being asked to evaluate. This specifically requires the forensic examiner to carefully consider the relevant insanity statute and generate questions to inform specific statutory requirements. For example, does the examiner need to consider only potential cognitive deficits (e.g., right vs. wrong) or must an inability to conform behavior also be considered (e.g., irresistible impulse)? A second a priori necessity is for the evaluator to have knowledge of specific variables relevant to the insanity defense. As an illustrative example, many states statutorily define mental illness. In the State of Georgia (O.G.C.A. 37–1-1 (12)), for example, mental illness is defined as a "Disorder of thought or mood which significantly impairs judgment, behavior, capacity to recognize reality, or ability to cope with the ordinary demands of life." Antisocial behavior and voluntary substance use are excluded. Many states have their own definitions of mental illness and some states provide no statutory definition. The evaluator must know the exact language of all relevant statues prior to evaluating a defendant for an insanity defense.

After acquiring the necessary a priori knowledge, the evaluator should begin the process of developing theories related to the defendant. Hypothesis development is foundational for proper criminal responsibility evaluations. Reviewing available discovery evidence provided by both the defense and prosecution enables the clinician to begin the initial data-driven process of determining a defendant's mental health or functioning at the time of the offense.

From that initial starting point, the next step in the insanity evaluation is data collection. Data collection is the *sine qua non* of insanity evaluations and involves clinical interviewing and a review of extant collateral data. The clinician should start by interviewing the defendant. As an important caveat, many jurisdictions will preclude use of the insanity defense if the defendant refuses to meet with court-ordered evaluators. Clinical interviews with the defendant to review history and information from around the time of the offense is essential; however, other interviews are often needed to obtain a complete picture of the defendant's functioning. Interviews from family members, treatment providers, roommates, witnesses, and at times, victims, often yield valuable information. Collection of collateral information will be reviewed in more detail in the next section of this chapter, but of particular import are records from mental health hospitalizations and substance abuse centers which can assist in determining if there is a nexus between mental illness and the criminal behavior. Such information helps place the behavior in question in a proper framework and provides a necessary historical context. For example, a middle-aged individual with no mental health hospitalizations may require different questions when compared to an individual with a documented history of psychosis and inpatient hospitalizations.

Once all relevant and available data is collected, the next step in the process is to analyze and interpret the data in the most objective way possible; however, this is highly dependent on the veracity of the data collected. Although the next section of this chapter will heavily focus on the review of data, as this can include data collected from social media accounts, the current section focuses on the evaluation of response styles (Rogers and Bender 2018) or the way(s) in which an examinee may respond to the interview. In the evaluation of criminal responsibility, malingering and defensiveness both warrant consideration. Malingering is defined by the Diagnostic and Statistical Manual of Mental Disorders, fifth Edition (American Psychiatric Association 2013) as "the intentional production of false or grossly exaggerated physical or psychological symptoms, motivated by external incentives such as avoiding military duty, avoiding work, obtaining financial compensation, evading criminal prosecution, or obtaining drugs" (p. 726). Evaluating response styles in malingering evaluations requires a nuanced approach and an awareness that defendants can utilize some sophisticated strategies to appear impaired. As outlined by Gottfried et al. 2016 individuals who feign in criminal responsibility evaluations typically rely on one of two primary strategies: general feigning and retrospective feigning.

General feigning is a strategy familiar to most clinicians, and involves an individual appearing highly impaired in many areas at present, and reporting similar difficulties, specifically having a significant mental disease or defect, at the time of the offense. This type of strategy is more straightforward, and a clinician can be assisted in their diagnosis by a host of general and specialized instruments. Instruments with embedded response style scales or instruments specially designed to detect feigning are both helpful in these situations. For instance, the imbedded validity scales on the Minnesota Multiphasic Personality Inventory-second Edition (MMPI-2; Butcher et al. 2001) or the Personality Assessment Inventory (PAI; Morey 1991) would be useful in detecting general malingering, as would specialized instruments designed to detect malingering like the Miller Forensic Assessment of Symptoms Test (M-FAST; Miller 2001) or the Structured Interview of Reported Symptons-second Edition (SIRS-2; Rogers et al. 2010). It is important to note that the MMPI-2, PAI, SIRS-2, and M-FAST have all demonstrated utility in detecting general malingering in the present. Some defendants engage in retrospective feigning; however, which refers to the endorsement of false or exaggerated past symptoms. Such examinees often present as generally asymptomatic in the present but report a bevy of symptoms when describing the time of the alleged offense.

As described by Gottfried et al. (2016), properly evaluating retrospective malingering can be complicated and requires a deeper dive into the person's symptoms at the time of the offense. Such an analysis is often more complicated by the current, asymptomatic clinical picture. In case example 2, we describe a case where an individual's alleged lack of capacity to use social media was part of a prior expert opinion related to both his competency to proceed to trial and criminal responsibility. Despite this prior opinion of another evaluator, two of the authors on this chapter discovered several uploaded YouTube videos of the defendant that he acknowledged filming and placing on the media site close in time to the alleged offenses. This data, while not dispositive of mental illness or sanity, was certainly useful in rebutting some claims of functional impairment. This exemplifies the potential utility of social media in supplying insights into one's overall level of functioning. Consider a worker's compensation case where an employee indicates a high level of disability resulting from a back injury related to a fall at work, but there are pictures on SNS showing him playing hockey and lifting weights. Although not as clear cut, social media evidence in criminal responsibility evaluations functions much the same way in that it points toward or away from mental impairment. To that end, social media can be a valuable source of information when considering malingering.

The final task for the clinician is to develop and form a clinical opinion related to insanity. This does not mean the clinician has to state their ultimate opinion in written form as this is an area of mental health practice that has remained contentious (Tillbrook et al. 2003; Rogers and Ewing 2003). However, the clinician must have obtained enough information to determine if the individual had the presence of a threshold condition (i.e., significant mental disease or defect) and if the presence of the disorder comported with applicable statutory definitions of insanity. The forensic examiner must carefully describe their evidence and its relationship to the psycho-legal question of criminal responsibility. Through a careful exploration of symptoms and legal standards, the examiner can provide evidence for their opinion. This is where social media can have an important impact and forensic examiners are encouraged to consider how social media can inform professional opinions on mental illness and insanity. Consider the initial example related to an individual posting increasingly bizarre anti-government posts on their SNS who is subsequently charged with a crime. Now consider the same charge absent the SNS postings, and whether that changes the equation for the clinician. For example, if there are several SNS posts with vacation pictures and no inkling of untoward attitudes toward the government, this may, at minimum, suggest alternative hypotheses other than mental illness for the alleged action.

2.4 Collateral Information in Insanity Evaluations

Collateral information is critical to the appropriate determination of criminal responsibility opinions (Packer 2009; Rogers and Shuman 2005). In evaluating collateral information in criminal responsibility, extant scholarship has addressed what areas should be considered. For example, Knoll and Resnick (2008) outlined several inquiries that should be made regarding a defendant's history as part of a comprehensive criminal responsibility evaluation. Their recommendations include records related to developmental history, academic performance, previous employment, military service, disability compensation, medical issues, mental health and treatment history, previous forensic evaluations, drug use and abuse history, and criminal history. Although the examiner should inquire about this information during interview with the defendant, collateral information is imperative to verify this information. For example, educational records are critical (though not always enough) to determining the presence of an intellectual disability. Interviews with family members and others familiar with the defendant often provide indispensable context to a defendant's history. As a caveat regarding criminal history, the evaluator must be careful not to report undetected crimes that defendants may divulge during interview, as our responsibility is to conduct an evaluation of criminal responsibility, not to serve as a criminal investigator for unsolved crimes.

In addition to history, the evaluator in criminal responsibility evaluations should obtain from the defendant their account of the alleged criminal behaviors. This involves asking the defendant to describe not only the events of the alleged offense, but also the events preceding and following the alleged behaviors. In addition to behaviors, the evaluator must attempt to ascertain the thoughts and feelings the defendant was experiencing during and around the time of the alleged offenses. Interviewing the defendant regarding these issues is the cornerstone of a criminal responsibility evaluation, but it is not enough as defendants may not provide an entirely accurate or complete account of events. There are several reasons for this potential lack of saliency, including but not limited to purposeful misleading to appear impaired, defensive responding, lack of memory as a result of intoxication or time passed since the alleged criminal act, or severe psychosis leading to misinterpretation of events. To that end, speaking to witnesses and reviewing discovery is often clarifying. Witnesses can provide critical information concerning a defendant's mental state at the time of the alleged events which can carry significant weight in proceedings. Green and Follingstad (2009) found mock juries valued third-party information over previous mental health records in rendering a verdict on criminal responsibility. Speaking to victims can also provide pertinent information regarding a defendant's mental state at the time of the offense; however, there are risks that must be thoughtfully considered prior to contacting a victim. For example, it is possible that speaking about the offense would lead to feeling revictimized or increasing trauma. Additionally, some attorneys may object to having victims interviewed and prefer evaluators use the official statements provided in discovery. Finally, a review of previous forensic evaluations may offer comparisons and contrasts to the current situation and can be useful in differentiating a bona fide from a feigned presentation. For instance, a defendant who is charged with Robbery reports that, at the time of the offense, he believed that he was wealthy and owned the bank he is charged with robbing and so was attempting to obtain his own funds. Prior forensic evaluations may substantiate or call this account into question if, for example, they reveal similar past behavior attributed to bona fide mental illness, or instead, indicate the defendant was previously malingering.

2.4.1 Social Media as Collateral Data in Criminal Responsibility Evaluations

This section of the chapter will provide information on the use of social media in developing opinions on criminal responsibility. In evaluations of criminal responsibility, social media is another form of collateral data. As such, its reliability should be highly scrutinized, while recognizing its potential import on informing opinions of criminal responsibility. For example, posts on social media platforms, whether they be on Twitter, YouTube, Facebook, Instagram, or elsewhere can provide a glimpse into the functioning and behavior of the individual at specific timepoints. Given the retrospective nature of criminal responsibility evaluations these snapshots in time can provide useful information. Consider recent trends of using social media to live stream; if a defendant was streaming during or near the time of the alleged offense, the video may be useful in evaluating an individual's ability to differentiate right from wrong or other insanity prongs; this is no different than reviewing Bodycam or Dashcam footage from police officers (Vitacco et al. 2018).

As will be described in both case examples below, social media can speak both indirectly and directly to criminal responsibility. For example, in one case, the defendant sent an instant message saying he needed to leave the area because of an incident. He was later implicated in a murder on the day he sent the message. Likewise, in the second case, the SNS information was related to a threshold condition (e.g., intellectual disability), but not directly related to criminal responsibility. Like all collateral information, specifically linking the collateral data and drawing inferences is the responsibility of the evaluator conducting criminal responsibility evaluation.

Despite the potential utility of social media in criminal responsibility evaluations, one of the important issues that forensic evaluators need to consider is the perception of credibility. Batastini and Vitacco (2019) sampled both forensic examiners and jury-eligible participants and found that SNS data is viewed as less credible than similar information reported by the defendant and located in medical records. Forensic examiners should be aware of how the credibility of their data may be perceived as they support their opinions of criminal responsibility. These findings suggest that evaluators should continue to go beyond social media to support their clinical opinions on insanity and social media should only be one small part of any criminal responsibility evaluation.

2.4.2 Ethical-Related Issues

Using social media in any forensic evaluation as a collateral source of information brings unique ethical challenges. This is especially true with regards to criminal responsibility as the evaluator may go back to find social media posted in close proximity to the time of the alleged offense. One challenging area is verifying that the posts were made by the defendant and that the posts have not been edited in any manner. Certainly, hacking or someone else writing SNS posts is a real possibility and could problematically lead the forensic evaluator astray. Consider the possibility that, after a defendant is arrested, someone with knowledge of the defendant's SNS accounts makes posts to make it appear the individual is mentally ill. Or, conversely, once arrested, someone removes bizarre postings from a defendant's SNS feed, making it appear an individual is less psychotic. Both are possibilities that must be considered when evaluating social media as a source of collateral information in a forensic context. If the individual who created the social media post cannot be independently verified, the evaluator is at-risk for using information that could undercut their opinion.

Explicit ethical guidelines have not been developed yet to deal with the use of social media in criminal responsibility evaluations. However, the Ethics Guidelines for the Practice of Forensic Psychiatry (American Academy of Psychiatry and the Law 2005) and the Specialty Guidelines for Forensic Psychology (American Psychological Association 2013) both require clear description of the use of collateral data which would include social media if used by the evaluator. As noted by Vitacco et al. (2018), evaluators must also carefully weigh the information they obtain from social media and make sure it has relevance to criminal responsibility. Likewise, it is important to exclude information from a report if it is irrelevant and/or prejudicial. For example, unless the relevance is clear, information about religious or political affiliations and practices, sexual orientation, and other similar personal information should not be included in criminal responsibility reports. The use of such information can serve as a red herring and distract the trier of fact. Perhaps more than any other collateral source, SNS are overloaded with information (e.g., personal interests, opinions, social connections); most of which is likely to be irrelevant to the issue of criminal responsibility. While care must still be taken when sifting through such data provided in discovery, it can be an even steeper, more slippery slope when evaluators go searching for themselves. Evaluators have a responsibility to stay focused on the psycho-legal question at hand, and should disregard data that is clearly immaterial.

A final consideration revolves around preserving potential data from social media platforms. For example, if in the course of their work the examiner comes across information from SNS that speaks directly or indirectly to the relevant psycho-legal issue, steps should be taken to make sure the data is saved in its original form to be used for later. If the examiner used such data in a criminal responsibility report, it is our contention the evaluator should find a way to preserve the data for their record and to support their use of such data. A more detailed discussion of other ethical considerations and recommendations for the use of social media in forensic mental health assessment generally is presented in Chap. 9 of this volume.

2.5 Conclusions

Insanity evaluations, due to the examiner needing to retrospectively evaluate a defendant's mental state, are intrinsically complicated. Using collateral information is essential to conduct a proper criminal responsibility evaluation. A burgeoning area of research is how to integrate social media into forensic evaluations, including those dealing with criminal responsibility. This chapter provides an outline of how to appropriately consider social media in forming opinions on criminal responsibility. When conducting these evaluations, such data can speak both directly and indirectly to constructs of relevance. Evaluators must be cognizant of distinct ethical issues that accompany the use of social media in criminal responsibility evaluations and take time to ensure its relevance. Over the next several years, forensic evaluators can expect the development of more formalized guidelines and training for integrating this type of data in specific forensic contexts, including criminal responsibility evaluations.

Case Profile 1

Type of Evaluation

Criminal Responsibility

Case Context

The defendant in this case, 35-year-old Mr. John Scott, was evaluated for approximately three hours in response to a Superior Court Order requesting an independent evaluation of his criminal responsibility at the time of the offense. He was charged with Murder in the shooting death of his uncle. Mr. Scott was evaluated in a private room at the local jail.

Sources of Information

1. A clinical interview with Mr. Scott
2. The following psychological tests administered to Mr. Scott:
    a. *Wechsler Abbreviated Scale of Intelligence—Second Edition* (WASI-II)
    b. *Wechsler Individual Achievement Test—Second Edition, Abbreviated* (WIAT-II)
    c. *Personality Assessment Inventory* (PAI)
    d. *Miller Forensic Assessment of Symptoms Test* (M-FAST)
3. Mental Status Evaluation
4. Georgia Bureau of Investigation Records
5. Detention Center Records
6. Mr. Scott's Criminal History
7. Records of SMS Messages sent via email
8. Records from the County Sheriff's Office
9. Records from Behavioral Health
10. Records from the Medical College
11. County School District Records
12. State Hospital Records
13. Screenshots of Facebook posts
14. Copy of Facebook messages

Relevant Background

Mr. Scott was born in Georgia and was raised by his biological parents along with his two sisters. He described his childhood as abusive and elaborated to explain he "received a lot of beatings with switching cords…irons." He lived with a family member for a couple of years as an adolescent, but ultimately returned home with his parents. He indicated having a diagnosis of Bipolar Disorder and some trauma from the "beatings." He said, "I was hearing voices real bad." Mr. Scott was unaware of any developmental delays he had as a child.

Mr. Scott attended public schools growing up, but according to school records, he received special education services for both educational and behavioral problems. He described intentionally setting a trashcan on fire in the backyard when he was in kindergarten and estimated getting into his first physical fight in the first grade. Mr. Scott was expelled in fifth grade for physically fighting his teachers. He also needed to repeat several grades as a result of academic difficulties. He left school in the tenth grade after being arrested for assaulting a teacher.

Mr. Scott supported himself primarily through Supplemental Security Income (SSI). As an adult, he worked odd jobs such as lawn work, or working in various clubs. He denied having any history of military involvement. Mr. Scott was never married and had been in one serious relationship in his life.

Mr. Scott had been psychiatrically hospitalized numerous times throughout his life beginning at the age of nine. His longest hospitalization occurred at a state hospital when he was 10 years old for being a danger to self and others. Reportedly, he made threats to kill his parents and then himself. A year later he was hospitalized again at a state hospital for headbanging and making additional threats to hurt himself. As a teenager, Mr. Scott was admitted to the Medical School Mental Health Unit for an evaluation due to "hearing voices." He was discharged after two days when it was determined that Mr. Scott was not having mental health symptoms. One year later Mr. Scott underwent another mental health evaluation after he complained about mood swings and was being argumentative with people. He was prescribed Depakote (for mood regulation) and asked to follow-up with outpatient treatment. Follow-up treatment, as noted by records, was sporadic. While incarcerated, Mr. Scott was being prescribed Depakote and Risperdal; the Depakote was being used to stabilize his mood and Risperdal was prescribed to help reduce the frequency of auditory hallucinations.

Regarding medical history, Mr. Scott had some heart issues that required surgery when he was three years of age. He described one instance of being intoxicated and breaking his wrist after he fell off the hood of a moving vehicle. He denied ever having a serious head injury or any other serious medical conditions.

Mr. Scott first consumed alcohol at the age of 18 and subsequently drank alcohol every weekend. He described himself as "not a big drinker" but admitted to having one conviction for Driving under the Influence (DUI) at the age of 19. Mr. Scott reported using marijuana for the first time at the age of 15 and continuing to smoke marijuana on a daily basis until he was incarcerated. He described smoking the same amount of marijuana every day, not experiencing symptoms of withdrawal, and never being told by family or friends he needed to stop smoking marijuana. He denied using all other illicit substances and denied ever participating in substance abuse treatment.

Behavioral Observations and Mental Status

Mr. Scott was dressed in standard-issued jail attire. His grooming and hygiene were adequate. He made an effort to appear cooperative; however, his responses were indicative of embellished and disingenuous experiences. He also put forth minimal effort in completing testing. Rapport was easily established and maintained throughout this evaluation. Mr. Scott made appropriate eye contact and his psychomotor movements were within normal limits (e.g., not excessive or restricted in any way). He spoke in a clear, audible voice that was easy to understand. He was oriented to person, place, time, date, and situation.

Mr. Scott described his mood as "pretty stable…pretty good mood." His affect (i.e., outward expression of emotion) was appropriate and consistent with the topics discussed. He denied symptoms of depression, mania, and anxiety at the time of the evaluation. Mr. Scott further denied experiencing suicidal and homicidal ideations. He described his appetite as "very hungry," which he attributed to his current regimen of psychiatric medications, as well as the portions and quality of the food he was receiving in jail. He denied changes to his energy level, describing it as "pretty average." He reported difficulty sleeping at night; which was likely due to frequent naps during the day.

Mr. Scott's thinking appeared logical and on-topic based on his coherent, relevant, and straightforward responses. However, he described instances in which his thoughts do not always make sense. He provided an example by explaining, "Sometimes it might be Friday and my thoughts say its Monday." He also noted he frequently does not think before he acts, which he attributed to these nonsensical thought patterns. Mr. Scott endorsed experiencing auditory hallucinations, estimating that they occur approximately once every week. He described hearing voices telling him "to do things." Although he noted the voices are "hard to ignore," he explained "I just don't listen and not do what they want." Mr. Scott also stated, "If I'm in a bad mood, the voices egg it [his bad mood] on." He did not appear to be responding to internal stimuli at any point during the evaluation. Mr. Scott did not endorse any overtly delusional beliefs but reported feeling paranoid both in jail and the community. For example, he described being in a store and a woman following him into different aisles, which he interpreted as the woman "probably there to set me up for something bad."

Mr. Scott's fund of general knowledge was adequate. Based on a series of immediate and delayed recall tasks, his immediate memory was intact, but delayed memory was slightly impaired. Mr. Scott demonstrated good abstract reasoning abilities, as he was able to accurately interpret the meaning of a common proverb, as well as identify similarities between word-pairings. Based on behavioral observations and his responses to mental status questions, there were no remarkable indications suggestive of mental illness.

Summary of Test Results

The *Wechsler Abbreviated Scale of Intelligence, Second Edition* (WASI-II) is an individually administered screening measure to assess intellectual functioning. Mr. Scott obtained a Full-Scale Intelligence Quotient (FSIQ) score of 63, which placed him in the first percentile, meaning 1% of peers his age would obtain an FSIQ score of 63 or lower. Based on this score alone, Mr. Scott is in the *extremely low* range of intellectual functioning. Mr. Scott's scores on the Verbal Comprehension Index and Perceptual Reasoning Index within the WASI-II were consistent with his FSIQ score, both falling within the *extremely low* range (scores of 67 and 63, respectively).

The *Wechsler Individual Achievement Test, Second Edition, Abbreviated* (WIAT-II) is an individually administered screening measure of academic achievement. Mr. Scott's overall composite score on this measure was 64, which is in the first percentile and falls within the *extremely low* range. Subtest scores on the WIAT-II were similar, with his score of 53 on the Word Reading subtest also falling in the *extremely low* range (age-equivalent = 10-years-old) and his score of 75 on the Numerical Operations falling in the *borderline* range (age equivalent = 11 years, 4 months). Lastly, Mr. Scott earned a score of 60 on the Spelling section (i.e., a task requiring the examinee to spell several words that are read aloud by the evaluator).

Mr. Scott's profile on the *Personality Assessment Inventory* (PAI), a 344-item assessment of an individual's personality and clinical symptomatology, was considered invalid. Specifically, Mr. Scott responded in a markedly inconsistent manner and attempted to present himself with unusual psychological symptoms and ailments that are extremely bizarre and unlikely. The extent of these distortions was significant enough that the other clinical scales measured on the PAI could not reliably be interpreted.

Given these indications of exaggerated responding, Mr. Scott was also administered the *Miller Forensic Assessment of Symptoms Test* (M-FAST). The M-FAST screens for a variety of intentionally disingenuous responses styles, such as endorsing unusual combinations of symptoms, reporting atypically severe and pervasive symptoms, and endorsing uncommon psychotic symptoms. Mr. Scott's total score on the M-FAST was 10. A Total Score of 10 is higher than the suggested cut-off score of 6, suggesting Mr. Scott was making an effort to feign symptoms of mental illness. Specifically, Mr. Scott endorsed experiencing extreme symptoms of mental illness that are very unlikely to occur even among psychiatric populations and reported experiencing combinations of symptoms that do not actually occur together in the context of genuine mental illness. Mr. Scott also described a progression of symptoms that was inconsistent with the course of a genuine mental illness.

Diagnostic Conclusions

Based on all available data, it was determined that Mr. Scott met criteria for the following diagnoses:

- Malingering (primary diagnosis)
- Schizoaffective Disorder (by history)
- Antisocial Personality Disorder
- Borderline Intellectual Functioning
- Cannabis Use Disorder, Mild, In a Controlled Environment

Summary of Data Relevant to Psycho-Legal Question

Records from the Sheriff's Office At approximately 7:08 P.M. the County Sheriff's Office received a call regarding a suspicious vehicle in a wooded area that was determined to belong to Mr. Alexander Ladd. Mr. Ladd could not be located at this time. There appeared to be smear marks all down both the driver and passenger side of the vehicle, suggesting someone had wiped the car down. No identifiable fingerprints were recovered from the vehicle and no signs of a struggle were apparent. In the vehicle, investigators found an address for Mr. Scott, who was determined to be the nephew of Mr. Ladd. When investigators went to interview Mr. Scott, he answered the door drinking a beer and said he had not seen his uncle in several years and that he did not have any information about his uncle or his uncle's whereabouts.

A friend of Mr. Scott, Mr. Johnson, contacted the County Sheriff's Office and told investigators that Mr. Scott sent a message to him on Facebook "that he had killed someone and he was going away for a while." Mr. Johnson logged into his Facebook account for investigators, who documented a message stating, "I killed a man and the law is looking for me." Mr. Scott then wrote that he loved Mr. Johnson and will miss him when he "goes away." Investigators also printed Mr. Scott's Facebook posts for the seven days prior to the alleged offense. Posts suggested Mr. Scott was occupying his time playing video games and meeting friends. Later that day, investigators located Mr. Scott and he was taken into custody without incident.

Upon entering Mr. Scott's home, investigators saw blood stains on the walls and carpet, and a piece of bloody carpet was found in a trash can. When being taken into custody, Mr. Scott reportedly made the statement, "This is about the Murder," and when officers did not respond, he stated, "Come on man, is this about the missing body?" At the Sheriff's Office, Mr. Scott was read his Miranda rights and signed a form expressing his understanding. Upon questioning, he initially denied knowing why he was at the Sheriff's Office, but then smiled and said, "he was messing around and knew he was there about the Murder." Mr. Scott told investigators his uncle stopped by asking about some money he owed. An argument ensued.

Mr. Scott said he then heard voices saying his uncle was there to hurt him and he acted on those voices.

Mr. Scott's Account of the Alleged Offenses During the Evaluation Mr. Scott provided an account of his mental state before, during, and after the alleged offenses. Prior to the alleged offenses, Mr. Scott was living alone and estimated consuming one gram of marijuana and drinking about 18 to 30 beers on a daily basis. He reported meeting with a psychologist once every month to work on anger issues and stated that he was prescribed Depakote and Saphris but ran out of both medications approximately one month before the alleged offenses. He endorsed auditory hallucinations "daily…every waking minute of the day" that would say "random stuff." On the day of the alleged offense, Mr. Scott woke up feeling intoxicated from the alcohol he drank the night before. He went online and saw that he received a message from his uncle, Mr. Ladd, who stated he was coming over to Mr. Scott's house to collect money. Mr. Scott knew his uncle may be upset with him because he did not have the money.

Mr. Scott recalled telling Mr. Ladd to get out of the house and that he was never getting paid. An aggressive verbal fight ensued. Mr. Scott described being scared due to childhood sexually traumatic events involving a peer and stated that he "couldn't think" due to being intoxicated on marijuana and alcohol. During the confrontation, Mr. Scott grabbed a gun and fired it toward Mr. Ladd but was unsure of how many times he discharged the weapon. The next thing he remembers was seeing his uncle dying in front of him. He then moved his uncle's car to the backyard and dragged his body into the trunk of the car. He then drove away, took money out of his uncle's wallet, and threw the body in a shallow creek several miles from his house. He wiped down the car to "get the moss off" and then ran back home. He explained feeling scared because, "I killed a man. I knew it wasn't right." Mr. Scott confirmed sending Mr. Johnson a message through Facebook telling him he killed a man and was likely going to prison. He said voices told him to send that message.

Clinical Forensic Opinion

While Mr. Scott has a history of mental illness, specifically Schizoaffective Disorder, his disingenuous presentation during this evaluation made it difficult to determine whether he genuinely suffered from symptoms of this disorder or not. However, even if Mr. Scott genuinely experienced Schizoaffective Disorder at the time of the offenses, there was no evidence to suggest his sense of reality or his behaviors were impaired at that time based upon his account of events. Based on interviews and review of Mr. Scott's social media, he was not significantly impaired by a mental illness at or around the time of the alleged offense. Mr. Scott's descriptions of the alleged offense and his behaviors before and after the alleged offense suggest he was aware it was wrong to kill another human being. He explained knowing it was wrong because "people get in trouble," "go to jail," and he messaged his neighbor that he would be "going away" for killing someone. Other actions, such as denying any involvement in the crime when first interviewed by the police, dumping the body in a creek, abandoning the car, and wiping the car's surfaces suggest he was attempting to avoid apprehension and detection for a wrongdoing. Given the totality of the evidence, it was opined that Mr. Scott *was* able to distinguish right from wrong at the time of the alleged offense and, therefore, could be held criminally responsible.

Recommendations

No specific recommendations were offered as part of this evaluation.

How Did Social Media Impact This Case?

Social media was brought into this case initially when a friend of the defendant contacted the police to inform them about the presence of a private message that was allegedly sent to him by the defendant implicating the defendant in a crime. The information provided through the defendant's social media account was able to be linked to the day and approximate time of the alleged offense. In doing this, the message had direct implications for ascertaining if Mr. Scott had the capability to determine if his behavior was wrong. This message indicated that on a cognitive level, Mr. Scott was aware he could be "going away" for murder. Likewise, previous postings on Mr. Scott's Facebook page indicated someone who was relatively organized and active in the community with peers.

Case Profile 2

Type of Evaluation

Criminal Responsibility

Case Context

The defendant in this case, 29-year-old Mr. Charles Mills, was evaluated for approximately three hours in response to a Superior Court Order requesting an independent evaluation of his criminal responsibility at the time of the alleged offenses.

He was charged with Armed Robbery, Aggravated Assault and Murder after he allegedly robbed a retail store and assaulted and fatally shot the store clerk.

Sources of Information

1. A clinical interview with Mills
2. Mental Status Evaluation
3. Results of the *Miller Forensic Assessment of Symptoms Test* (M-FAST)
4. Georgia Bureau of Investigation Records
5. Mr. Mills' Criminal History
6. Detention Center Records
7. Records from the County Sheriff's Office
8. Mental Health records from a psychiatric hospital and outpatient provider
9. Four prior forensic evaluations
10. County School District Records
11. Review of defendant's YouTube, Facebook and Instagram Accounts including:
    a. 6 YouTube videos
    b. 2 Facebook accounts
    c. 3 Instagram accounts

Relevant Background

Mr. Mills was born in Florida and was raised primarily by his biological mother. His biological father was involved sporadically throughout his life. Mr. Mills was temporarily placed in foster care on three to four occasions during his childhood due to verbal and physical abuse by his mother. He moved to Georgia shortly before his current incarceration to live near an ex-girlfriend and her children. He reported that he does not have any biological children but assisted in the upbringing of his ex-girlfriend's children and considered them to be his own.

Mr. Mills reported considerable behavioral difficulties throughout his childhood. School records showed that he was placed in an Emotionally Handicapped program for behavioral problems in elementary school (e.g., crying outbursts, aggression, hyperactivity). He was diagnosed with Attention Deficit Hyperactivity Disorder (ADHD) in elementary school and was treated with Ritalin and later Adderall. Mr. Mills continued to receive a variety of services throughout school (e.g., placement in separate classrooms and educational programs, time to cool-down as needed, use of Individual Education Plans [IEP's], etc.), but records suggest that the majority of interventions were not effective. Mr. Mills fell behind in math and reading due to significant disruption in his education caused by his behaviors such as missing time from class due to suspensions. He eventually graduated from high school, although commented that he was "surprised" he did so considering his ongoing behavior problems.

Mr. Mills' work history was sporadic and types of employment ranged from construction to fast food. He was last employed several months prior to his incarceration. He never received social security benefits and did not have a military history.

Regarding medical history, Mr. Mills reported being stabbed in the head seven or eight years prior to the current evaluation. He stated that he received staples to treat his head wound and experienced minor memory problems shortly after the incident. He also noted one incident when he punched out a car window and claimed that he subsequently woke up in a hospital. He denied any lasting impacts from either incident.

Mr. Mills reported that he first drank alcohol at nineteen years of age and subsequently drank once every other month. He stated that, outside of periods of confinement, he used several drugs regularly including marijuana, cocaine, and Ecstasy. He began using these substances between seventeen and nineteen years of age and continued to use marijuana up until his current incarceration, including on the day of the alleged offenses. Mr. Mills denied use or abuse of any other substances. He also denied ever receiving substance use treatment but noted that he once had his stomach pumped for alcohol poisoning. He endorsed a history of two convictions for possession of marijuana and one conviction for possession of cocaine.

Mr. Mills had an extensive criminal history dating back to his juvenile years, with records reflecting more than 20 charges. These charges included various drug-related charges, possession of weapons, Robbery, Assault, and Armed Robbery. He was convicted or plead guilty to the majority of these charges. In 2017, Mr. Mills was opined incompetent to stand trial on two counts of Armed Robbery. Two evaluations were completed at that time, with one evaluator opining that psychosis impaired his competency abilities while another opined him incompetent due to an Intellectual Disability. After treatment in a psychiatric facility, a third evaluator opined that Mr. Mills was restored to competency. The competency finding was contested and the court ordered the original evaluator to provide an updated evaluation. Without reevaluating Mr. Mills, the original evaluator opined that Mr. Mills was incompetent to stand trial due to an Intellectual Disability and not restorable. The court concurred with this opinion and Mr. Mills was released to the community with outpatient mental health treatment, after which he moved to Georgia without notifying authorities in Florida.

Behavioral Observations and Mental Status

Mr. Mills was dressed in standard correctional attire and was handcuffed at the wrists. His hygiene and grooming were adequate. He was cooperative throughout the interview; however, during the competency portion of the interview, he became notably less engaged. When asked about the change in his presentation, he expressed fatigue with the evaluation and reported having a headache. The evaluators offered to return on another day to complete the evaluation, but Mr. Mills agreed to proceed. He demonstrated improved effort following that interaction. During the course of the interview, he took two breaks which lasted approximately five minutes each. Mr. Mills clearly communicated to the evaluators and appeared to understand the communication of the evaluators. He spoke at an appropriate pace and volume and there was no apparent disturbance in his thought processes. His affect was primarily flat, although generally congruent to the topics discussed. Mills did not at any point in the evaluation appear to be responding to internal stimuli.

Mr. Mills described his current mood was "aggravated," and that he experienced periods of aggravation every few days. He described this aggravation as tenseness in his body that did not "mess with (him) emotionally." Mr. Mills endorsed intermittent insomnia but stated that his energy was good. He denied any disturbance in his appetite, although reported that he has never had a large appetite. He denied any other mood symptoms, including thoughts of self-harm.

During the interview, Mr. Mills spontaneously endorsed auditory hallucinations. Specifically, when discussing his job history that involved an altercation with a coworker, he stated that he thought the coworker was "coming at me with a hammer." Mr. Mills was asked why he thought that, and he laughed and replied, "John said." He then described that he hears a male voice whom he calls "John" and stated that "John," watches over him and helps him, such as telling him to watch everyone. Mr. Mills provided the example that he was involved in an altercation with another inmate two days prior to the evaluation because the voice informed him that the other inmate was going to attack him. Mr. Mills reported that he hears one male voice and stated that the voice does not ever instruct him to hurt others. At a different period in the interview, however, he stated that he hears "voices all day every day." He stated that his medications have variable efficacy in treating the auditory hallucinations. Regarding any other symptoms of psychosis, Mr. Mills described some paranoia which he related to what "John" tells him but denied any other symptoms such as visual hallucinations.

Given Mr. Mills' report of frequent auditory hallucinations, he was asked to notify the examiners if he was actively experiencing a hallucination during the evaluation. He was also specifically queried on two occasions if he had experienced any hallucinations during the interview. On one occasion after providing an interpretation of a common parable, Mr. Mills commented that "John" told him another answer. He was asked if "John's" answer was the same as his own answer and was asked to tell the evaluators what "John" said. He commented that "John's" answer was "not the same," but circumvented the question regarding what specifically he heard. He was prompted to answer the question multiple times and eventually provided the evaluators with the same response he previously had with minor variation in wording. He did not provide any other examples of auditory hallucinations which he reportedly heard during the evaluation.

Mr. Mills was screened for other symptoms including anxiety and trauma-related symptoms. He reported that the voice he hears makes him to "think the worst," but he denied any other issues.

Lastly, given Mr. Mills' prior diagnosis of an intellectual disability, the evaluators screened Mr. Mills for deficits in his adaptive functioning. He reported that he was capable of budgeting money for purchases, although never learned how to pay bills. He stated that he never needed to learn such skills because he always lived with someone. Mr. Mills was asked why he always lived with someone and he reported feeling "afraid" to live alone and commented that he used to "see things" when he was "ten or eleven" years old such as "red eyes" which would be "gone when the light on." He also stated that he watched "too many scary movies." Mr. Mills denied experiencing any problems attending to other tasks of daily living such as personal hygiene, which was consistent with the evaluators' observations and jail records. Throughout the course of the interview, Mr. Mills used adequate vocabulary and did not appear to have any difficulty understanding the communication of the evaluators. For example, he did not ask the evaluators to use simpler language or explain any concepts to him. Further, he spontaneously used various terms such as "double jeopardy" of which he demonstrated a good understanding.

Summary of Test Results

Given concerns regarding potential feigning, Mr. Mills was also administered the *Miller Forensic Assessment of Symptoms Test* (M-FAST). The M-FAST screens for a variety of intentionally disingenuous response styles, such as endorsing unusual combinations of symptoms, reporting atypically severe and pervasive symptoms, and endorsing uncommon psychotic symptoms. Mr. Mills was somewhat fatigued when he began the M-FAST and reported that he had a headache. Although he expressed a desire for the interview to be over, he agreed to continue with the evaluation rather than the evaluators returning on another day. Mr. Mills' score of 5 on the M-FAST was below the suggested cut-off score of 6 and so was not indicative of feigning.

Diagnostic Conclusions

Based on all available data, it was determined that Mr. Mills met criteria for the following diagnosis:

- Antisocial Personality Disorder

Summary of Data Relevant to Psycho-Legal Question

Records and Interview Video from the Sheriff's Office Police responded to a report of an armed robbery at a retail store and found a deceased female victim, later identified as the store clerk, with a gunshot wound to her abdomen. The register was noted to be open and empty. Surveillance video showed Mr. Mills entering the store around the time of the alleged offenses and witnesses reported that Mr. Mills had a bag of money later that evening. Evidence, including blood spatter analysis, wounds and other markings found on the victim, and analysis of the trajectory of the bullet, indicated that the victim had been bludgeoned on the head prior to her death and was kneeling on the floor when she was shot at point-blank range.

During interview with investigators, Mr. Mills at first declined to discuss the alleged offenses. He demonstrated caution when answering questions and directly stated to investigators on multiple occasions that he could not answer certain questions because the information could be incriminating and everything could be used against him. Mr. Mills admitted to being at the store but denied any wrongdoing. Later in the interview, he admitted to shooting the victim, although reported that the gun accidentally fired. He stated that his plan was to rob the store and he had no intention to shoot the victim, but as he was waving the gun around in front of the victim, it accidentally fired. He reported that he thought the gun was on safety. He expressed remorse about the incident and became tearful when talking about the likelihood that he would spend the rest of his life in prison for his actions. Investigators confronted him about the evidence suggesting that the victim was shot at point-blank range while kneeling and that she had been struck in the head; however, Mr. Mills denied any such actions.

Mr. Mills' Account of the Alleged Offenses During the Evaluation Mr. Mills reported he could not remember much of the details of the alleged offenses. He stated that he intended to rob the store clerk and while demanding money from her, the gun accidentally fired. He denied purposefully assaulting the store clerk or shooting her at close range. He reported that after taking the money, he called a friend to pick him up and he left the scene. He stated he was hearing the voice of "John" around the time of the alleged offenses which he described as making him feel generally paranoid. He did not, however, endorse feeling afraid of the store clerk at any point. He further did not endorse any command hallucinations or other symptoms at the time of the alleged offenses. Mr. Mills reported he had smoked marijuana earlier in the day of the alleged offenses but denied being under the influence at the time of the incident.

Clinical Forensic Opinion

Although Mr. Mills was previously diagnosed with Intellectual Disability and Schizoaffective Disorder, it was the opinion of the evaluators that Mr. Mills did not meet criteria for either of these disorders. Indeed, the only diagnosis rendered by the evaluators was Antisocial Personality Disorder. The evaluators did not observe any indications of an Intellectual Disability including impairments in intellectual functioning (e.g., deficits in vocabulary, understanding, processing speed) or adaptive functioning, nor did records reveal any such issues. Mr. Mills denied involvement in the alleged offenses, although he reported that he was hearing the voice of "John" at that time, he did not in any way relate the voice to the alleged offenses. Further, his current report of auditory hallucinations was questionable, and not consistent with records (i.e., he had never reported hearing "John" before the evaluation). Additionally, even if Mr. Mills were experiencing similar symptoms at the time of the alleged offenses, there is no indication that these symptoms would have precluded his ability to distinguish right from wrong. Rather, available information suggested that Mr. Mills fled the scene, hid the money at a friend's house, gave the weapon to another individual to hide, and lied to investigators about his involvement on multiple occasions. All of these behaviors suggested that he was attempting to conceal his involvement in the alleged offenses and thus understood his actions to be wrong. Social media revealed that Mr. Mills was previously in possession of a weapon illegally given his videos showing him in possession of a gun while he was on probation and also revealed that that he had a history of gang involvement. This suggested that Mr. Mills' behaviors at the time of the alleged offenses were not limited in scope to that one incident and motivated by mental illness at that time, but rather had been ongoing for several years. This is further corroborated by Mr. Mills' lengthy criminal record, including previous charges and convictions for similar crimes such as Robbery, assault charges incurred during a robbery, and Armed Robbery. These prior arrests should have also facilitated Mr. Mills' understanding of the legal wrongfulness of his actions at the time of the alleged offenses given that he had been convicted of similar charges in the past (i.e., knowing that he could be arrested for Armed Robbery). In sum, there was no indication that Mr. Mills could not distinguish between right and wrong at the time of the alleged offenses. Rather, the available information suggested that he *was* able to distinguish right from wrong at the time of the alleged offenses and, therefore, can be held criminally responsible.

Recommendations

No specific recommendations were offered as part of this evaluation.

How Did Social Media Impact This Case?

Social media was brought into this case from a prior evaluation during which Mr. Mills reportedly noted a variety of adaptive functioning deficits. The prior evaluation indicated that Mr. Mills could use the Internet for basic tasks such as viewing Facebook but was so impaired because of his intellectual deficits that he was not capable of more complex tasks. The evaluators conducted a search for Mr. Mills and discovered that he had his own YouTube channel where had uploaded multiple videos. The videos were primarily of him rapping, some of which were reportedly raps that he wrote himself. Further search revealed that Mr. Mills had multiple Facebook and Instagram accounts which he updated with various posts and used appropriate language. This was in stark contrast to the description of him in his prior evaluation as being unable to perform anything but very basic daily tasks and having considerably impaired intellectual functioning. Additionally, Mr. Mills was depicted holding a gun in several videos and the content of his raps primarily focused on criminal activity such as shooting and robbery. At the time when the videos were posted, Mr. Mills would have been on probation and prohibited from possessing a weapon. He frequently flashed gang symbols in the videos and talked about being a "soldier" in a gang. Thus, the content of the videos suggested a history of interest and engagement in risky behaviors, again rather than Mr. Mills' behaviors at the time of the alleged offenses being limited to that instance and attributable to a mental illness.

References

American Academy of Psychiatry and the Law. (2005). Ethics guidelines for the practice of forensic psychiatry. Retrieved from http://www.aapl.org/ethics-guidelines.

American Law Institute. (1985). *Model penal code and annotations*. Washington, DC: Author.

American Psychiatric Association. (2013). *Diagnostic and statistical manual of mental disorders* (5th ed.). Washington, DC: Author.

American Psychological Association (2013). Specialty guidelines for forensic psychology. Retrieved from https://www.apa.org/practice/guidelines/forensic-psychology.

Batastini, A. B. & Vitacco, M. J. (2019, March). Perceived credibility of social media data as a collateral source in forensic mental health assessment. In A. B. Batastini (Chair), *Applications of technology in psychology-law contexts*. Symposium at the annual meeting of the American Psychology-Law Society, Portland.

Butcher, J. N., Graham, J.R., Ben-Porath, Y.S., Tellegen, A., Dahlstrom, W.G., & Kaemmer, B. (2001). *Minnesota Multiphasic Personality Inventory-2 (MMPI-2): Manual for administration and scoring* (rev. ed.). Minneapolis: University of Minnesota Press.

Cirincione, C., Steadman, H. J., & McGreevy, M. A. (1995). Rates of insanity acquittals and the factors associated with successful insanity pleas. *Bulletin of the American Academy of Psychiatry & the Law, 23*(3), 399–409. Retrieved from.

Clark v. Arizona, 126 S. Ct. 2709 (2006).

Frederick, R. I., Mrad, D. F., & DeMier, R. L. (2007). *Examinations of criminal responsibility: Foundations in mental health case law*. Sarasota: Professional Resource Press/Professional Resource Exchange.

Gottfried, E. D., Schenk, A. M., & Vitacco, M. J. (2016). Retrospectively assessing for feigning in criminal responsibility evaluations: Recommendations for clinical practice. *Journal of Forensic Psychology Practice, 16*(2), 118–128.

Green, E. P., & Follingstad, D. R. (2009). Third-party information in retrospective assessment of NGRI: Impact of source and supportive versus contradictory content. *Journal of Forensic Psychology Practice, 9*(1), 35–56.

Knoll, J. L., & Resnick, P. J. (2008). Insanity defense evaluations: Toward a model for evidence-based practice. *Brief Treatment and Crisis Intervention, 8*(1), 92–110.

M'Naghten case, 8 English Reporter 718 (1843).

Melton, G. B., Petrila, J., Poythress, N. G., Slobogin, C., Otto, R. K., Mossman, D., & Condie, L. O. (2018). *Psychological evaluations for the courts: A handbook for mental health professionals and lawyers* (4th ed.). New York: Guilford Press.
Miller, H. A. (2001). *Miller-forensic assessment of symptoms test (M-FAST): Professional manual.* Odessa: Psychological Assessment Resources.
Morey, L. C. (1991). *Personality assessment inventory professional manual.* Odessa: Psychological Assessment Resources.
Morse, S. J., & Bonnie, R. J. (2013). Abolition of the insanity defense violates due process. *Journal of the American Academy of Psychiatry and the Law, 41*(4), 488–495.
Packer, I. K. (2009). *Evaluation of criminal responsibility (best practices in forensic mental health assessment).* New York: Oxford University Press.
Parsons v. State, 81 Ala. 577, 2 So. 854, 60 Am. Rep. 193 (1887).
Perlin, M. L. (2017). The insanity defense: Nine myths that will not go away. In M. D. White (Ed.), *The insanity defense: multidisciplinary views on its history, trends, and controversies; the insanity defense:*. (pp. 3–22, Chapter xii, 441 Pages). Santa Barbara: Praeger/ABC-CLIO.
Plato. (1859). The Laws: B. IX. C. 8. In (trans: Burges, G.). *The works of Plato: A new and literal version, chiefly from the text of stallbum, volume V containing the laws* (pp. 372). London: Henry G. Bohn.
Ray, I. (1838). *A treatise on the medical jurisprudence of insanity.* Boston: Charles C. Little and James Brown.
Rex v. Arnold, 16 How. St. Tr. 695 (1724).
Robinson, D. N. (1996). *Wild beasts & idle humours: The insanity defense from antiquity to the present.* Cambridge: Harvard University Press.
Rogers, R., & Bender, S. D. (Eds.). (2018). *Clinical assessment of malingering and deception.* New York: Guilford Publications.
Rogers, R., & Ewing, C. (2003). The prohibition of ultimate opinions: A misguided enterprise. *Journal of Forensic Psychology Practice, 3*, 65–75.
Rogers, R., & Shuman, D. W. (2005). *Fundamentals of forensic practice: Mental health and criminal law.* New York: Springer Science & Business Media.
Rogers, R., Sewell, K. W., & Gillard, N. D. (2010). *Structured Interview of Reported Symptoms (SIRS) and professional manual.* Odessa: Psychological Assessment Resources.
Tillbrook, C., Mumley, D., & Grisso, T. (2003). Avoiding expert opinions on the ultimate legal question: The case for integrity. *Journal of Forensic Psychology Practice, 3*(3), 77–87.
Vitacco, M. J., Gottfried, E. D., & Batastini, A. B. (2018). Using technology to improve the objectivity of criminal responsibility evaluations. *Journal of the American Academy of Psychiatry and the Law, 46*(1), 71–77.
Winslow, F. (1843). *The Plea of insanity in criminal cases.* London: H. Renshaw.

Chapter 3
Competency to Stand Trial

Robert E. Cochrane and Kristina P. Lloyd

Competency to stand trial (CST) evaluations are by far the most frequently requested evaluation in criminal courts by judges, defense counsel, and prosecutors with estimates upward of 60,000 occurring each year in the United States (Poythress, Bonnie, Monahan, Otto, & Hoge, 2002). As a result, courts have become accustomed to reading reports and hearing testimony about the bases on which experts reach their opinions. This includes observations of the defendant, statements made during clinical interviews, results from psychological testing, reports from family or other collateral sources, and details from available records (e.g., medical, police, school). What forensic evaluators and courts are now beginning to grapple with is what to make of the social media defendants either produced (or allegedly produced) or has been reported about them on Social Networking Sites (SNS). The question for clinicians and the court to address is: are these data to be considered like any other collateral data?

Social media via blogs, websites, YouTube, Facebook, Snapchat, Twitter, or any of the numerous other outlets have become part and parcel of the technology culture in which we now find ourselves. Some studies have found that over 75% of Americans use SNS on a regular basis (Pew Research Center, n.d.). The use of SNS has become so ubiquitous to our communication and is so ingrained that it is no wonder forensic evaluators are confronting what to do with these communications by defendants. Unfortunately, as this is an emerging question there is a paucity of scientific guidance to assist in navigating this question. Nonetheless, we can utilize what we know from the law, professions ethics, and guidelines for best forensic and assessment practices to help inform us when it comes to the use of SNS in competency evaluations. With those resources, we must ask ourselves several questions about SNS data. This includes questions about obtaining, using, and considering SNS information. This chapter will focus on these issues as they relate to CST evaluations.

R. E. Cochrane (✉) · K. P. Lloyd
Federal Bureau of Prisons, Federal Medical Center, Butner, NC, USA
e-mail: rcochrane@bop.gov; klloyd@bop.gov

A. B. Batastini, M. J. Vitacco (eds.), *Forensic Mental Health Evaluations in the Digital Age*, https://doi.org/10.1007/978-3-030-33908-1_3

3.1 Should SNS Data Be Utilized in CST Evaluations?

Some might argue that SNS data has little place, or little to offer, when it comes to evaluating a defendant's competency to stand trial. In fact, are we not primarily concerned about the functional abilities of the defendant in the present moment? How does communication a defendant made on social media at some point speak to these abilities? Unless communicated contemporaneously during the evaluation, how useful will social media communications really be? Others may contend that fully understanding a defendant's personality, diagnoses, and how they communicate in different contexts is critical to completing a thorough and well-supported competency evaluation. One of the cornerstones of any forensic assessment, including competency evaluations, is the use of multiple sources of data (American Psychological Association [APA] 2013). The great extent by which multiple sources are utilized distinguishes forensic assessment from other clinical practices and helps ensure the evaluation process has greater thoroughness, objectivity, and neutrality. Given the goal of CST evaluations is to determine the defendant's actual abilities, this can only be accomplished if all potentially useful data sources are considered, including SNS information. Assessing whether clinical presentations or communications are consistent across time and sources may be vital to a CST evaluation. Further, the utility of SNS data can be considered like other sources when an evaluator balances how much weight to give the information. In fact, neglecting to obtain and utilize SNS data may indicate the forensic evaluator failed to use sufficient sources of information in conducting the competency evaluation.

The Federal Rules of Evidence, specifically Rule 702 (1975) indicates evaluators can offer opinions based on data that is *reasonably relied* on in the profession. Most states have similar rules of evidence (Wroth 1985). Based on limited survey data, it appears evaluators are using SNS as a collateral source relatively frequently in cases and report it as being useful (Coffey, Batastini, & Vitacco, 2018). Further, among those who have conducted CST evaluations, over two-thirds consulted SNS at least once (Coffey et al. 2018). The question may not be *whether* SNS data is being relied upon, but rather in what ways it is and should be used.

3.1.1 How Should SNS Data Be Obtained?

If an evaluator decides SNS data would be useful to a CST evaluation, care must then be taken so the data is obtained in an ethical and legal manner. If the SNS information is relevant to and part of discovery material provided by counsel, the evaluator will likely have little compunction about reviewing and at least considering the data. After a careful review, the evaluator may decide not to give the data much, if any, weight. If information from social media posts was contained in the discovery packet, it would likely not create discomfort for the evaluator. However, other situations will require evaluators to solicit or search for SNS data themselves.

In many respects, forensic evaluators conducting CST evaluations are "mental health investigators" who often directly obtain data (e.g., medical records, third party contacts) that is used to understand and speak to the defendant's current mental state and abilities. However, to what lengths can or should an evaluator go in obtaining a defendant's social media information? These waters can get muddy when it comes to social media sites. Again, law enforcement may uncover and provide some of this information to evaluators. However, in many cases a defendant's social media may not be directly relevant to the prosecution, but could be extremely important to the CST evaluation. A case in point would be YouTube videos made by a potentially delusional defendant who informs you of the footage during the CST exam. Assume the evaluator learns the posting was made just prior to the arrest. The defendant indicates it contains his "philosophy" of law, which he is no longer willing to discuss with anyone but his attorney. The evaluator suspects the contents may directly speak to the defendant's understanding of his charges and ability to converse rationally with his attorney. In this situation, should the evaluator perform searches to discover the videos? Is the defendant's consent needed to obtain these videos? There may not be expectations of privacy with YouTube posts, but what about postings made on a defendant's Facebook page or other site?

3.1.2 How Should SNS Data Be Considered and Used?

If utilized, another consideration for the forensic evaluator must be *how* the SNS data will be used and considered in the CST evaluation process. Will it serve to buttress or refute other sources of data? Will the information address the content and quality of the defendant's thinking? Or will the evaluator simply utilize it during the interview process to question and potentially confront the defendant? There are several potential ways in which social media can be utilized in CST evaluations, which will be discussed in the next section of this chapter. Many of these are relevant to forensic mental health evaluations, and some are specific to CST evaluations. Regardless, evaluators will need to be thoughtful about their approach, staying consistent with best practices and complying with relevant standards and statutes.

First, and as discussed in further detail in Chap. 1, evaluators need to establish the *authenticity* of social media. As an example, what if a defendant denies having posted a message on social media that was attributed to him by a prosecutor? Should the evaluator assume the legal authorities have verified or authenticated authorship, or should the evaluator take additional steps to determine the veracity and reliability of the SNS information? If so, how should an evaluator determine its reliability and accuracy? These questions, of course, are not specific to CST, and more guidance on how to address these is presented in Chap. 9.

Next, evaluators must determine the *clarity and usefulness* of the data. Some information from social media may be questionable, whereas others may be obvious and of little concern to a CST evaluator. For instance, a YouTube video depicting a defendant making several clear statements may give the evaluator few concerns.

However, a cryptic Tweet from the defendant to an alleged victim may have different meaning or implication. Take a case in which the defendant tweeted to a local politician "I know what you have done and the house of cards will crash down hard on you. I have the power!" The defendant also tweets "I see in you. It's there. U r not meant for this world." These tweets are far from clear and require clarification if the evaluator is to determine its relevance for the CST evaluation. Through probing questions during clinical interviews and review of additional collateral data, the evaluator may determine these statements are indicative of a delusion the defendant holds about having supernatural powers to read the minds and intentions of others. The delusion undermines the defendant's competency by leading him to make irrational decisions in court. For example, he insists on testifying about his ability to know what the alleged victim was thinking and planning due to his clairvoyance.

Third, and perhaps most directly relevant to CST, evaluators will need to determine whether the social media information speaks to the defendant's *true state of mind* within relatively close proximity to the CST evaluation. Many individuals use social media in ways other than to communicate their true thoughts and feelings. SNS are replete with posts and media that express individuals' creativity, fantasies, and desires. As noted elsewhere in this book, many people intentionally misrepresent themselves to impress, manipulate, or otherwise influence others. Evaluators would be mistaken to assume communications on a media platform, which largely allows one to be anonymous, are a true reflection of an individual's beliefs or quality of speech.

Finally, the *Specialty Guidelines* (2013) and recommendations by many experts in the field (e.g., Pirelli et al. 2016) speak to the importance of corroborating all data sources. For social media, this can be done in several ways. Perhaps the simplest means is by speaking directly with the defendant about the SNS data when conducting the CST interview. This will hopefully result not only in corroboration, but greater meaning and understanding of the data in its context. Other methods may include speaking with third parties with direct knowledge of the posts/texts/blogs, etc., or perhaps obtaining records (e.g., diaries or journals) that describe the media posts. Data gleaned from these additional sources may suggest the defendant has greater legal knowledge and ability than was initially thought. For instance, if the defendant's brother states the defendant wrote the bizarre social posts in question while highly intoxicated, this may have little bearing on his current CST. Or perhaps additional writings, such as journal entries, reveal language deficits, impoverished vocabulary and grammar, or other impaired communication that raise concerns about the defendant's ability to effectively work with counsel.

The next section of this chapter will address clinical applications of SNS data in competency evaluations. The referral source and setting in which the evaluator works may have implications for how SNS data is utilized. How evaluators corroborate and document the SNS information is also discussed. The third section of this chapter will address several important ethical and legal questions evaluators must consider before soliciting or obtaining SNS information for a competency evaluation. This includes whether informed consent is needed and whether there are any expectations of privacy. There will also be discussion as to how social media of a potentially inflammatory nature may bias or impact the evaluator. The final section will include two case examples that highlight the applications of SNS data, several legal and ethical implications, and recommended best practices when using SNS data in CST evaluations.

3.2 Clinical Applications

One consideration with regard to the use of SNS, is how and when to use the information from social media in our evaluations. As the use of social media becomes more integrated into everyday life of most of the population, the question asked of evaluators is whether this information should be collected and considered as a standard part of collateral information in CST evaluations. Just as evaluators may routinely interview family members about the functioning of a defendant, should evaluators review of SNS be a routine part of a clinical case conceptualization? It is our opinion that if information from websites like Facebook or Instagram is considered during an evaluation, then this information should be considered as a type of collateral information. The *Specialty Guidelines* (2013) suggest, when possible, evaluators should use additional sources to corroborate or contradict information provided during a forensic evaluation. We consider information from social media networking sites a potentially helpful source of information when conducting a competency to proceed evaluation.

3.2.1 Using SNS as Collateral Material in CST

Competency evaluations necessitate a clinical interview and clinical observations as part of the process. Clinical interviews include information such as educational background, employment history, medical conditions, to name a few. Information from SNS can be helpful as supplemental information gathered during the clinical interview. For example, if a defendant indicates he is presently a minister and has his own congregation to whom he preaches, this may be verifiable though the church website or Facebook page. The absence of such a page does not necessarily mean the defendant is not a preacher, but other means of verifying this information would be needed. Alternatively, if a defendant describes himself as having an active social life, his Instagram page can serve as a way of corroborating this information and whether his social life is primarily virtual. Social media sites should not be considered the *only* way to verify clinical information, but are one potentially helpful information source.

The use of information from SNS can also be useful to determine if a mental illness has been long standing. Most states and the federal government require that if a defendant is found not competent to stand trial, it be due to the presence of a mental disease or defect. In determining if a threshold condition (e.g., mental illness) is present, the postings made by a defendant on social media may lend support or refute the presence of a mental illness by suggesting a person is falsely representing themselves (e.g., malingering). Consider the defendant who asserts he is the victim of voice-to-skull technology (i.e., believing the government is communicating with him via satellite directly to his brain). If the defendant extensively posted to his Facebook page about constantly being subjected to this kind of technology and the manner in which it affects him, this may lend credence to his self-report of delusional material. This information potentially supports that he has a threshold condition that renders him not competent to proceed. However, should a defendant report he has believed in voice-to-skull technology for many years, but there is no evidence of this on any social media publishing, it may cause the evaluator to question if these beliefs are truly held or a recent acquisition, and that the defendant is attempting to malinger a mental illness. If there is no other evidence of a mental disease or defect (other than the defendant's self-report), the evaluator may conclude the defendant is malingering. In CST evaluations, this information may be used to support the opinion that a defendant does (or does not) have a threshold condition required for a finding of not competent to proceed. Information from SNS can also provide suggestions regarding the mental health impairments of a guarded defendant. In the voice-to-skull technology example, an evaluator may be able to offer some helpful and previously unknown information to the retaining party, if the social media information is shared.

3.2.2 SNS to Evaluate Present Functioning

Undergoing legal proceedings is an inherently stressful process. When evaluators are working with a defendant to assess their competency to stand trial, it is an evaluation of their *present* functioning. A defendant may be experiencing significant stress due to his current legal situation. Information about his functioning prior to arrest can provide valuable information about the type of symptom(s) to be targeted. For example, consider the defendant who presents as apathetic, uninterested, and is in bed for a significant portion of the day and night. The attorney has complained the defendant "won't talk to me. He just sits there and stares at me. He doesn't read the information I give him. I've asked him if he is depressed and he said no." Social media postings may paint a picture of a defendant who was vibrant, active, and energetic prior to his arrest. An astute clinician may suggest a psychiatric consultation and consider depression is currently limiting his ability to engage with others, including his lawyer. The information from social media can provide important information about a defendant's baseline functioning and how this may have changed due to current stressors.

Adjudicative competency evaluations also require a functional assessment of the skills of a defendant (e.g., does the defendant possess the ability to make rational decisions about his or her case). The use of social media sites can be helpful in this regard by providing information about the skills and abilities of the defendant. For example, consider the defendant who has a documented history of requiring specialized education services and described "barely graduating high school" due to his poor writing ability. However, a review of the defendant's Twitter feed shows he was making well-articulated postings with a college level vocabulary prior to his arrest. This could suggest the person was embellishing or malingering intellectual deficits. Or, if the defendant verified he made the posts but used dictation software on his cell phone rather than typing out the posts, this could provide valuable information about the defendant's ability to communicate orally rather than by written word. This suggests the defendant may be able to follow courtroom proceedings, but may struggle to read case associated documents. As such, defense counsel working with the individual may need to rely on a different approach when communicating with such a defendant.

An important consideration when using information from SNS is to consider how much weight the information should be given. A preliminary step is to ascertain whether the defendant actually made the postings attributed to him. If the defendant indicates he made the postings, the next consideration is how much weight should be attributed to the postings. As CST evaluations are focused on present functioning, the timeliness of the posting is crucial. While a defendant may evidence symptoms of a mental disease or defect in old SNS postings, if that is not his present state, the information from SNS may be irrelevant. However, their presence at least suggests an area of inquiry for CST evaluators. Evaluators will have to make this determination on a case-by-case basis, just as they would for other collateral information. If the defendant posted information on multiple social media sites, was the information across the sites generally consistent across sites? For example, if a defendant has posted several educational type videos on YouTube about the legal system that are factually correct, this suggests that at one time, he understood the legal system. Information should be considered as to whether it is convergent or divergent from other collateral or self-reported information (e.g., has the defendant posted about and described during interviews his sovereign citizen views). Additionally, how much weight to give the information, should be considered. This will likely vary by the type of information gathered, the case specifics, and the other collateral information provided. For instance, say a defendant appears in several online videos that were taken just prior to the CST evaluation. In the videos he can be seen talking at length in a logical and coherent fashion with no mention of unusual or delusional content. The evaluator may put considerably more weight into this data point than perhaps the psychological test results, clinical interviews, or medical records.

3.2.3 SNS Audience

Information from social media websites is clearly different from information that is self-reported to the evaluator by the defendant. During a clinical interview, the defendant is providing information directly to the evaluator during a one-to-one interpersonal experience. Defendants may consciously or unconsciously modify, filter, or shade their information based on their perceived reactions by the evaluator. However, information posted on SNS sites is not the same type of interpersonal experience as a clinical interview. One notable difference is the audience. In contrast, a social media post is most often intended for and received by a much wider audience. The person making the post may not even know whom the viewers or respondents will be. Another notable difference is time delay between when the defendant receives a response to the statement he or she made to the evaluator as compared to the time it takes for him or her to receive a response to the social media post. During a clinical interview, the evaluator may provide immediate verbal or non-verbal feedback to the defendant's statement. It may be to ask a follow up question, take a note, or to respond with silence. This differs from the information shared in a social media post in which it may take several minutes, hours, or even days to receive a response. As such, the information shared in a social media post may be somewhat different to that presented during a clinical interview and therefore, may have additive value to the information gathered during the clinical interview. For example, if a defendant posts views online about nanobots that have been implanted in his body, other community members may not respond to his assertions for several days. However, if his views are then repudiated by others, he may stop making these posts. This is different from an interviewer who does not dismiss the views, but asks follow-up questions. An interviewer may be provided more detailed and in-depth information from the defendant than is posted on SNS. If an evaluator *only* reviewed SNS information a belief system may appear far-fetched and superficial. However, a clinical interview may reveal a complex set of delusions. When these sources of information are used in conjunction, a richer, more detailed CST opinion can be formulated.

3.2.4 How to Collect SNS Information

Another consideration is if SNS information is requested but not provided, should evaluators attempt to obtain it on their own? Unlike hospital records that require a signed release of information, SNS sites are often easily accessible. If evaluators elect to pursue the SNS data, should they obtain permission from the retaining party? At what lengths should an evaluator go to obtain access to SNS sites for the defendant? If the information is publicly available, this makes is relatively easy to access and review the material. However, if the page access is limited and can only be garnered by approval from the defendant, how should an evaluator approach this? Should he or she ask the defendant for permission? Should the evaluator "friend" the defendant? If so, does this need to be addressed as part of informed consent? If the "friend request" is accepted, has this created a multiple relationship and blurred the lines or professional roles with the defendant? If the case is court ordered, has this shifted the role of the evaluator to an advocate for the defendant?

Unless extenuating and highly unusual circumstances exist, the authors would strongly advise evaluators against "friending" a defendant to gain access to his or her SNS pages. Requests for access to these pages can be made directly to attorneys in the course of a request for collateral materials.

Another area to consider is the physical location of the defendant. For example, if a defendant is in custody and has been for several months (or years), are his or her Facebook postings as relevant as a defendant who is actively posting on SNS because he or she remains in the community on bond? Providers may be faced with other unique challenges when a defendant is not in custody and has access to the internet and SNS. When outpatient CST evaluations are performed, providers may want to inquire about a defendant's current access and contemporaneous communications via these sites. Since SNS correspondence includes evolving disclosures, some online communication will not be part of the official record or discovery. Given CST evaluations are focused on current mental state, the information may prove very useful in discerning diagnoses and the understanding of legal concepts. Take, for example, a defendant who sends daily Tweets complaining about his prosecution, including court dates, admitted evidence, and filed motions. The evaluator will likely find this 'grist for the mill' so to speak, topics in which she wishes to explore and clarify with the defendant. Comments or tweets may also provide independent evidence that supports (or refutes) hypotheses related to competency. For example, imagine the defendant tweets his reasons (with law citations) that the judge is biased against him because of rulings that were made during several pretrial conferences. The defendant provides a list of rational reasons he does not think the judge had been a neutral party in the case. He also includes case law that support his assertions. In interviews with the CST evaluator, the defendant reported he has a strong understanding of the legal system and is ready to move forward now that his medication dosage was corrected. In this case, SNS data support the defendant's statements that he can consider his case clearly and is competent. While it may not be prudent to make the aforementioned tweets, the information contained in the SNS postings suggests the defendant can read, interpret, and apply case law to his personal situation.

3.2.5 Competency Restoration

Some evaluators are tasked with competency evaluation and restoration of competency. Information from social media sites may provide valuable information about a defendant's baseline functioning, when treated and untreated with medication, and when not involved in the legal system. Evaluations completed for the federal government for competency restoration require evaluators opine as to whether there is a substantial likelihood the defendant can be restored to competency. At times, this is can be difficult to ascertain, especially if the defendant is presently refusing treatment. However, a historical review of social media (in addition to treatment records and interviews) may provide valuable information for evaluators about the defendant's functioning when adequately treated. In a case one of the authors completed, the defendant arrived for competency restoration in a manic phase. At the time of his arrival, he was disheveled and not wearing shoes because he refused to wear them. His speech was disorganized as did not make sense. However, his SNS postings evidenced a man that was articulate, well groomed, and was an active participant at his church and in his community. In this case, the information from SNS data provided a wealth of information about the defendant's functional abilities when adequately treated.

3.3 Legal and Ethical Concerns

Few studies regarding SNS data in forensic assessments have been produced, but some guidance and considerations for using internet data have been offered. Pirelli, Otto, and Estoup (2016) describe the use of SNS/internet data as another form or collateral information at the disposal of forensic practitioners. They explain that while the *American Psychological Association's Ethical Principles of Psychologists and Code of Conduct* ([EPPCC] APA 2017) and *Specialty Guidelines* (2013) do not prohibit the use of this type of information, practitioners should be cognizant of the ethical and practical implications involved. They raise some excellent points about SNS data utility, the informed consent process, and formulating opinions, reports, and testimony. Kaslow et al. (2011) also touched on some of these issues, including privacy concerns, best interest of the client, and trust. Much of their discussion focused on how SNS access affected the relationship between therapist and client, but some topics were relevant to forensic professionals, such as respect for the evaluee's autonomy. These authors discuss how in a treatment relationship, a clinician's decision to obtain client information may be dictated by their theoretical orientation. For instance, someone from a psychodynamic perspective may not want to contaminate the relationship or transference/countertransference that takes place in session by knowing additional information presented on social media. This can be distinguished from a CST evaluator, who is not primarily concerned with the mental health or well-being of the defendant, but rather determining facts and truth (i.e., correct diagnoses, ability to proceed to trial). The relationship between evaluator and defendant is important, but there is not the same kind of ongoing, therapeutic relationship found between therapist and client. Therefore, a CST evaluator will likely feel more inclined to pursue information that may shed light on the psycholegal issues.

This section of the chapter will expand on those discussions, specifically examining the legal and ethical contours of using SNS data in CST evaluations. Three primary areas will be addressed: informed consent, reliability and relevance of SNS data, and evaluator bias.

3.3.1 Informed Consent

As noted in Chap. 1, psychologists have an ethical obligation to respect the autonomy and decisions of the persons with whom they work. The *EPPCC* (2017) and *Specialty Guidelines* (2013) both state that individuals be informed of the nature of the service provided. This would arguably include what is involved in the CST evaluation, such as interviews, testing, and review of collateral data (i.e., SNS data). However, does the provider need the defendant's consent to obtain data, including SNS data? In court ordered CST evaluations consent is not typically required to obtain data and complete the assessment. The client is not the person undergoing the assessment, but rather the court itself. Nonetheless, as will be discussed, it would be wise for providers to *notify* defendants that SNS data may be examined and the purpose for doing so. To facilitate integrity, transparency, and respect for the individual, evaluators should explain how SNS material may speak to the individual's mental condition, capacity for understanding, and ability to effectively communicate and make decisions.

In many cases prosecutors have legally obtained relevant SNS data, which is part of the discovery material forwarded to the CST evaluator. The defendant had no choice in the release of the information, some of which may be highly personal and embarrassing. In these cases, the evaluator may want to address any SNS data that is pertinent to the diagnostic formulation and/or competency opinion. For instance, imagine a defendant recently sent Instant Messages (IM) to friends on Facebook about the government tracking his movements with Nano technology inserted into the fillings of his teeth. However, during clinical interviews he attempted to conceal this and denied having any such thoughts or ideas of persecution. What should an evaluator do in such a situation? Most would probably agree that, at a minimum, the evaluator should further question the defendant about this discrepant information. Even though not obligated to do so, informing the defendant about the IMs and other data within the discovery may serve to demonstrate openness and build trust. Also, taking the time to establish greater rapport may serve to decrease the defendant's discomfort in sharing his fears with a person he recently met. This in turn may increase the likelihood of greater self-disclosure and therefore more accurate conclusions.

The situation may be different, however, if the CST evaluation is not court ordered, but rather, requested by defense counsel. Given many defendants referred for CST evaluation suffer from various mental disorders, it is no surprise some of these individuals will not have the capacity to consent to the evaluation. In these cases, evaluators are encouraged to take "reasonable steps" to protect their rights and welfare (*EPPCC* Standard 3.10, 2017) and consider notifying the defendant's attorney. It would be sensible for an evaluator to discuss with the attorney at the outset what is typically included in a CST evaluation. If the evaluator customarily seeks or reviews SNS data, then informing counsel this data will be sought by the evaluator is essential. Otherwise, the retaining attorney may not be able to fully advocate for their client by explaining to the evaluator why certain SNS media should not be sought or acquired. For instance, the attorney may be concerned the SNS information may lead to additional criminal charges and would provide little to no relevant information for competency purposes. What steps should be taken in such cases when defense counsel does not want the evaluator to search the internet for SNS data? Would this be any different than if the attorney asked the evaluator not to contact a family member or another collateral source? Thoroughness and gathering third-party information are hallmarks of forensic assessment. Accuracy can be affected if evaluations are stymied or limited in some ways. The evaluation may still be able to be completed, but this limitation would need to be explained to the retaining attorney and acknowledged in the report and during court testimony.

In some cases, the evaluator may not know about, or even know how to obtain, relevant SNS data unless the defendant discloses this and provides enough detail for it to be located. Certain data may not be relevant to a prosecution, and therefore not part of discovery, but may be paramount to the psycho-legal question of competency. If a defendant shares that he frequents SNS, the evaluator may determine obtaining that data may provide useful information that will serve to clarify the diagnostic picture, or provide information regarding functional capabilities related to competency. In these situations, passwords may be required, evaluators may have to create accounts, and/or further steps may need to be taken to get the information. For example, say a defendant hosts a website and manages a blog espousing he is a "Sovereign Citizen" and believes in "Redemptionist and Strawman" theories about the United States government. In order for the evaluator to access the blog, the defendant may have to provide the evaluator his or her login information since the forum is only available to "members." The evaluator believes the probative value of the communications will likely outweigh any prejudicial effects or logistical hurdles. There is concern the defendant may have delusional beliefs causing him to be unwilling to work with defense counsel. The defendant's statements suggest he wishes to pursue a legal strategy at trial that will, by all accounts, fail. Should the evaluator proceed and work with the defendant to obtain the SNS data? If so, what cautions should be taken?

As discussed in earlier chapters, it is important to inform the client (attorney) that SNS material, along with other collateral data, may be germane to the assessment and therefore sought. If the attorney is not informed at the outset or prior to the evaluator obtaining the information, the SNS data may become discoverable to the prosecutor, depending on the jurisdiction. If the attorney objects to investigating for SNS data, the evaluator must then decide whether a fair, complete, and accurate evaluation can be completed. This would be consistent with *Specialty Guidelines* 11.01 (2013) pertaining to accuracy and the withholding of relevant evidence. Of course, in a court ordered or government hired assessment, the evaluator may choose to seek the material without consent of the defendant or notifying the parties involved. Another consideration pertains to the personal and collaborative nature of this type of exchange between the defendant and CST evaluator. If a defendant discloses or requests the evaluator go online and review his SNS communications, this should cause the evaluator to pause and reflect on whether this approach to obtaining data in any ways blurs the lines or roles which CST evaluators are warned to make clear. These authors have had defendants encourage them to review YouTube videos and other material they have reportedly produced and placed online. One such defendant believed the evaluator would be convinced he was not mentally ill once his videos were reviewed. To the contrary, his rambling, nearly incoherent descriptions about the Central Intelligence Agency (CIA) using mind control on him only confirmed he did not have the ability to rationally discuss the allegations or evidence in his case. In this and similar cases, consent was not required but implicit *permission* was provided in order to access the material. In another case, the defendant indicated the evaluator would have to send him a "friend" request in order to get access to his Facebook page. The defendant insisted on his competency and believed because he too was a "psychologist and surgeon," the evaluator would agree with his positions after reviewing his Facebook page. While the boundaries and roles of the professional relationship were fully explained and understood at the outset, it was determined that accessing his Facebook material in that fashion created a potential role confusion that outweighed any benefits of obtaining the material. However, there may be circumstances when an evaluator feels confident such confusion would not take place and proceeds to secure the data in that manner.

3.3.2 Reliability and Relevance

As described in the first chapter, CST evaluator are encouraged to base their opinions on sufficient data and to use reliable and valid procedures (*EPPCC*, Sect 9.01 and 9.02). How does one determine whether SNS media and communications are reliable? A defendant certainly may claim to have written or produced material on social media that, in fact, he did not. Or a prosecutor may believe a defendant communicated something on a SNS that was actually done by someone else. Beyond authenticating authorship, one must establish whether the communications accurately reflect the defendant's true thoughts and feelings. Finally, ascertaining the relevance of the SNS data is necessary before including it in reports and testimony.

Competency evaluators must first take reasonable steps to corroborate and verify authorship of any social media communication upon which they have relied. This could come through the defendant's self-report, third party statements, law enforcement investigative reports, or other documentation. Oftentimes it is difficult to know who wrote, uploaded, or edited comments, video, or social posts. Pseudonyms and usernames frequently do not correspond to actual identities. And even when they do, others may have access and the ability to make social posts in place of the defendant or even alter the postings after arrest or incarceration. This can complicate how to consider the data. For instance, a defendant may deny making posts a prosecutor attributes to him on Twitter. Even if it is solidly established the posts originated from his account, he may claim his account was hacked or others had access to his username and password and made posts in his name. Should the evaluator dismiss the SNS information in such cases without any further corroboration? What if the defendant acknowledged making the posts to police investigators, but then later retracted it? Evaluators will have to make difficult judgments about authorship before assuming it was written by the defendant.

Another complication for evaluators occurs when the defendant reports the statements he made online do not reflect what he actually believes. This often occurs when the communications include threats, sexual content, or otherwise embarrassing information. A defendant may indicate he made the statements during the course of "fantasy" or role-play, or perhaps during a period of intoxication. Or he may claim to have been bragging, exaggerating, or intentionally misrepresenting himself. Determining which statements are accurate and reflect the evaluee's true feelings – current ones or online ones – presents a challenge. Additional collateral data may be required before an evaluator is comfortable concluding the social media is an accurate portrayal of the defendant's true thinking. For example, if the defendant's family and work colleagues all report he often made similar statements during the course of routine conversations and while conducting his affairs, the evaluator may conclude his online persona reflects what he genuinely thinks and feels. However, the accuracy of the content may not be the only information that is useful to an evaluator. How the person speaks, or the *quality* of the communications may be just as, if not more, important than the content that is present. Available audio or video social media can illuminate the defendant's capacity for clear communication, a necessary competency ability for effectively assisting counsel.

Even if SNS data is considered a reliable and an accurate reflection of the defendant's thinking, the CST evaluator must determine whether the information is *relevant* to the diagnostic and legal questions at hand. *Specialty Guideline* 11.04 (2013) encourages practitioners to "limit discussion of background information that does not bear directly upon the legal purpose of the examination or consultation." As has been mentioned, online reflections and communications can be highly personal and reveal much about the defendant that can needlessly embarrass and/or prejudice the fact finder. Also, much online content about or from a defendant may be too dated to be relevant to his current mental state. For example, if the defendant's mental condition is clearly established through other means, and his mental state is known to fluctuate considerably as a result of treatment, the information obtained from SNS may be of limited value. It may also not be relevant to report online content when it is apparent that the defendant was inebriated, or when his presentation is no different from how he presents in the CST interview. There are, however, many circumstances in which SNS media of the defendant has great relevance - when it conflicts with other data, when knowledge is conveyed, when communication is impaired, when delusional content is voiced, and many others. One of the authors evaluated a middle-age defendant who was a psychiatrist suspected of having bipolar disorder. The man insisted he was not mentally ill and downplayed suggestions by family and his attorney that he had been behaving erratically leading up to his arrest. He had sufficient legal understanding, knew the allegations against him, and appeared fully capable of working with counsel. However, his wife noted he had several "episodes" in recent years of grandiosity, lavish spending, sleep disturbance, and other signs of a potential mania. Several of his blogs, emails, and a web page he designed contained comments of a conspiratorial nature. They also consisted of outlandish claims he made about having found a cure for substance addictions. After reviewing the material, it became apparent that while his condition was presently in remission, he likely had manic episodes that qualified for a bipolar I disorder diagnosis. Knowing this allowed the evaluator to inform the court that while he appeared competent to stand trial, without prophylactic treatment he was at increased risk for relapse which could compromise his competency as the case moved forward.

3.3.3 Evaluator Bias

Maintaining objectivity is one of the primary goals of forensic evaluators who conduct CST evaluations. While there is no APA ethical standard related to objectivity and avoidance of bias, the *EPPCC* Principle related to integrity cautions psychologists to "promote accuracy," which arguably includes attempts to avoid biased assessments. The *Specialty Guidelines* (2013) encourage forensic practitioners to "strive for accuracy, impartiality, fairness, and independence."

A variety of different biases have been identified in the literature as it relates to forensic practice. For example, Murrie et al. (2013) asked evaluators to review materials of a risk assessment case. Half of the participants were told they were retained by the prosecution, while the other half were told they were retained by the defense. Those who were informed that they were hired by the prosecution had significantly higher risk scores than those thought to be hired by the defense. The study provides the strongest methodology demonstrating support for an allegiance bias among evaluators. There is no reason to think this would be any different for those conducting CST evaluations versus risk assessments.

There has been recent interest in the study of how to combat evaluator biases. Neal and Brodsky (2016) surveyed forensic psychologists about bias awareness. Some of the challenging situations identified by forensic practitioners included disliking or feeling sympathy for the defendant, disgust or anger toward the offense, and preexisting values. It is no stretch to say reviewing provocative SNS material could trigger or heighten strong emotions, resulting in bias among CST evaluators. Unlike reading words on a page, visual and auditory information can have a significant emotional impact that may create bias.

Take for example what occurred on January 19, 2019 at the Lincoln Memorial in Washington, DC, when a confrontation ensued between a group of Catholic school teenagers, Native Americans, and Hebrew Israelites. The incident made national headlines and stirred strong reactions when a video surfaced appearing to show a teenager, a President Trump supporter wearing a "Make America Great Again" hat, provoke a confrontation with a Native American man. Many jumped to conclusions about the motivations and behaviors of the teenager. It was only after additional videos and reports became available was there a more accurate understanding of that day's events. Could this not happen to an evaluator who relies on video or SNS information about a defendant? While something may appear to be "caught on tape" and tell the whole story, the context and nuances of the individual's actions or speech may not have been fully captured. If an evaluator has certain political leanings or strong feelings about certain behavior, one video, blog, or statement by a defendant may confirm the evaluator's initial erroneous hypothesis about the person. The case above shows how an isolated video can bias opinion, but also how images, statements, and video can serve to correct or reduce bias by providing greater context. This should serve to caution forensic practitioners when they review SNS material, especially if they have a strong reaction to what they have seen or heard.

Bias may also come into play when the evaluator has little or no experience with social media. Lacking familiarity and appreciation for the context of these communications may distort the evaluator's perception of the content, tone, or intent of the speech. For instance, users on Snapchat send messages to people that may not be sent to someone in another application because the photo or message deletes itself after you open it (unless the recipient screenshots it, to which the sender is informed). A CST evaluator unfamiliar with this application may make false assumptions about a defendant who frequently uses this app. For instance, an evaluator may conclude the defendant is rather "tech savvy" or intelligent because he uses Snapchat, when in fact it is so ubiquitous among millennials and Generation Z that it speaks little to one's communication or cognitive abilities. One author had this experience when evaluating a 22-year old defendant charged with distribution of child pornography. The defendant had utilized what the author assumed were sophisticated SNS downloading programs to conceal the illicit material from detection by the authorities. While the defendant presented with impairments suggesting a possible intellectual disability interfering with his understanding and legal decision making, his supposed SNS savviness caused this author to question whether he was embellishing his deficits. However, it was later discovered that the software programs in question required very little technical knowledge and understanding but were widely utilized. In fact, there were many more programs "on the market" that could have been used by the defendant had he possessed greater skill and ability.

So how does one remain impartial, unbiased, and independent when reviewing SNS material for which one is unfamiliar or that is potentially inflammatory? In the Neal and Brodsky (2016) study they identified twenty-five potential debiasing strategies. Some of the strategies were ineffective, such as introspection, while others were effective and consistent with other empirical data. Some effective approaches included didactic education, "forcing functions," and slowing down strategies. Evaluators should make attempts to reduce bias and enhance objectivity by following recommended procedures. This may include any number of actions, such as: intentionally examining a defendant's strengths and positive qualities; speaking with and getting feedback from colleagues; reviewing transcripts instead of watching videos; or only reviewing SNS material that one believes directly speaks to the CST matter. Since CST evaluations are primarily focused on present abilities, in many cases SNS data may be less needed or important in reaching decisions on competency. For this reason, evaluators may wish to avoid superfluous or potentially prejudicial material found in SNS.

Summary and Recommendations When conducting CST evaluations practitioners will have to decide whether SNS media exists for a defendant, and if so, whether and how to use it. There are practical as well as ethical and legal implications when using any third-party information. This is especially true for social media produced by or about a defendant. Social media can present complicating scenarios for evaluators and caution should be taken before relying upon this information. The purpose of this chapter was to assist CST evaluators in reflecting on and utilizing a sound approach to SNS information in their assessments. To that end, we suggest evaluators conducting CST evaluations take the following steps when using SNS information:

1. Determine if consent is needed and obtain the data in a legal and ethical fashion.
2. Verify the authorship.
3. Determine the reliability and clarity of the SNS data.
4. Determine whether it represents fantasy/fiction or the defendant's true thoughts.
5. Corroborate with other sources and the defendant.
6. Question the meaning and context with the defendant.
7. Examine how the data may have impacted or biased your assessment.
8. Determine the data's relevance to the diagnostic and competency questions.

There is no reason SNS data cannot be considered and used like any other form of third-party information. In fact, if it exists and is not utilized, questions could be raised about whether the CST evaluation lacked thoroughness. However, if evaluators utilize caution, social media can aid in reaching clear diagnostic and competency opinions.

Case Profile 1

Type of Evaluation

Competency to Stand Trial

Case Context

Mr. Daniel Thomas was a 37-year old man who was undergoing an evaluation of his competency to stand trial. The evaluation took place within an inpatient prison hospital over the course of several weeks. He was charged with several counts related to impersonating a federal official.

Sources of Information

1. Clinical interviews with Mr. Thomas
2. Court Order, dated 10/30/2018;
3. Criminal Complaint, dated 06/28/2017;
4. Indictment, dated 07/12/2018;
5. Criminal Docket, printed 01/02/2019;
6. Competency Evaluation by Dr. Franklin, dated 10/26/2018;
7. 276 pages of discovery material, including investigative reports;
8. Incident/Investigation Reports from the Village of Montgomery Police Department, dated 11/12/2015 to 12/01/2015;
9. Federal Bureau of Prisons records from 06/27/2018 to 05/24/2019;
10. Medical records from Local Community Hospital, dated 11/13/2015 to 01/22/2016;
11. Medical records from State Hospital – Celebration, dated 10/26/2017 to 10/28/2017;
12. Medical records from Blank Health System, dated 01/13/2019;
13. Psychological Evaluation by Dr. Thomas, dated 10/19/2015;
14. Psychological Evaluation by Dr. Jones, dated 10/27/2015;
15. Psychological Evaluation by Dr. Smith, dated 10/29/2015;
16. Psychiatric records from Dr. Gonzalez, dated 01/29/2015 to 05/26/2018;
17. Review of Mr. Thomas's social media material including personal websites, Facebook, Instagram, Youtube, and Amazon Video on 03/12/2019;
18. Telephone interviews with Mr. Thomas's mother, Jane Thomas, from 03/11/2019 to 05/16/2019;
19. Telephone interview with Mr. Thomas's acquaintance, Frank Burns, on 04/02/2019;
20. Telephone interview with Mr. Thomas's acquaintance, Alan Foster, on 04/08/2019;
21. Telephone interview with Mr. Thomas's civil attorney, Kyle Wooley, on 04/22/2019.
22. The following psychological tests (and relevant versions) were administered separately to Mr. Thomas and his mother:

    a. Adaptive Behavior Assessment System Third Edition (ABAS-3)
    b. Conners' Adult ADHD Rating Scales – Self-Report: Long Version (CAARS-S:L and CAARS-O: L)

Relevant Background

Mr. Thomas is single, never married, and was most recently living with his parents. He has lived independently at intervals when provided financial support. He graduated high school and earned a certificate in sports management at a state university.

He has never maintained steady employment. He has no prior criminal history nor a history of alcohol or substance abuse. Besides asthma that is well controlled with treatment, he is physically healthy with no history of head trauma, seizures, or other significant ailments.

Mr. Thomas was identified as having mental health problems from a very young age. Diagnoses he received by the time he was a teenager included Asperger's, Tourette's syndrome, bipolar disorder, and schizoaffective disorder. He was described by family and treatment providers as having "grandiose" beliefs, ideas, and plans for many years that persisted despite engagement in various psychiatric and psychological treatments. These included claims he was a sports agent who had several professional athletes as clients, he produced several realty television programs, he was "semi-famous" on YouTube and other social media outlets, he had millions of dollars in sports memorabilia, and he started various companies and product lines (e.g., hair gel, skin cream).

The most notable concern related to his competency was the potential delusional beliefs he had about being an authorized federal agent, the basis for the criminal charges. The prosecution alleged he personally printed out and constructed official-looking badges and credentials and displayed those on social media. Mr. Thomas denied having done anything illegal and indicated he was unfairly targeted because he was suing Twitter for several million dollars after his account was terminated for posting inappropriate content.

Behavioral Observations and Mental Status

At first, Mr. Thomas presented as calm and alert. He was dressed appropriately but mildly disheveled. He was oriented to the city and facility, but not the state. He knew the date. He was pleasant and cooperative, and his speech was clear; however, his thoughts wandered at times and he made several grandiose statements about being law enforcement personnel and having a high IQ. Conversely, he acknowledged having trouble "comprehending things." He had some difficulty providing details and a coherent narrative. His affect was odd and labile. At one point during the initial interview he described his cell mate at a prior facility having committed suicide (which was later not substantiated), at which point he began crying and stated he has been "traumatized." His sleep has reportedly been poor for some time. Earlier he began laughing uncontrollably while describing the prior forensic examiner getting into psychology "in order to get laid."

Mr. Thomas frequently presented as demanding and inappropriate with staff. Staff noted that he would enter the nurses' station despite prompts that he was not allowed to do so without being invited. He received one incident report for threatening bodily harm for sending a threatening email to his attorney and two for assaulting without serious injury.

During subsequent clinical interviews, aspects of Mr. Thomas's mental status varied considerably. On some occasions, he presented as calm and clear. His speech increased in rate when he spoke of his complaints, but it remained coherent and understandable. He could be interrupted and did not speak over the evaluator. On other occasions, Mr. Thomas became visibly agitated, rocked in his seat, and raised his voice. He was resistant to limit-setting in these interviews and spoke over the evaluator. During these times he did not appear to self-initiate strategies to calm himself, but when strongly redirected to pause and collect himself, he was able to do so. In addition, he laughed loudly and unrestrainedly at times that were incongruent with the topic of conversation (e.g., when asked what a less serious charge than his would be, he replied "a notary violation"). Mr. Thomas's level of cooperation also varied. At times he appeared eager to provide information or to prove the extent of his legal knowledge. However, he often engaged in evasive responses as well, providing incorrect answers and then laughing, or denying that he had ever made particular statements. His sleep and appetite varied. He complained of getting too little sleep due to the ambient noise and light on a particular locked unit, but noted this improved after he was moved to different unit. He variably reported gaining/losing too much weight, but records revealed no significant changes. His personal hygiene ranged from fair to disheveled.

During the course of the CST assessment, Mr. Thomas frequently bragged about and highlighted many accomplishments. For example, he stated, "I'm famous as a reality TV star and sports marketing agent." He added that he has signed many famous athletes and received his Association of Tennis Professional (ATP) tour card in 2009. However, he stated some have claimed he is a fraud and he is suing them for breach of contracts. However, he also sought to explain and clarify what he believed were misperceptions the authorities and others had about him. For example, he denied ever claiming to be a federal law enforcement officer, but rather was a "leading member" of several fraternal organizations, such as volunteer firefighter and police groups (e.g., Neighborhood Watch). In order to determine the veracity of his claims, the evaluator first reviewed the available records and spoke to his mother, with whom he was reportedly very close. His mother indicated her son was "very delusional" and recounted several of the claims noted above. She affirmed he had extensive baseball memorabilia but doubted its value. She also corroborated he has made several online videos and received a sports agent certificate after completing courses at a local university (from where he claimed to have earned a degree and was a university "alumni"). Mr. Thomas' mother noted that while he is fairly intelligent and can initially appear convincing, he has never had the ability to follow through or succeed in his ventures.

Summary of Test Results

To supplement extensive testing conducted by prior examiners, Mr. Thomas and his mother each completed the Adaptive Behavior Assessment System Third Edition (ABAS-3). The ABAS-3 is a comprehensive assessment of adaptive abilities needed to effectively and independently carry out skills needed to care for oneself, interact with others, and complete necessary tasks.

Mr. Thomas' General Adaptive Composite (GAC) and Conceptual and Social adaptive domain standard scores fall in in the extremely low range (all at or below the second percentile), as rated by both himself and his mother. While Mr. Thomas rated his own skills in the Practical adaptive domain in the low range (sixth percentile), his mother rated his abilities in this domain in the extremely low range (0.2nd percentile). Mr. Thomas' scores and his mother's scores in the GAC and all adaptive domains were significantly different. However, the magnitude of the difference between these ratings is not particularly rare compared to other individuals of his age. His self-ratings indicate a rare and statistically significant strength of his practical skills (e.g., taking care of himself, managing his health and safety, using community resources) over his social skills and his conceptual skills (i.e., communication, academic skill, ability to be self-directed). Mrs. Thomas's ratings of her son indicate a relatively rare and statistically significant strength of her son's social skills over his conceptual and practical skills. It is interesting to note that Mr. Thomas indicated on 54 items that he is not able to perform particular behaviors because he does not have the skills to do so or has some limitation in performing the behavior. By contrast, Mrs. Thomas indicated on only one item that her son cannot perform the behavior. In sum, although the severity of the ratings differed between Mr. Thomas and his mother, both sources of data are supportive of impairment in his adaptive functioning either due to a deficit in skill or his performance of the skill.

The Conners' Adult ADHD Rating Scales (CAARS) was also administered. The CAARS are a set of easily administered self- and observer-rated instruments to assess for symptoms and behaviors related to Attention-Deficit/Hyperactivity Disorder (ADHD) in adults ages 18 and up. Mr. Thomas was administered the CAARS - Self-Report: Long Version (CAARS-S:L), and his mother completed the CAARS Observer: Long Version (CAARS - O:L). Mr. Thomas' Inconsistency Index was elevated (score of 9), so the results of his self-report are considered with caution. Although Mr. Thomas's ratings of symptom severity were less severe than his mother's ratings, they both reported a similar pattern of impairment. Data from both sources indicate Mr. Thomas experiences clinically significant symptoms of ADHD, including both inattentive and hyperactive-impulsive symptoms.

Diagnostic Conclusions

Based on all available data, it was determined that Mr. Thomas met criteria for the following diagnoses:

- Autism Spectrum Disorder, Level 1
- Attention Deficit-Hyperactivity Disorder, Combined presentation
- Bipolar I Disorder, Current or most recent episode hypomanic
- Narcissistic Personality Disorder
- Tourette's Disorder

Summary of Data Relevant to Psycho-Legal Question

As part of the discovery, printed copies of Mr. Thomas's website pages were obtained, where he purportedly made several unsubstantiated claims. This included postings about his affiliation with federal law enforcement and credentials he allegedly manufactured. While those claims and allegations were up for some dispute, the discovery did not contain any evidence that challenged his many other claims. Two acquaintances of Mr. Thomas were also contacted. Both individuals characterized Mr. Thomas as frequently embellishing the truth and misrepresenting their relationship. For example, one was a law enforcement officer who recognized Mr. Thomas's disabilities and "took him under [my] wing" as part of a volunteer police officer program. This lasted for less than two weeks and Mr. Thomas had no official duties with the department. However, he later falsely and publicly claimed that he and the officer were "partners in the war on drugs" and completed many assignments together.

Mr. Thomas insisted he could prove his claims if the evaluator obtained material he has produced online. He specified several items that could readily be verified. For example, he said he is rather well known for several realty shows he produced and starred in, as well for being a regular guest on the show of a famous radio personality. At that point of the evaluation, it was clear Mr. Thomas was fairly bright and had a good factual understanding of the proceedings. Further, his speech and the form of his thinking was within normal limits. The primary concern as it related to his competency dealt with whether or not he had delusional beliefs that impacted his ability to make rational decisions and work with his attorney. The working hypotheses included that his claims were true, delusional, or party true and partly delusional. If there was some truth to his claims, it could certainly be the case his claims were simply grossly exaggerated for personal gain. In order to test the hypotheses, it appeared necessary to obtain additional data. Online searches and speaking to additional third parties familiar with Mr. Thomas's activities appeared the only viable way this could be done.

Prior to searching social media Mr. Thomas was questioned about the extent of his social media presence, in order to ascertain where to find the material he reportedly produced. He readily described the material, including videos he had produced on Amazon Prime and YouTube. In the search, the evaluator discovered he had in fact produced several videos, some of which were worthy enough to be distributed by Amazon. The videos were "reality tv" in nature, where Mr. Thomas discussed his great successes despite his disabilities (i.e., he repeatedly stated he had Tourette's, bipolar disorder, and Asperger's). He also called in and spoke several times to a national radio personality, who seemed to engage Mr. Thomas in much debate and argument on political issues. After reviewing all the content, the evaluator wondered whether Mr. Thomas was perhaps being exploited by these media sources, and/or he was taking advantage of his disabilities for personal gain and notoriety. Mr. Thomas initially characterized himself as being a major contributor and writer for the radio program and stated his videos had an enormous following or viewership.

Clinical Forensic Opinion

The area of competency that remained of greatest concern for Mr. Thomas was his ability to assist counsel in his defense. Discussions with him about the evidence and pleas resulted in irritation, some hostility, and rigid opinions as to how he wished to proceed. Also, his ability to remain calm and coherent during court proceedings was of some concern. When extremely agitated, anxious, and embarrassed, Mr. Thomas had difficulty controlling his emotions. In the past this included verbal and physical outbursts. However, he demonstrated good ability to calmly discuss these topics on occasion. In addition, Mr. Thomas may have difficulty testifying coherently in a stressful situation such as a trial, and where contradictory information to his rigid thought patterns is presented. To further complicate matters, Mr. Thomas asserted several times he would intentionally "lose it" on the stand and "look crazy" and not be able to testify due to his "delusions, fantasies, and grandiose beliefs." While on one hand he saw himself as incapable of proceeding, on the other hand he viewed himself as highly intelligent and wanted to challenge the allegations.

Overall, Mr. Thomas appeared to have an adequate factional knowledge of court proceedings. Although he had some misunderstandings, he demonstrated the ability to retain corrective feedback. Though some gaps in knowledge may remain, there was no evidence to suggest he would not be able to learn new information with the assistance of an attorney. His ability to rationally understand his legal situation was more complicated to determine. At baseline, his difficulty with attention, narcissistic personality, and rigid patterns of thinking make it hard for Mr. Thomas to hear and consider information that may be damaging to his sense of self or that contradicts his personal desires, which change frequently. However, when directed to engage in calming techniques and communication skills, he is able to interact appropriately, consider new information in his decision-making processes, and engage in more rational evaluation of his options. In sum, although his abilities to demonstrate rational understanding of his legal situation and to work to assist his attorney may be difficult for him, he has demonstrated the capability to do so with some assistance.

Recommendations

The following considerations may be useful for Mr. Thomas in moving forward with his legal proceedings. He should continue taking his medications as prescribed and comply with other treatment recommendations. In interviews, he has been responsive to firm limit setting and redirection when he begins to digress or perseverate on a given topic. This practice would be helpful in maintaining appropriate interactions with his attorney. Finally, he has demonstrated some benefit from practicing emotion regulation and distress tolerance skills (i.e., acting mindfully, pausing and observing thoughts and feelings before reacting). Continued practice of these skills would benefit Mr. Thomas in tolerating the stress of legal proceedings.

How Did Social Media Impact This Case?

Watching and reviewing the SNS data was useful in accomplishing three things. First, it helped establish that, in fact, Mr. Thomas was the creator and participant of material that had some considerable viewership. The SNS data, which included a website, audio recordings, and YouTube and Amazon Prime videos, clearly depicted him in images, voice, and video. Further, Mr. Thomas was very familiar with the content. Therefore, there was never any question about authorship.

Second, the review helped put the material and Mr. Thomas's claims in better perspective. While Mr. Thomas had some level of "success," his media and online following was not nearly as grand as he reported it to be. For instance, the Amazon videos were very brief, of non-professional quality (in the evaluator's opinion), and were not viewed by a large audience. Also, Mr. Thomas did not help write or contribute in any substantial way to the radio program. The program simply allowed him to call in multiple times to engage in debate on political topics. He was never paid in that role or for any of the online videos he produced.

Third, reviewing the material allowed the evaluator to question Mr. Thomas in greater detail about his thinking and reasoning. At first, it was not clear how much of what he said in the videos reflected genuine beliefs versus statements designed to entertain and lead to greater viewership. During interviews, the evaluator was able to test not only the nature of his beliefs, but how rigidly he held those views. Mr. Thomas initially described being a "celebrity" and important producer with strong conviction. However, when gently challenged about the significance of his roles and contributions, he acknowledged not having made any money, written or co-produced anything for the radio program, or had the number of viewers he previously claimed. It became apparent that, while Mr. Thomas's reported activities had a firm foundation in reality, he grossly embellished his importance and success. His claims became muted and more in line with what truly occurred once challenged and pressed for greater detail. His presentation was not consistent with rigidly held delusions, rather he demonstrated considerable flexibility and willingness to acknowledge the overstatements he made. It appeared Mr. Thomas's strong need to be recognized led him to exaggerate his accomplishments. What was also apparent was that Mr. Thomas had a strong need to be recognized, which led him to exaggerate. Further, he acknowledged his grandiose and bombastic presentation style was designed for attention and "shock value."

Amidst Mr. Thomas's many reports, he also claimed to be a famous "porn star" and cited pornographic websites where he has performed. Interestingly, upon a routine medical examination as part of his inpatient CST evaluation, staff noted Mr. Thomas had a penile implant. Mr. Thomas indicated having enlargement done to promote his pornographic career. While the implant was present, his claim of pornography fame had questionable veracity given reports by his mother, his lack of any wealth, and other questionable claims. This claim created a more interesting, but problematic situation and raised some ethical and personal concerns. On the one hand, it may have been useful to establish whether Mr. Thomas's claims were true. But would this mean the evaluator would have to search pornographic websites and view pornography? If one were to proceed in that manner, could the salacious material prejudice the evaluator's view of Mr. Thomas or negatively impact the opinions? What if the evaluator was repulsed or had strong emotional reactions to what was viewed? If so, questions could be raised about the neutrality and objectivity of the evaluator.

One option to avoid the possible bias (or the perception of bias) was to ask a third party (perhaps an assistant or colleague) to briefly review the sites in order to verify or refute his claims. This would allow the evaluator to at least determine whether his report had any basis in reality or required any further follow up. A final option, as this evaluator saw it, and the one ultimately taken, was to not explore whether Mr. Thomas had a pornography career. Given Mr. Thomas made numerous grandiose claims which were verifiable through SNS data, it did not seem necessary to turn over yet another stone. Whether a false statement by Mr. Thomas or not, at that point there were several examples and a clearer picture of his clinical presentation. Further, the pornography claim had no direct bearing on his competency or thinking about his case. While evaluators do not always know when something will turn out to be probative until they review it, one must consider the potential prejudicial effects and whether additional data is necessary to reach one's opinions. In this case, it was deemed unnecessary and potentially prejudicial.

Case Profile 2

Type of Evaluation

Competency to Stand Trial

Case Context

The defendant in this case, 35-year-old Mr. Randall Scott, was ordered by the District Court to undergo a period of hospitalization and treatment to determine whether there was a substantial probability his competency to stand trial could be restored in the foreseeable future. The evaluation took place within an inpatient prison hospital over the course of several months. Mr. Scott was charged with Communicating Threats.

Sources of Information

1. Clinical interviews (ongoing)
2. Evaluation of Competency to Stand Trial-Revised (ECST-R; 09/16/13)
3. Court Order, dated 06/06/13

4. PACER information
5. Criminal Complaint, dated 02/27/13
6. Forensic Evaluation by Kathleen Harris, Ph.D., dated 05/20/13
7. Copies of Donald Trump's Facebook page
8. Copies of Mr. Scott's Facebook page
9. Compact Disc containing a video of Mr. Scott's interview with law enforcement officials, dated 02/26/13
10. Criminal History
11. Livingstone College Transcript
12. National Crime Information Center (NCIC) criminal history
13. Telephone interview with Angelina Bowen, sister of Mr. Scott
14. Telephone interview with Phillip Carroll, Defense Counsel for Mr. Scott
15. Telephone interview with Mark Fletcher, AUSA

Relevant Background

Mr. Scott readily provided information about his personal background. The information he provided was consistent with information reported by Dr. Harris.

Mr. Scott reported he was born in Colorado Springs, Colorado, to the non-marital union of Justin Bowen and Angelina Scott. He noted his parents married shortly after he was born and he is the oldest of eight children. His youngest sibling is currently 14-years-old. Mr. Scott was "not sure" when he met his developmental milestones, but indicated he did not believe he was delayed in meeting them. He described his parents as "strict, but I got whooping's. They were strict, but also lenient. They were fair." He indicated he never experienced or witnessed any abuse. Mr. Scott reported his mother died in 2008 from cancer. He described he has a "good relationship" with his family and was in close contact with them prior to his arrest. His father continues to reside in Colorado. When asked if his father might visit him, Mr. Scott indicated he would not want his father to visit because "it is weird for them to think of me as a mental patient." He indicated his father is employed in the t-shirt screening business.

Mr. Scott indicated he has never been married and has no children. However, for a period of time he was under the impression that he had two children. He stated that on two occasions, shortly after he began dating a woman she informed him she was pregnant. Paternity tests subsequently indicated he is not the father of either child. He described that he considers himself to have been a parent to both children. He indicated he has had three serious relationships in his life. Two were the aforementioned relationships and the third ended last year, but was 5 years in duration. He indicated his most recent relationship ended due to his legal issues. When asked about friendships, Mr. Scott noted he had friends growing up, "but they weren't really my friends. There were just playing on my intelligence. Any idea I had they were trying to sketch it away from me." He provided several examples in which he believed his friends were trying to steal his business ideas or girlfriends from him.

Regarding his education, Mr. Scott reported he graduated from Livingstone College in Pueblo, Colorado with a Bachelor of Arts in History. He described himself as a B student who was active in extracurricular activities. However, his transcript indicates he earned a Grade Point Average of 2.4, which is approximately equivalent with a D average. Mr. Scott's Bachelor of Arts in History was conferred on 05/05/03. He noted that in high school he lettered in Football and Basketball and participated in Chess Club, Science Club, and Debate Club. He reported he was in a fight during the sixth grade with another student who was bullying him. As a result, he was suspended for 6 days. He noted this is the only time he was in trouble at school.

Mr. Scott reported he was employed as a teacher, but resigned due to a "misunderstanding about the curriculum." He explained he was teaching the curriculum, but "it was the extra stuff I brought to the table that got me out of favor with the principal." He noted he was showing videos to students about "how to break a slave." He acknowledged the videos were graphic and may not have been appropriate for school. Mr. Scott stated he has also worked to start a magazine, in a group home, as a counselor and mentor, and as a dispatcher for a car transport company. He stated he has never been fired from any job. He reported he has no military history.

Mr. Scott reported he has several criminal convictions, which is consistent with his criminal record from National Crime Information Center (NCIC). He stated he was arrested for Possession of a Stolen Vehicle and given probation. He was also convicted of Possession with Intent to Sell and Deliver Cocaine and again given probation. Mr. Scott stated he was arrested for Assault on a Female, but these charges were dismissed. He reported he has never been sentenced to prison.

When asked about his medical history, Mr. Scott indicated he experienced a concussion when he played football in college (approximately age 20). He also noted he was unconscious on one occasion from alcohol and believes someone put something in his drink. He noted he experienced asthma as child and used an inhaler, but no longer experienced these difficulties.

Mr. Scott maintained he had no history of mental health problems and never received any kind of treatment. He reported he began using marijuana at age 15 and stopped in 2010. As noted, he has a prior conviction for selling cocaine, but reported he did not use cocaine. Mr. Scott described himself as an occasional drinker. When asked about treatment for addiction, Mr. Scott indicated he had received treatment for gambling addiction because he was online gambling.

During a telephone interview with Angelina Bowen, Mr. Scott's sister, she reported her brother has no history of mental health difficulties. She reported that when he was arrested and sent for a mental health evaluation, the family was "shocked." She noted Mr. Scott was living with her at the time of his alleged activities and subsequent arrest. She noted he was helpful around the house, took care of her children, and appeared "fine." She reported he went to the library for long periods each day and she assumed he was trying to find employment. He did not mention his Facebook activities to her. Ms. Bowen noted Mr. Scott shared his belief that he and Richelle Carey were "soul mates." Ms. Bowen stated she wanted to believe his statements, but found them unusual.

Behavioral Observations and Mental Status

Mr. Scott's mental status was largely stable and unchanging during this evaluation period. His hygiene and grooming were well maintained. He was alert and correctly oriented to his person, place, situation, and time. Attention and memory functions were assessed as grossly intact. His speech was normal in rate, rhythm, and volume. No articulation deficits were present. He reported he was not experiencing any perceptual disturbances and did not appear to be responding to internal stimuli. No mood disturbances were endorsed or observed. Affect was euthymic. He reported he had no thoughts to harm himself or anyone else. Eye contact was appropriate.

One significant change in Mr. Scott's mental status was the presence of delusions. Initially, Mr. Scott expressed delusions that he was part of a Facebook game controlled by engineers at Facebook in which he was forced to participate. He believed there was a game because his personal Facebook page became filled with information from newscasters, political figures, and other media sources. This information filled his page so that he was no longer receiving updates from his friends. He believed this was happening because he had a "page of privilege" and because he was a "person of privilege." This privilege allowed him to make posts on the pages of celebrities (e.g., Donald Trump and George W. Bush) and this ability was special to him. Most other Facebook users were not able to post on celebrity pages like Mr. Scott. As part of Mr. Scott's special abilities, he was able to make "reads" from the information that was on the sidebar of his page. Mr. Scott espoused his belief that he had special information/secrets that he could not share with others, which he learned through Facebook. As part of his delusions, he believed he had a special connection to several media personnel (e.g., Dan Abrams and Richelle Carey). These individuals were feeding him special information about breaking news. For example, he believed he was the individual to break news that Michael Strahan was hired for the Kelly and Michael show. Mr. Scott believed that by going through this Facebook game he had "become a better human being" and he did not "live like people in the world. People that are here. The criminal aspect. There is a lustful aspect. I don't look at people with lust. I don't judge people. I have a lot of knowledge from what I learned from Facebook."

Mr. Scott also had delusions about his relationship with Richelle Carey. He explained that her profile kept coming up on his page, meaning that he and Richelle Carey were soul mates and he was going to be married to her, even though he had never met or corresponded with her.

Over the course of several months, Mr. Scott was informed the evaluator considered these beliefs delusions and not reality based. Initially, he was resistant to this information, however over time the rigidity of Mr. Scott's beliefs loosened and at the completion of his evaluation he disregarded those beliefs. While Mr. Scott does not articulate that he was experiencing a mental illness with delusions, he has indicated he was mistaken. When asked about the change, he stated, "When three doctors all tell you are wrong, you gotta listen."

During his stay at the facility, Mr. Scott frequently went to recreation, the library, or watched TV. He went to the dining hall for meals and to laundry to exchange his clothing. Mr. Scott navigated the institution without difficulty. He lived with a cellmate without complaint and worked with staff easily. He was polite and cooperative with both inmates and staff.

Summary of Test Results

Mr. Scott was not given any psychological assessment measures during his hospitalization.

Diagnostic Conclusions

According to the *Diagnostic and Statistical Manual of Mental Disorders, Fifth Edition, (DSM-5)*, by the American Psychiatric Association, Mr. Scott's diagnosis is as follows:

Delusional disorder, mixed type, first episode, in partial remission

The diagnosis of delusional disorder, mixed type, first episode, in partial remission has been assigned to Mr. Scott based on the presence of referential and grandiose delusions. Referential delusions are when an individual believes that certain gestures, comments, or environmental cues are a special message for him or her. In Mr. Scott's case, he believed he was receiving special messages in Facebook. Grandiose delusions are defined as when an individual believes he or she has exceptional abilities, wealth, or fame. Mr. Scott believed he was a "person of privilege" and as a select Facebook user he could post on the celebrity pages. As Mr. Scott experienced both referential and grandiose delusions with no one being prominent over the other, he is assigned the mixed type specifier. The essential feature of delusional disorder is the presence of one or more delusions that persist for at least one month. There is evidence to suggest Mr. Scott was experiencing these delusions from 02/27/13, when a criminal complaint was filed based on his Facebook posts, until approximately 11/14/13. During interviews after 11/14/13, Mr. Scott disregarded his delusions and therefore, is considered to be in remission.

One distinguishing feature of delusional disorder is if hallucinations are present, they are typically not prominent and are related to the delusional theme. Mr. Scott has repeatedly denied experiencing hallucinations and does not appear to be experiencing perceptual disturbances. Individuals with delusional disorder typically do not experience marked impairment in their daily functioning apart from the delusion. As noted, Mr. Scott does not have significant impairments in his life, with the exception of his limited ability to find employment. Family members expressed surprise about his Facebook activity and his beliefs associated with it. He has maintained familial and romantic relationships, suggesting limited impairment. No impairments, other than those related to competency, were observed while he was hospitalized. In order to meet the criteria for this disorder, mood symptoms (depression or mania) are relatively brief. Mr. Scott did not display any symptoms consistent with a mood disorder. Finally, the disturbance is not due to the effects of a substance (e.g., drugs or alcohol) or due to a medical condition. Mr. Scott has endorsed limited use of drugs or alcohol. Consistent with his report, he was arrested for selling cocaine approximately 10 years ago. He noted he stopped using marijuana four years ago and is an occasional drinker, suggesting his delusions are unlikely to be associated with substance use. As noted, he did not require medical intervention while at the FMC.

Mr. Scott's diagnosis is consistent with Dr. Harris's assessment. However, as Mr. Scott now disregards his beliefs he is considered to be in partial remission.

Summary of Data Relevant to Psycho-Legal Question

Mr. Scott was charged with Communicating Threats. The criminal complaint alleges he posted the following messages on Facebook:

- "We pray for Favor in supplying a candidate at the [redacted] Elementary School in [redacted] in demonstrating full concentration in killing as many children as possible in our dedication and love to the Devil for all time. Where we hope to sustain our Reign of Evil for all time."
- "We pray for Favor in supplying a candidate at [redacted] Middle School in killing as many kids possible in the Name of the Devil for all time. As we hope to secure our alignment and service to the Will of the Devil for years to come in providing our Blood in the Evils of the Devil for generations to come. As we serve the Devil for all time. On Both Knees We pray with Confidence to the Devil! AMEN!"
- "Richelle Carey and I pray for Favor in planting a Bomb at the [redacted] Arena in showing our Love and Dedication to the Purpose of the Devil. We pray for Favor in making sure we demonstrate a form of Evil in attack in planting a Bomb or Candidate at the Cosmos Club downtown in killing people in the surprise of Evil showing up at any time. We Pray for Favor in activating both plans if possible in showing our dedication and want in displaying our appetite for evil in the Image of the Devil. On Both Knees We confidently pray to the Devil! AMEN!"
- "Richelle Carey and I pray for Favor in making sure we hit a target in planting a Bomb at Privilege Night spot where hundreds of students will be sure to go in securing our purpose in priority. We pray for Favor in supplying a candidate to make sure we hit targets and increase our Reign of terror on People for years to come in forming our family in the Evils of the Devil for all time."

Several other similar postings were alleged to have been made by Mr. Scott. The criminal complaint also indicated that at the time of his arrest, Mr. Scott admitted to law enforcement to making the threats. During his interview, Mr. Scott admitted to making the threats from library computers by posting messages from his Facebook account. He asked investigators if they were familiar with the Sandy Hook school shooting. When they responded they were familiar, he stated words to the effect that "it was all about the body count."

As part of the discovery, Mr. Scott's Facebook pages were obtained. Additionally, the Facebook pages where he made comments (e.g., Facebook page of Donald Trump) were also obtained.

Clinical Forensic Opinion

Mr. Scott's attorney, Mr. Carroll, was interviewed regarding his concerns about Mr. Scott's competency related deficits. Mr. Carroll described that Mr. Scott did not appear to understand the consequences of his postings. When discussing the case, Mr. Scott was focused on his beliefs and did not appear able to understand how his postings might be viewed by others. Additionally, Mr. Scott's focus on his delusions interfered with discussions about his legal case.

With regard to the issue of competency to stand trial, Mr. Scott was administered the Evaluation of Competency to Stand Trial - Revised (ECST-R), which is a structured interview to assess the defendant's factual understanding of the court proceedings (FAC), rational understanding of the current legal circumstances (RAC), and ability to consult with counsel (CWC). In addition to assessing competency to stand trial, the ECST-R also provides a systematic screening for a defendant's feigned psychopathology as a deliberate attempt to avoid being found competent for proceedings. Mr. Scott obtained scores in the normal range on his factual and rational understanding of the proceedings. Further, his rational ability to consult with counsel and overall rational ability were also in the normal range. There was no evidence of feigned incompetency or endorsement of atypical psychological experiences.

Consistent with Dr. Harris's report, Mr. Scott demonstrated a good understanding of the factual elements related to his case and legal proceedings. He correctly identified the responsibilities of the judge, defense counsel, and prosecution. He correctly named his charges and explained the meaning of the charge against him. He identified the role of the jury and contrasted that with a bench trial. Mr. Scott clearly identified the dangers of speaking to the prosecutor without his attorney present.

Mr. Scott demonstrated a rational understanding of the courtroom procedures. He could compare and contrast the best and worst potential outcomes in his case. He did not appear to have any delusional beliefs about the courtroom. He described how he should conduct himself while in court and to date had been able and willing to comport his behavior to the expectations of the courtroom.

Mr. Scott did not appear to have any irrational beliefs about his attorney, who he correctly identified. He described a scenario in which they had differing opinions and how he worked with his attorney to find a mutually agreeable solution. His expectations of his attorney were realistic. There is no evidence that he has delusional beliefs about his attorney.

At the time the ECST-R was completed (09/16/13), psychotic symptoms were evident during clinical interviews. Even though Mr. Scott correctly recited the charge against him, he could not appreciate how this charge applied to him. When asked to describe how the charge of "Communicating Threats" related to him, he provided delusional information about Facebook. During initial interviews, Mr. Scott's delusions affected his ability to work with his attorney. He could not engage in a meaningful discussion about legal strategy.

The evaluator discussed Mr. Scott's mental illness with him at length. He was provided information about his mental illness, the reasons for his diagnosis, and how his mental illness negatively affected his competency to stand trial. During this period, Mr. Scott's views on Facebook became malleable and he eventually rejected them outright. At the completion of the evaluation period, Mr. Scott was able to meaningfully discuss the allegations against him and consider a variety of legal options. He no longer perseverated on his delusions. This was a significant change from his presentation during Dr. Harris's evaluation and when he first arrived at the facility. This change is attributed to the remission in his mental illness.

The evaluator concluded Mr. Scott does not currently suffer from a mental disease or defect that would preclude him proceeding to trial. During clinical interviews, Mr. Scott demonstrated an understanding of the legal process. He was able to give a coherent and thorough overview of his involvement in the legal system, to include the proceedings related to the instant offense. There is no evidence to suggest that Mr. Scott does not understand the legal process, charges against him, or how to assist in his defense.

Recommendations

No specific recommendations were offered as part of this evaluation.

How Did Social Media Impact This Case?

The SNS data was helpful in this case for two main reasons. First, the basis for Mr. Scott's present charges was the information he was alleged to have posted online. Mr. Scott reported to the evaluator and to law enforcement that he was the author of the SNS data and provided explanation of his meaning in the posts. Generally, the standard for competency includes "sufficient present ability to consult with his lawyer with a reasonable degree of rational understanding" and a "rational as well as factual understanding of the proceedings against him." [*Dusky v. United States*, 362 U.S. 402 (1960)]. Assessing for a factual understanding for the judicial system and well as case-specific material is one component of competency assessment. In this case, showing Mr. Scott his Facebook posts and discussing how they formed some of the evidence that would potentially be used at a trial, was an essential part of the evaluation. Discussing this material with him provided a way to evaluate his ability to discuss, understand, and retain this information. In addition to providing information about Mr. Scott's factual understanding, discussion about his posts provided information as to how Mr. Scott might work with an attorney.

Mr. Scott's Facebook pages also provided valuable information about his past and present mental health functioning. During interviews, he and the evaluator looked at the pages together and discussed his delusional beliefs. Without discussing this material with Mr. Scott, his delusional belief system and how his mental status changed over time would not have been fully understood. For example, Mr. Scott's Facebooks pages from 2 years prior to the alleged offense were substantially different in content and style than the posts from 2013. During the initial stages of my evaluation, Mr. Scott remained delusional and provided extensive information about his belief system. He explained how he could "make reads" from the sides of the pages and asserted he was in a romantic relationship with a well-known journalist. This was helpful when forming the diagnostic impressions. Likewise, when Mr. Scott began to reject his delusions, he and the evaluator reviewed the Facebook pages together and he articulated that his writing did not make sense. For example, he questioned why he capitalized words in the middle of the sentence when that was not needed (e.g., providing our Blood in the Evils of the Devil). Of note, his Facebook posts from prior to the onset of his mental illness were generally logical and grammatically correct. Reviewing and discussing his postings aided in the assessment of how his mental status changed over time, which in turn aided in determining if he continued to have a threshold condition.

References

American Psychological Association (2013). Specialty guidelines for forensic psychologists. Washington, DC. Author.

American Psychological Association. (2017). *Ethical principles of psychologists and code of conduct*. Washington, DC: Author.

Coffey, C. A., Batastini, A. B., & Vitacco, M. J. (2018). Clues from the digital world: A survey of clinicians' reliance on social media as collateral data in forensic evaluations. *Professional Psychology: Research and Practice, 49*(5–6), 345–354. https://doi.org/10.1037/pro0000206.

Dusky v. United States, 362 U.S. 402 (1960).

Kaslow, F. W., Patterson, T., & Gottlieb, M. (2011). Ethical dilemmas in psychologists accessing internet data: Is it justified? *Professional Psychology: Research and Practice, 42*(2), 105–112. https://doi.org/10.1037/a0022002.

Murrie, D., Boccaccini, M., Guarnera, L. A., & Rufino, K. A. (2013). Are forensic experts biased by the side that retained them? *Psychological Science, 24*(10), 1889–1897. https://doi.org/10.1177/0956797613481812.

Neal, T. M. S., & Brodsky, S. L. (2016). Forensic psychologists' perceptions of bias and potential correction strategies in forensic mental health evaluations. *Psychology, Public Policy, and Law, 22*, 58–76. https://doi.org/10.1037/law0000077.

Pew Research Center, (n.d.). Retrieved from https://www.pewresearch.org/fact-tank/2019/04/10/share-of-u-s-adults-using-social-media-including-facebook-is-mostly-unchanged-since-2018/
Pirelli, G., Otto, R. K., & Estoup, A. (2016). Using internet and social media data as collateral sources of information in forensic evaluations. *Professional Psychology: Research and Practice, 47*(1), 12–17. https://doi.org/10.1037/pro0000061.
Poythress, N., Bonnie, R. J., Monahan, J., Otto, R., & Hoge, S. K. (2002). *Adjudicative competence: The MacArthur studies*. New York: Springer.
Testimony by Expert Witnesses, Article VII C.F.R. § 702 (1975).
Wroth, L. K. (1985). The federal rules of evidence in the states: A ten-year perspective. *Villanova Law Review, 30*(6). Available at: http://digitalcommons.law.villanova.edu/vlr/vol30/iss6/4.

Chapter 4
Violence Risk and Threat Assessment

Kirk Heilbrun, Victoria Pietruszka, Jennica Janssen, and Keisha April

The process of conducting mental health evaluations to inform legal decision-making has advanced considerably in the last three decades. Paralleling these advances have been very substantial advances in one type of appraisal sometimes conducted as part of forensic mental health assessment (FMHA): risk assessment for violence and other criminal offending (see, e.g., Melton et al. 2018; Otto and Douglas 2009). Despite these considerable advances, however, there is one respect in which FMHA development has apparently not kept pace with our larger society. This area involves social networking sites (SNS) and other Internet-based forms of communication and information-sharing. This chapter focuses on one aspect of risk assessment and social media: the use of the evaluee's SNS data as a form of collateral information that can inform risk assessment conducted in a forensic context.

4.1 The Nature of Risk Assessment

There are five important aspects of risk assessment generally: context, purpose, population, parameters, and approach. We consider each of these aspects in this section. This summary on the five aspects of risk assessment is drawn from more extensive discussion elsewhere (see Heilbrun 2009).

K. Heilbrun (✉) · V. Pietruszka · J. Janssen · K. April
Drexel University, Philadelphia, PA, USA
e-mail: kh33@drexel.edu

A. B. Batastini, M. J. Vitacco (eds.), *Forensic Mental Health Evaluations in the Digital Age*, https://doi.org/10.1007/978-3-030-33908-1_4

4.1.1 Context

Risk assessment is not a specific kind of FMHA. Rather, it is an appraisal that may be conducted in various contexts, including legal, clinical, school/workplace, and threats to protectees (those who are under the protection of an organization such as the United States Secret Service, which is responsible for protecting the president, vice-president, and their families). For present purposes, the distinction between risk assessment and threat assessment mainly concerns whether a specific target—individual(s) who would be victimized by the violent behavior—has been identified. This is typically not the case in risk assessment but is an important feature of threat assessment; in the following discussion, we consider threat assessment as a form of risk assessment. In legal contexts, the risk assessment is part of an evaluation conducted to assist the court in legal decision-making or to assist an attorney in preparing a case. Clinical contexts, by contrast, involve assessing risk to guide interventions intended to reduce the likelihood that an individual will harm others (though not of relevance to this chapter, "risk assessment" in standard clinical settings is often used more broadly to also include evaluations of self-harm). In school and workplace contexts, both decision-making and intervention may be guided by risk assessment. The decision involves whether the individual will continue in that setting; if so, the intervention can be guided by the findings of the risk assessment. Finally, threats to protectees are within the domain of those who work to ensure the safety of designated figures through investigation and appraisal of threat seriousness. The United States Secret Service provides a good example of this kind of professional activity. Later in this chapter, we discuss risk assessment as part of FMHA in two different cases: (1) federal sentencing and (2) juvenile transfer. Risk assessment may also be relevant to help address clinical-legal questions in other kinds of FMHA, including capital sentencing, competence to stand trial (for hospitalization purposes), mental state at the time of the offense (for both hospitalization and release), civil commitment, and juvenile commitment.

4.1.2 Population

Examinees can, of course, belong to many different populations based on their individual characteristics, with age, sex, mental health status, and setting (e.g., hospital, prison, community) being among the most prominent. Identifying the population(s) to which the individual belongs is necessary not only for clarity; it also means that the base rates of the outcome of interest can be specified and used as part of the risk assessment. Such base rate identification and application are among the most important contributions that have improved the risk assessment accuracy (see, e.g., Monahan and Steadman 1994), particularly when combined with the greater structure associated with the risk assessment process over the last two decades (Monahan 2008).

4.1.3 Parameters

This term encompasses additional considerations beyond the examinee's demographics that should be both specified and included within a risk assessment: nature and frequency of target behavior, whether the appraisal is to be given as a probability estimate or risk category, where the behavior might occur, over what period, and the relevant risk and protective factors. Prior to the development of specialized risk assessment tools (see, e.g., Otto and Douglas 2009), it was particularly important to specify these parameters at the outset of a risk assessment. One of the advantages of using a validated risk assessment tool is that many of these parameters are already defined—and the user must simply determine whether the tool fits the present risk assessment needs.

4.1.4 Approach

There are currently three approaches to risk assessment that have received support by the field: actuarial, structured professional judgment, and anamnestic. Actuarial approaches involve specifying predictors and outcomes in a way that can be measured, conducting empirical research that is sufficient to allow the statistical relationship between predictors and outcomes to be estimated in an accurate and stable fashion. Empirically-derived information is then used to create a measure that estimates the outcome of a given probability by combining the predictors using a predetermined "formula." Structured professional judgment also specifies items and outcomes to be considered but does not combine the item scores in a formulaic way. Rather, it calls for the evaluator to make an informed judgment based on the totality of the information provided; in this respect, there is discretion and flexibility that is not associated with actuarial approaches. The accuracy of both actuarial and structured clinical judgment approaches appears comparable, and both are superior to "unstructured clinical judgment"—which is distinctly less accurate (Heilbrun et al. 2009a). This difference is likely attributable to the higher level of structure associated with the more accurate approaches (Monahan 2008). Anamnestic assessment (see Melton et al. 2018) involves applied behavior analysis—using the individual's own history of the target behavior to identify individualized risk and protective factors. It is less desirable as a primary risk assessment approach when there is a specialized tool available, but useful when there is not. It is also useful for individualizing risk assessment.

4.1.5 Applicability

The final consideration to be addressed as part of risk assessment involves the fit between the present question and the available appraisal approaches. This is particularly relevant when a specialized risk assessment tool is being considered. To what extent does the tool include the population to which the evaluee belongs? Are the outcomes specified by the tool comparable to the outcome of interest for present purposes? If there is a preference for actuarial versus structured professional judgment, does the tool conform to the preference? Further, when there is no available specialized risk measure, is the anamnestic approach to be used as a primary approach to risk assessment?

4.2 The Nature of Social Networking Sites

A more thorough review of social networking and Internet-based information is provided in Chap. 1 (this volume). For present purposes, SNS will also include online tools that connect individuals to various social networks. Traditional SNS platforms include social media sites like Facebook, where users can connect and share their profiles with friends and family, and Instagram, where users can post photos and messages that can be seen by other users or "followers." Other platforms that have a social element but have not necessarily been considered as "social media" will also be considered. These include online dating applications (e.g., Bumble, Coffee Meets Bagel, Hinge, Plenty of Fish, Tinder), online communities (e.g., Twitch, which connects individuals to others with similar interests and allows them to establish virtual social networks while interacting through live chat) and forums (e.g., Reddit, also connecting people with similar interests through posts). A common thread among these platforms is that individuals can use them to make interpersonal connections and conduct social interactions.

Privacy protections, which function to limit access of unauthorized individuals to the content posted on various platforms, vary across such platforms and fall under three levels. The first tier includes publicly-accessible profiles. For example, any information posted by an individual on a public Facebook profile can be viewed unless a user changes applicable protections to create stronger privacy restrictions. If a user shares a Reddit account username, then anyone can access their history if it has not been deleted or posted in a sub-Reddit with heavier user restrictions. In the second tier, information on social media platforms is private but may be accessed through other means. This includes password-protected private Facebook pages that may nonetheless have a work-around, or restricted sub-Reddit pages. Finally, some SNS are inaccessible to the general public. This includes websites such as those contained on the deep web, which is not indexed by search engines—and may contain content that is otherwise regulated by law.

For present purposes, we focus on SNS that convey written information or pictures that is either publicly accessible or has second level privacy protections. In some cases, material with third-level protections may become available to an evaluator because it is provided along with other records provided to the evaluator to conduct the FMHA. We will not discuss the prospect of the evaluator's obtaining such information independently, however, simply because it is our view that evaluators should stay within applicable law in obtaining materials to inform FMHA (see Chap. 9, this volume, for further discussion on recommendations).

4.3 Contributions of Social Media to Risk Assessment

Risk assessment can be used for a variety of purposes. One basic aspect common across uses involves the importance of obtaining accurate information about the individual. Without accurate information regarding thoughts, feelings, and behavior, the risk assessment process is poorly informed and likely to be of limited validity.

Certainly, the challenge of obtaining accurate information is longstanding when the evaluee has external reasons for distorting information. Individuals who are evaluated for future risk as part of their legal proceedings, for example, face outcomes such as incarceration or other loss of liberties and financial loss as consequences of such proceedings. Others in school or workplace settings may face different but still adverse outcomes depending on the findings of the risk assessment. For these reasons, the field has long accepted the notion that self-report is not assumed to be accurate in FMHA (Melton et al. 2018), and the evaluator should obtain information from different sources that include self-report—as well as psychological testing and specialized measures (particularly tools with validity indicators), and third party information such as records and collateral observers (Heilbrun et al. 2009b).

It is in this third area—records—that SNS data offers the greatest contribution to FMHA generally and risk assessment more specifically. The cornerstones of evidence law are reliability (encompassing behavioral scientific constructs of both reliability and validity) and relevance (Melton et al. 2018). Verifiable written content, pictures, and videos offer documentation that is not adversely affected by memory or motivation. In this respect, social media provides information that is likely to be much more reliable than that obtained through interviews, psychological testing, or specialized tools. One disadvantage is that the presumed author may not have actually written the material; faked material may be more likely in high-profile cases. Another disadvantage of this information is that it may be less relevant than something obtained by directly targeting the areas of interest through questioning and testing. But relevance can often be appraised in a straightforward fashion. SNS content with little or no bearing on the assessment of risk can be selectively disregarded when the evaluator is using a structured approach to risk assessment, focusing only on domains with empirically-supported relevance to risk and protective factors.

SNS provides an effective means of documenting behavior, therefore. But how well does it reflect thoughts and feelings? Probably no more than any other accurate documentation of an individual's behavior. But there is one particularly important caution to be considered when using SNS content: individuals' posts and pictures may be influenced by the social context in which they were made. For example, an adolescent boy who posts a picture of himself and three others flashing gang signs and brandishing weapons on Facebook might be displaying evidence of gang involvement and a propensity toward harming others—or he might be influenced by the context of the others and the moment into posing in a way that exaggerates his antisocial interests. But such evidence should at least serve as a reasonable basis for developing hypotheses, asking questions, and offering documentation in the face of adamant denials.

4.4 Using Social Media in Risk Assessment: Ethical Considerations

The use of social media in FMHA, and the ethical questions associated with such use, are relatively new considerations for the field. A recent book on ethics in forensic psychology practice (Otto, Goldstein, & Heilbrun, 2017), for example, had little to say about the role of social media—referencing only how it might be used to obtain collateral interviews by balancing openness and discretion. This appears to reflect the limited attention to this area from the field of forensic psychology. While collateral information is frequently sought through Internet searches conducted as part of FMHA (Pirelli et al. 2018), most of the discussion on this point has been provided by forensic psychiatry (e.g., Glancy et al. 2015; Metzner and Ash 2010; Neimark et al. 2006; Recupero 2008, 2010). In particular, the question of Internet searches is addressed in the current practice guidelines of forensic psychiatry:

> Internet searches regarding the evaluee can also provide useful information. Social networking sites and other Internet social forums may contain information about the evaluee that conflicts with data provided by the evaluee or others, warranting further examination to contextualize this apparent conflict. An evaluee's online persona may constitute impression management or posturing, as people often behave or present themselves differently online than in person. It is also possible that the online information is more accurate than what the evaluee is telling the police and experts (Glancy et al. 2015, p. S10).

This underscores two points. First, it is important for the field of forensic psychology to devote both general and discipline-specific attention to this question. Second, such discussion should be sufficiently detailed to cover particular kinds of FMHA and its components. This is an important rationale for this book. We now consider the ethical aspects of using social media in the course of risk assessment.

There are two sources of ethics guidance to be considered in weighing the role of social media as part of risk assessment conducted by psychologists: the *Ethical Principles of Psychologists and Code of Conduct* (APA 2017) and the *Specialized Guidelines for Forensic Psychology* (APA 2013). Neither makes specific reference to social media as it might be used in FMHA, or in risk assessment. But when SNS is considered as part of the information that may be used in any psychological assessment, the EPPCC underscores the same point about relevance that was noted earlier in this chapter: "Psychologists include in written and oral reports and consultations, only information germane to the purpose for which the communication is made" [APA 2017, 4.04(a)].

Both the EPPCC (APA 2017) and the SGFP (APA 2013) contain information relevant to the reliability of any component of risk assessment, including the use of SNS as collateral records. A psychologist conducting a risk assessment should know enough about SNS to understand matters such as authorship, posting, and privacy. There are no guarantees, of course, that someone who allegedly posted a comment or uploaded a picture is the individual who actually did so, but an evaluator should be sufficiently knowledgeable about SNS to understand what would be required for a third party to impersonate the person being evaluated in making a post. This is covered under EPPCC Standard 2.01(a): "Psychologists provide services, teach, and conduct research with populations and in areas only within the boundaries of their competence, based on their education, training, supervised experience, consultation, study, or professional experience" (APA 2017). This is particularly important when working with images and language relevant to violent behavior, as the vividness and emotional tone associated with such content can be prejudicial to the extent that it can potentially overwhelm other content that is less vivid or emotional.

A source's reliability also depends on its scientific and professional status. This is clear under EPPCC Standard 2.04: "Psychologists' work is based upon established scientific and professional knowledge of the discipline" (APA 2017). A similar point is underscored by EPPCC Standard 9.01(a): "Psychologists base the opinions contained in their recommendations, reports, and diagnostic or evaluative statements, including forensic testimony, on information and techniques sufficient to substantiate their findings" (APA 2017).

Material in the SGFP is consistent with that from the EPPCC on this point. In SGFP Guideline 2.05, the following is noted:

Forensic practitioners seek to provide opinions and testimony that are sufficiently based upon adequate scientific foundation, and reliable and valid principles and methods that have been applied appropriately to the facts of the case. When providing opinions and testimony that are based on novel or emerging principles and methods, forensic practitioners seek to make known the status and limitations of these principles and methods.

Clearly, both the EPPCC and the SGFP contain ethical support for using SNS as collateral information in risk assessment, with relevance and reliability important considerations in whether and how it is used. It might be tempting to assign a disproportionately large amount of credibility to SNS images for certain domains of risk assessment. For example, when considering whether substance abuse should apply, whether on an actuarial or SPJ measure, the viewing of an image of a clearly-intoxicated individual might influence the evaluator to conclude that the presence of substance abuse is justifiable. But such images, even when they are clearly relevant, must still be considered for their reliability. Is this actually the person? Is this image representative of behavior that occurs with requisite frequency? SNS information must still be treated with the same rigorous scrutiny that should be applied to other collateral information used in risk assessment.

The third ethical consideration concerns authorization for the access of SNS as part of risk assessment. The SGFP (2013) contains material relevant to authorization for the use of social media. When SNS is considered as a form of collateral information, the following is applicable: "Forensic practitioners strive to access information or records from collateral sources with the consent of the relevant attorney or the relevant party, or when otherwise authorized by law or court order" (APA 2013, Guideline 8.03). To minimize intrusion upon an individual's privacy, the EPPCC emphasizes relevance: any material used in written and oral reports and consultations should use "only information germane to the purpose for which the communication is made" and "only for appropriate scientific or professional purposes and only with persons clearly concerned with such matters" (Standard 4.04; APA 2017).

When evaluating an individual who does not have the legal capacity to decide whether to participate in the assessment, a psychologist is guided by the EPPCC to proceed as follows under Standard 3.10:

(b) For persons who are legally incapable of giving informed consent, psychologists nevertheless (1) provide an appropriate explanation, (2) seek the individual's assent, (3) consider such persons' preferences and best interests, and (4) obtain appropriate permission from a legally authorized person, if such substitute consent is permitted or required by law. When consent by a legally authorized person is not permitted or required by law, psychologists take reasonable steps to protect the individual's rights and welfare.

The importance of authorization—either through informed consent or court order—is expanded when considered in an ethics context. Authorization via informed consent (for evaluations that are not legally mandated) or court order (for legally compelled evaluations) remains important. We do not suggest that social media has a distinct status that allows access only through specific permission or specific authorization by a court order. When considered as a form of collateral information, the authorization to access SNS should be covered by a broader agreement to participate in the risk assessment, or under a broader court order to undergo risk assessment. However, the language included in the notification of purpose or the request for informed consent should be expanded to include SNS when relevant. This language modification should also describe any intent on the evaluator's part to review publicly-accessible SNS data. For evaluees who do not have the legal capacity to consent necessary to authorize access to their social media accounts, permission should be sought from the guardian or substitute decision-maker.

We do not suggest, however, that this is specific to SNS or other Internet data. Permission from a substitute decision-maker should *already* have been obtained when the risk assessment is conducted at the request of the individual's attorney. The attorney may be legally authorized to provide this limited permission in the context of the litigation for adults who may not have the legal capacity to make such a decision, or adolescents who are under the age of majority.

4.5 Analysis of Cases: Social Media in Risk Assessment

Neither of the following cases is genuine. Both draw upon elements of real cases, but each has been "hybridized" (see Heilbrun et al. 2014), combining material from different cases to create a product that is meaningful but not genuine. Both cases have also been deidentified.

Case Profile 1

Type of Evaluation

Juvenile transfer to adult criminal system for adjudication (or waiver of juvenile court jurisdiction).

Case Context

This case involved an adolescent male who allegedly conspired with individuals representing radical Islam through organizations such as ISIS and Al Qa'ida to harm the Pope during his visit to the United States. The youthful defendant was being considered for transfer into the (federal) criminal system. To address relevant questions involving public safety and rehabilitation needs, the evaluators conceptualized the risk assessment to include conclusions regarding both risk level and risk-relevant needs. In addition to the usual "general offending" outcome that we typically use in risk assessment in transfer cases, we also considered the risk of serious harm to others as part of radical Islamic activity.

The evaluee, David Satar, was a 16-year-old Asian male (D.O.B. 7-26-1998) who was charged with one count of attempting to provide material support to a designated foreign terrorist organization and two counts of providing material support to terrorists. Assistant United States Attorney Andrew Ewing requested a mental health evaluation to assist in the determination of appropriateness for waiver of juvenile court jurisdiction.

David was evaluated for approximately 7 h on November 3, 2014 at the Department of Youth Services Center (DYSC) in Worcester, Massachusetts. In addition to a clinical interview, David was administered a risk assessment tool for use with adolescents (the Structured Assessment of Risk Violence in Youth, or SAVRY), a measure of overall intellectual functioning (the Wechsler Adult Intelligence Scale–fourth Edition, or WAIS-IV), a structured inventory of symptoms of mental and emotional disorders specifically designed for use with adolescents (the Massachusetts Youth Screening Instrument, second Edition, or MAYSI-2), and a standard objective test of mental and emotional functioning for adolescents (the Minnesota Multiphasic Personality Inventory-Adolescent, or MMPI-A).

Sources of Information

Collateral interviews were conducted with David's parents, Alice Satar and Alec Satar for approximately 2.5 h on November 5, 2014, and with David's high school soccer and tennis coach, Richard Andrews, for approximately 30 min on November 14, 2014.

The following documents, obtained from Mr. Ewing's office, were reviewed as part of the evaluation:

1. Federal Bureau of Investigation (FBI) report of interviews with Worcester Police Department, Worcester High School, and Worcester Board of Education;
2. FBI audio and video recording of meeting between David Satar, Jr., and FBI Confidential Human Source;
3. Worcester Police Department Operations and Incidents Reports;
4. David Satar Jr.'s Middle School and High School Records;
5. David Satar Jr.'s Ninth Grade Personal Journal;
6. Portions of David Satar Jr.'s YouTube, Facebook, and Twitter Profiles and Postings;
7. Department of Children & Families (DCF) Reports;
8. Youth Consultation Service (YCS) Records; and
9. Psychiatric and Diagnostic Evaluation Reports.

Relevant Background

Family History David Satar was born on July 26, 1998 to Ms. Alice Satar and Mr. Alec Satar, who are married. David reported that he has one biological sister, Kirsty (age 12). David and Mr. and Ms. Satar reported that, whenever angered as a child, David would physically harm Kirsty and his parents. According to YCS records, David once attempted to kill his sister by choking her and threatened to kill his father with a knife. David reported that he was removed from his home on several occasions between 2007 and 2014. As noted in his DCF record, David and Kirsty were removed from Mr. and Ms. Satar's physical and legal custody and temporarily placed in foster care in 2007 due to excessive parental use of corporal punishment, which included the use of shoes, spoons, belts, jump ropes and sticks as punishment. David and Kirsty were returned to their parents' care approximately two weeks later, with continued DCF supervision. According to DCF records, David was again removed from his home in July 2008, due to oppositional/ defiant and aggressive and threatening behaviors towards his mother and sister, and was placed at the Holley Center. YCS reports indicate that David was compliant and demonstrated continued improvement during his time at the Holley Center and successfully completed the residential program in June 2010, upon which he returned to live with his family. Between 2011 and 2014, David was placed at three different youth residential programs and currently resides at DYSC, as of August 2015.

Ms. Satar added that with DCF out-of-home placements and his maturation, David's relationship with his sister has improved.

When asked about family strengths, David replied, "sometimes we watch TV together." When asked about family challenges, David referred to his anger management problems, multiple removals from his home, and having therapists enter his home. David reported that until one to two years ago, "whenever I didn't get what I wanted, I would get angry" and resort to using physical violence against his family. According to Ms. Satar, when David was in second or third grade he reported to a guidance counselor that he had no love for his family and that he wanted to "stab his family members." David denied ever having witnessed domestic violence between Mr. and Ms. Satar. He also denied experiencing any sexual abuse; however, Ms. Satar and DCF records indicated that David was exposed to pornography on a neighbor's computer during childhood. David reported being physically abused by his parents "once or twice" as a child for misbehaving. DCF records indicate that DCF became involved with the family following allegations of parental physical abuse against David and Kirsty in 2008 to which both Mr. and Ms. Satar admitted to the use of corporal punishment to discipline their children. David also noted that he physically assaulted his sister on multiple occasions when he was "little," and once "gave her a black eye." Since being placed at DYSC, David reported a recent improvement in his relationship with his parents and sister. He reported his family visits him weekly and he feels closer to them than when he was first arrested.

Medical and Mental Health History David stated that he had never received a behavioral health diagnosis. Ms. Satar, by contrast, reported that David had been evaluated by several psychiatrists throughout his childhood and that they had suggested several diagnoses, such as Delusional Disorder and Schizotypal Personality Disorder. She added, "I was never told exactly what his problem was." Prior evaluation records, between 2007 and 2011, indicated that David had received, from various clinicians, diagnoses of Delusional Disorder, Oppositional Defiant Disorder, Depressive Disorder, Obsessive Compulsive Disorder, Impulsive Control Disorder, Attention Deficit/Hyperactivity Disorder-Combined subtype, Mood Disorder NOS, possible Reactive Attachment Disorder, Anxiety Disorder-NOS, Bipolar Disorder, Schizoaffective Disorder, Adjustment Disorder with Disturbances in Mood and Conduct, and/or Autism Spectrum Disorder. In a more recent psychological evaluation (dated 1-13-15), the evaluating psychologist concluded that David's "history of social ineptness, lack of empathy and emotional distance" is commensurate with an Autism Spectrum disorder diagnosis. In a psychiatric evaluation (dated 3-15-15) conducted with David while at DYSC, the evaluating psychiatrist described him as "a seriously emotionally disturbed youngster who has had a psychotic disorder since childhood…" and indicated that he had met diagnostic criteria for schizophrenia since age 8.

David stated that he had heard one psychiatrist at a group home once describe his behavioral health problems as "anxiety" and "delusions." He was asked if he thought, based on previous psychiatric evaluations, that he had schizophrenia—to which he replied, "maybe." When asked what symptoms of schizophrenia he observes in himself, he commented, "I would go through phases in life and base my whole life around it." As an example of these phases, he used his transition from moderate to extremist Islam and said that when he transitioned to being an extremist he felt as though he had found "the truth." Several of David' psychiatric evaluations conducted between 2007 and 2011 commented similarly on his affect, body language, and communication skills. David's evaluating physician from a February 12, 2010 psychiatric evaluation said that David's speech had "abnormally choppy rhythm, answering sentences one word at a time." Another psychological evaluation (dated 10/19/2010), conducted when David was 11, described his presenting affect as "very blunted and preoccupied." This evaluation also noted, "David also had verbalized some misunderstanding of other people's feelings. He does not understand the context of threatening to kill people and how that could make them angry with him."

David said that when he was younger he received in-home and outpatient psychotherapy and underwent several psychological evaluations. Mr. Satar stated that between 2007 and 2008 David was admitted on multiple occasions to the Psychiatric Crisis Inpatient Center for his homicidal behavior towards his parents and sister and destruction of property at home. Records indicate that David's DCF case worker referred him to Massachusetts Psychological Services for individual and family counseling to address his sexually inappropriate behavior, as part of which he received individual and family therapy on a weekly basis from November 2009 to March 2011. When asked if he thought therapy was helpful, David replied, "a little…It helped me stop getting angry. I started behaving better." Mr. Satar stated that David and his family received DCF behavioral health services from February 2007 until November 2013. Both David and Ms. Satar reported that several clinicians had recommended that he take medication to address his emotional distress. David said that he never took the medications because he felt he "didn't need them." Ms. Satar added that she and Mr. Satar decided against giving David medication because they were fearful of side effects and did not want medication to interfere with his academic performance. David reported that he was "too stubborn" to take medications that a psychiatrist once recommended, but that he would consider using medications now if it would "make it easier for me to think about things."

Educational History David reported that he attended one elementary school. He reported that his grades were in the A to B range and his attendance was regular. In third grade, he said, he would get into fights with other students on a monthly basis and had to sit for multiple lunch detentions. David denied failing or skipping any grades in elementary school, having an IEP, or participating in any after-school activities. David reported that he attended one middle school. He described his attendance as "good" and "regular." He described his behavior during middle school as "mostly good" and reported getting involved in one fight in fifth grade with a male student who was bullying him. He said that he mostly earned As and some Bs, was enrolled in all honors classes, and joined the National Junior Honor Society in eighth grade. Ms. Satar reported that David's middle school teachers would tell her that they were "happy to have a student like him." Ms. Satar added that David was diligent about his school work, never asking for assistance in completing assignments, and that his anger never kept him from going to school. As reported in a psychological evaluation (dated 11/23/2007), David was administered the Wechsler Abbreviated Scale of Intelligence, on which he earned a Full-Scale IQ of 123, placing him in the 94th percentile and Superior Range of intellectual ability for same-aged peers. David reported that he attended Worcester High School for ninth grade and described his attendance as "regular." Worcester High School records note that David received a three-day out-of-school suspension for "touching a girl." David further explained that he had seen other kids touching girls in class and thought it would be "funny" if he did so as well. He stated that he apologized to the girl and met with his guidance counselor weekly until the end of the year. David's Worcester High School records indicate that David was enrolled in honors courses and received mostly A's and B's—and one C—for his courses. David stated that he played soccer and tennis while in ninth grade. His soccer and tennis couch, Mr. Richard Andrews, reported that David "never missed practice" and that he was "very smart."

When asked during the present evaluation what he aspires to do in the next five to 10 years, David said he wanted to attend a Muslim college in California (Zaytuna College) to study Islam. He said that he would like to become an imam, build a mosque, and teach others about Islam. He added that he might like to become a farmer. He reported that he would probably attempt to achieve these goals while living in the United States within a Muslim community and does not know if he would ever really move to another country.

Substance Abuse History David and Mr. and Ms. Satar all reported that David does not use alcohol or drugs. DCF records report no evidence of substance use by David or other family members.

Social History David reported only having friends in school, and no close friends. He stated that his friends at school are both girls and boys, all close to his age. Mr. Andrews said, "Socially, he (David) did not have a group of friends he hung out with. He only hung out with kids at practice. He was totally solo." Mr. Satar commented, "he has to spend time with friends at school" as "he never hung out with friends outside of school." According to a DCF assessment conducted on May 19, 2014, David "does not have any friends and has poor social skills." David wrote in his journal (dated 8/18/2013) that he tries "to interact with everyone. Sometimes it feels like I might make people go away because I annoy them. I want to change somehow to make people like me more because sometimes I feel lonely."

David stated that he was interested in super heroes when he was in the fifth grade, and Star Wars in sixth grade. Ms. Satar commented that David would enter phases in which he would be obsessed with acting like whomever or whatever he admired. David said that he now enjoys listening to lectures on Islam, playing videogames, reading, and playing soccer and tennis. He also described spending "a lot" of time on the computer. He added that he had never had a girlfriend, but had originally wanted (as he wrote in his journal) 15 wives and 30 children. He said during the present evaluation that he would now like at least four wives, as the Quran allows.

David stated that he converted to Islam at 13-years-old. He said that during seventh grade he was interested in Al Qa'ida and would talk about it in school. Ms. Satar commented that when David was in seventh and eighth grades, his feelings for Islam were "very strong" as evidenced by his learning Arabic and telling people "he was a prophet" and that when he was born "he was supposed to go to a Muslim family and instead, Satan sent him to his current family." Mr. and Ms. Satar stated that they were confused as to how David could have become interested in Islam, as they did not raise him in a religion and he had no Muslim friends. Mr. Satar said that David might have been exposed to Muslim students and staff when he attended school in Albany, NY. Ms. Satar said that David may also have obtained information on Islam from his phone, as "he always kept busy with the phone." She reflected on David's conversion to Islam and commented, "I think he wanted something in life that made him feel like he had a purpose and he could be a hero." She noted that she and Mr. Satar were not upset that David wanted to become Muslim as they thought it would provide him peace given all his anger; however, they never thought he would turn to ISIS.

David reported that he transitioned more towards modern Islam in the eighth grade, but returned to conservative Islam in ninth grade. It was in ninth grade, he stated, that he grew interested in ISIS from watching the news and reading material on the Islamic State. David stated that he came to support ISIS because he realized that "they were the only ones enforcing the sharia and defending Muslims." When asked if he supports war and jihad, David replied that he is "OK" with both because it "benefits people in the Islamic State…they can hear the message of Allah and become better people." David reported during the present evaluation that he "wanted to move anywhere in the Islamic State." When asked why he wanted to do this, David replied, "People are living in the Islamic State and have everything they need and the only thing they have to worry about is the US dropping bombs on them." He stated that he will still hold his current ideas and beliefs in 20 years.

David stated that prior to his arrest, he primarily learned about Islam through Islamic extremist online propaganda. He commented, "I was always learning by myself and I formed my own version of Islam through the internet. My first version (of Islam) wasn't good enough; it was deviant…I twisted the facts I got. When I first converted, the Islam I knew was from the extremists." He did say that before his arrest, he met regularly with an imam but that he would often argue with him, as the imam's Islamic practice "contradicted what I believed (from the internet)." He described himself as initially "stubborn" in his beliefs about what Islam represented. David added that he had met with a different imam while at DYSC. In these meetings, he said, the imam provided him with reading materials on refuting ISIS and education on the different schools of Sunni Islamic law. David said that meeting with this imam has led him to consider if what he originally thought about ISIS is "wrong" and that ISIS does not represent "real Islam." Further, David was asked if he believed that ISIS soldiers and others' support of ISIS is delusional; David commented that ISIS leaders may say things that can be misconstrued as delusions and that leaders may "be trying to take advantage of people." When asked if he thought his previous convictions about joining ISIS were delusional in nature, he replied, "I would think they were delusions."

Offense History David reported that he had not been arrested prior to his current charges. However, both he and Mr. and Ms. Satar indicated several contacts with Worcester Police between 2007 and 2014, including incidents of child abuse of David and Kirsty by Mr. and Ms. Satar, assaultive and threatening behavior by David against his family members, and one incident in which David ran away from home after a disagreement with his family and returned a few hours later. According to the Affidavit, the Worcester Police Department was dispatched in May 2013 to Worcester Middle School after a school security officer alerted law enforcement to David's desire to "follow Al Qa'ida websites and may be becoming radicalized." As stated in Worcester Police Department records, law enforcement arrived at Worcester High School on March 15, 2014 after David's English teacher reported to police that he had written a paper for class stating that he "wanted to join ISIS."

David is currently charged with one count of attempting to provide material support to a designated foreign terrorist organization and two counts of providing material support to terrorists. The Affidavit further states that, beginning in the spring of 2014, David had been inspired by Islamic State of Iraq and the Levant (ISIL) and was planning a violent attack during the Papal visit to New York in September 2015 and that he believed this and other attacks he was planning "would support ISIL's objectives, and/or travel outside of the United States to fight on ISIL's behalf." The Affidavit explains that David planned to use a sniper rifle to assassinate Pope Francis and planned to use a homemade weapon of mass destruction during the Papal public mass to kill and injure attendees. These records also note that David frequently used social media to openly express his desire to join ISIL, that he told law enforcement that he would "gladly serve ISIS anywhere and anytime," and wrote on social media that he "would have my turn soon." Records indicate that given David's online activities and statements in support of ISIL, law enforcement instructed two undercover federal employees to contact David through social media and an FBI Confidential Human Source to interact with him in person to gather more details of his plans for a terrorist attack.

Behavioral Observations and Mental Status

David Satar presented as a 16-year-old Asian male of average height and medium build who appeared his stated age. David's speech was clear and relevant, but he spoke in a slow and halting tone. He reported that he prefers to text his thoughts as it is difficult for him to "think of what to say" if he must speak in person. He denied having any auditory, visual, or motor problems, or head injuries, throughout his lifetime. David appeared reserved, acted withdrawn, and demonstrated blunted affect throughout much of the evaluation. However, he was cooperative and able to exert good effort and complete all required tasks.

Summary of Test Results

On a measure of overall intellectual functioning (the WAIS-IV), David was measured as performing in the Average to High Average range (Full Scale IQ = 110), placing him in the 75th percentile relative to others his age. He measured in the High Average range for verbal tasks (VCI = 118; 88th percentile). He scored in the Average range for processing speed (PSI = 94; 34th percentile), performance tasks (PRI = 109; 73rd percentile) and working memory (WMI = 108; 70th percentile), relative to same-aged peers. David's verbal capacities may be considered relative strengths on which to build.

On a structured inventory of symptoms of mental and emotional disorders specifically designed for use with adolescents (MAYSI-2), David denied any symptoms. He was asked multiple times if he had noticed any changes in his mood, thoughts, or behaviors within the past few months that MAYSI-2 items best captured, but denied such changes. His lack of endorsement is inconsistent with his extensive mental health records that document severe fluctuations in mood, impulse control issues, inappropriate sexual behavior, bizarre thought patterns, and homicidal ideation towards his family in the past.

David completed the MMPI-A as part of the original evaluation to measure his current mental and emotional functioning. David was cooperative and attentive while completing the MMPI-A. His responses yielded a valid profile (Welsh Code 236/40 51:879# L"K′ + -/F:), but suggest that results are only a marginally valid description of David's current functioning because of his response style, which involved a tendency to deny unusual thoughts and experiences in a naïve, rigid fashion. As a consequence, the clinical scales may underestimate the extent and severity of behavioral health symptoms that are present. Individuals with such profiles tend to deny psychological distress, minimize faults, and lack self-awareness. His responses suggest that he is likely to take an inflexible and rigid approach to problems, project an excessively positive self-image, lack tolerance towards others' failings, and struggle to cooperate fully with treatment. His adolescent clinical scales are within normal limits, which is somewhat atypical for adolescents in correctional settings (although this may be partly a function of his response style, just described). His clinical profile did contain elevations for some personality characteristics that are consistent with individuals who tend to be pessimistic and unable to experience pleasure, with few or no friends. With regard to interpersonal relationships, his responses suggest that he has problems with social relationships and prefers being alone. David did endorse content suggesting a desire to succeed in life.

Diagnostic Conclusions

No specific diagnoses were made as part of this evaluation.

Summary of Data Relevant to Psycho-Legal Opinion

The SAVRY was completed based on information obtained from David and collateral sources as part of the current evaluation. The SAVRY is a structured risk assessment tool for use with adolescents that aids in determining an adolescent's future risk for violence. David's current level of risk, which is based upon the presence and absence of various risk and protective factors, appears to be high for future violence relative to other youth being considered for decertification.

There are a number of strengths or absence-of-deficits that should be noted. David does not experience the following: history of nonviolent offending; past supervision/intervention failures (DCF records indicate that David attended all DCF-mandated therapy sessions and YCS documents report that he was cooperative and engaged in treatment during his out-of-home placement; David reported that previous therapy helped him not get angry as much and made him more social); history of self-harm or suicide attempts; early caregiver disruption; poor school achievement; peer delinquency; poor parental management (DCF records indicate that Mr. and Ms. Satar, with the assistance of DCF involvement and therapy, actively invested in David's behavioral health treatment); community disorganization; substance-use difficulties; Attention Deficit/Hyperactivity difficulties; and low interest/commitment to school.

However, he presents a high risk of re-offense based on the presence of nine particularly strong risk factors: (1) history of violence (history of physically assaulting his family members and causing property damage); (2) early initiation of violence (history of aggressive and threatening behaviors toward family; fights with other children); (3) childhood history of maltreatment (David and his sister were removed from the home due to substantiated claims of child abuse); (4) stress and poor coping (when under stress David would become aggressive and physically destructive); (5) negative attitudes (David stated that he is supportive of war and jihad; FBI records note that David used social media to promote ISIS propaganda and speak with ISIS supporters as he devised and planned his attack during the papal visit); (6) risk taking/impulsivity (prior neurological reports indicate David's profile is consistent with Impulse Control Disorder; however, David stated that he now "thinks things through;" DCF records indicate that David engaged in inappropriate sexual behavior with peers); (7) anger management problems (between 2008 and 2014, David received intensive outpatient behavioral health services and was removed from the home on multiple occasions due to his aggressive behaviors towards his family); (8) low empathy/remorse (on several occasions, David denied feeling remorseful after injuring his family or causing damage when he was angry; David reported that, should he be released and arrested again for terroristic activities that he will not be concerned as he "did it for the right cause"); and (9) poor compliance with rules (David stated that he realizes the goal of the juvenile justice system is to "change" him, but he noted that he feels that it will not be able to do so and that he will continue to hold the same religious beliefs and ideals 20 years from now).

Clinical Forensic Opinion

In our opinion, based on all of the above, David has treatment/rehabilitation needs in the following areas:

1. Ongoing evaluation and treatment for behavioral health needs;
2. Training and counseling in anger management and social skills;
3. Continued emphasis on positive and appropriate peer relationships and involvement in structured activities; and
4. Continued interactions with an imam regarding traditional Islamic beliefs and practice.

David should be considered at high risk for future violent offending and with multiple rehabilitation needs. Some of these needs could be addressed in the juvenile justice system. Although there are no recognized interventions for addressing radical Islam in the juvenile justice system, informal meetings with a community-based imam appear to be helpful to David in gaining perspective about ISIS and encouraging him to practice his faith as part of a traditional Islamic community. David's extensive mental health history and mid-adolescent age position him to be developmentally underprepared with the psychosocial maturity and cognitive capacities necessary to exercise clear and rational decision making. However, David now shows less resistance to the idea that his previously held religious beliefs may have been flawed as well as to the possibility of his having a behavioral health disorder that could be helped with psychotropic medication. He has treatment needs related to his anger management, social skills, engagement in structured activities and positive peer relationships, and further evaluation of underlying psychological distress potentially related to an anxiety disorder and/or personality disorder, such as schizotypal personality disorder. David's academic performance in classes and cognitive strengths in verbal reasoning could be positive assets on which to build his engagement in structured activities and involvement with positive and prosocial peers. David possesses strengths that may positively influence continued development, including having supportive parents who are invested in his rehabilitation and other active protective factors (e.g., his interest in sports and spiritual commitment). David appears more amenable to certain kinds of intervention within the juvenile justice system (e.g., behavioral health treatment, religious counseling). It is strongly recommended that David continue to receive counseling from a community-based imam to further and maintain his cognitive and psychosocial maturation regarding his religious beliefs and means of practicing his Islamic faith. Given his previous radicalized belief system, difficulties living with his family in the community, and compliance in previous residential group homes, however, David likely will need long-term, highly structured interventions in a high security residential placement, where he can receive specialized mental health services. It is also noteworthy that he appears comfortable interacting digitally, which has implications that are both positive and problematic. He was apparently persuaded by much of what he read and learned from the internet with respect to radical Islam, so the unmonitored access to certain internet sites could be highly problematic. However, he probably has the potential to interact with rehabilitative individuals online rather than face-to-face, which could increase his access to individuals who could assist in his ongoing rehabilitation.

Recommendations

There are three areas in which David has treatment/rehabilitation needs that the juvenile justice system may be able to address to reduce David's risk for future offending. These areas include: (1) further evaluation and ongoing psychiatric management and behavioral treatment of David's current mental health needs; (2) training and counseling specific to anger management and social skills; and (3) a continued emphasis on positive and appropriate peer and adult relationships and involvement in structured activities.

First, David may require further evaluation and treatment of his mental health needs. Although he denied any current psychological problems on the MAYSI-2 and MMPI-A, his response style suggested that he minimizes psychological distress and lacks awareness regarding his own behavior. Since 2007, David has undergone several diagnostic evaluations from different providers for his aggressive behavior towards his family, inappropriate sexual behavior, and anger and irritability. These evaluations have yielded various diagnoses to explain David's symptomatic profile. Accordingly, David may benefit from further evaluation and treatment. Individual and family therapy may assist in establishing positive relationships between David and his family. Psychopharmacological intervention has been previously recommended by evaluating clinicians. Coupled with counseling, medication intervention may contribute to improving David's mental and emotional functioning, especially at home.

Second, David has treatment needs in the areas of anger management and social skills. When asked how he handles anger, David responded, "I don't really get angry." However, he as a history of physical aggression toward his sister, his parents, and property. People who call him a "terrorist" irritate him and his anger tends to linger after he fights. In addition, David groped a female classmate after observing other kids in class touch girls and thought it would get him positive attention from classmates. Skills-based training and counseling in anger management and social skills may allow David to expand his current skills for remaining calm and effectively communicating his needs with his family, peers, and other adults in stressful situations.

Third, David would benefit from involvement in more positive peer relationships and structured activities. He does not have any good friends and rarely speaks with peers. David described a desire for friends, but noted his peers perceive him as weird. He spends most of his time each day on the computer. FBI records indicate he used multiple social media accounts to promote ISIL propaganda and communicate with other ISIS supporters. Interacting with positive mentors and prosocial peers in structured activities may decrease David's fervent desires to move to the Islamic State and promote his investment in his life here in the United States.

The juvenile system is structured to provide rehabilitative interventions to youth to reduce the risk that they will reoffend by committing crimes motivated by more commonly-observed influences (e.g., monetary gain, property, functioning as part of an antisocial group, anger/jealousy/revenge). Although this system is not established to reduce the risk that a youth who describes himself as committed to radical Islam will attempt to commit further acts of holy war, it appears David's informal weekly sessions with an imam may be changing his views about Islam and ISIL. During our evaluation, was beginning to view ISIL as "not Islam." Additionally, he described a desire to develop a good working knowledge of the Islamic faith and practice by attending a Muslim university in the United States.

How Did Social Media Impact This Case?

Social media data were an important part of this evaluation. These data were obtained from the U.S. Attorney's Office, which provided them as part of the referral. This meant that the evaluation was court-ordered, with the prosecution making this request as part of the transfer motion in rebuttal to the defense transfer evaluation. Since the authorization to proceed with the evaluation was subsumed under court order, it was not necessary to seek the youth's assent, or the permission of his attorney or parent, to review them.

SNS data in this case were particularly relevant because of the defendant David's use of social media (and other internet-based material) in developing his views about radical Islam. David was described by his mother as "always on his phone," and he talked about his exposure to Islamic propaganda and its role in helping him develop his "own version of Islam." His interest in Al Qa'ida websites was reported by a school security officer to the federal authorities. He used social media to express his desire to join ISIS and indicate that he "would have my turn soon" after being contacted on SNS by undercover federal agents. Clearly this information was relevant to his behavior and thinking in becoming a proponent of radical Islam.

The question of the reliability of the SNS data in this case—whether it reflected an accurate accounting of his behavior, and the meaning of this behavior in the context of risk assessment—is more complex. The SNS data were used for several purposes. They provided behavioral descriptions, helped develop hypotheses, and targeted areas for investigation. David himself confirmed the accuracy of the SNS data through direct questioning during the interview. The most challenging question involved what had contributed to his seeking and/or responding affirmatively to those promoting radical Islam on SNS. Was it developmental immaturity? Behavioral health deficits? The desire for promised rewards? A serious religious conversion? These SNS data did appear authentic, both because they had been obtained and validated by law enforcement officials and because David acknowledged their accuracy. With the question of accuracy addressed, we were able to give more credibility to the SNS information than typically we would have with most collateral information. This both created a solid foundation and allowed us to develop a line of questioning that was valuable in addressing the issues particularly salient for reoffense risk. The SNS data helped disentangle three possibilities just cited, leading to a better-informed risk assessment.

Case Profile 2

Type of Evaluation

Risk assessment for purposes of determining federal sentencing.

Case Context

In this case, Tara Schmidt, a young adult female, was charged with the federal offense of stalking via electronic communication an older man who had conducted an alumnus interview as part of Ms. Schmidt's application for admission to graduate school in criminology. The evaluator was retained by the defense to conduct a federal sentencing evaluation, and SNS data was provided to the evaluator as part of the discovery. Ms. Schmidt provided informed consent to participate in the evaluation. As we discussed earlier in this chapter, we did not ask her specifically about reviewing any particular content within the records. We anticipate expanding our consent process in future cases to more specifically reference SNS data when they are part of the records.

Tara Schmidt was a 27-year-old white female (D.O.B.: 11/26/1988) who was charged with one count of stalking via electronic communication (18 U.S.C. § 2261A). A request for a mental health evaluation to provide the defense with information relevant to sentencing, pursuant to United States Sentencing Guidelines, was made by court-appointed counsel.

Ms. Schmidt was evaluated for approximately 0.5 h on December 4, 2015 at the Federal Detention Center in Butner, North Carolina. She responded to the initial portion of a clinical interview before we ended the session due to the arrival of her parents for a family visit. The evaluation resumed on December 11, 2015 for 4 hours. In addition to completing the clinical interview, Ms. Schmidt was administered a standard screening instrument for symptoms of mental and emotional disorder (the Brief Symptom Inventory, or BSI) reported at two times: [1] during the most recent 7 days, and [2] during the Federal Bureau of Investigation's (FBI) search of her apartment on February 21, 2017. She also completed an objective measure of mental and emotional functioning (the Minnesota Multiphasic Personality Inventory, second edition, or MMPI-2) and a standard measure of risk and need factors for adult offenders (the Level of Service/Case Management Inventory, or LS/CMI).

Sources of Information

The following documents, obtained from Ms. Schmidt's attorney, were also reviewed as part of the evaluation:

1. Screenshots of Email Chain Regarding Tara Schmidt's New York University School of Criminology Alumni Interview with Alex Grimes (dated between 2/2/2012 and 2/20/2012);
2. Screenshots of Twitter Account for "Alex Grimes" (created on 2/1/2013);
3. Screenshots of Pinterest Account for "Alex Grimes" (created on 2/1/2013);
4. Screenshots of Wordpress Blog for "Alex Grimes" (created on 2/1/2013);
5. Records of Three LinkedIn Accounts for "Alex Grimes" (created on 2/3/2013, 2/10/2013, and 3/15/2013);
6. Screenshots of Emails from Alex Grimes Regarding Unrequested Pizza Deliveries (dated 5/19/2013, 5/20/2013, and 5/21/2013);
7. Screenshots of Backpage Post by "Alex Grimes" (dated 5/19/2013);
8. Screenshots of Voicemails Received by Alex Grimes from Unknown Phone Numbers (calls dated from 2/2/2013 to 3/10/2013);
9. Better Business Bureau Complaint Filed by "Georgia Schmidt" against Alex Grimes (dated 5/16/2013);
10. Records of Craigslist Posts Associated with georgiaschmidt123@gmail.com (posts made on 9/20/2013, 9/21/2013, and 9/24/2013):
11. Screenshots of gradcafe posts alleging assault by Alex Grimes (dated 9/24/2013);
12. Screenshots of Reddit posts alleging assault by Alex Grimes (dated 9/25/2013);
13. Screenshots of medhelp.org forum posts alleging assault by Alex Grimes (dated 9/26/2013);
14. Screenshots of YouTube Account for "Alex Grimes" (dated 12/30/2013);
15. Screenshots of LinkedIn Profile for Tara Schmidt (dated 12/30/2013);
16. Screenshots of Two Twitter Accounts Alleging Assault by Alex Grimes (created 2/20/2014);
17. Screenshots of Wikipedia Page for Alex Grimes (dated 2/25/2014);
18. Screenshots of Facebook Profile for Tara Schmidt (dated 3/5/2014);
19. Federal Bureau of Investigation Electronic Communication Request to Open Computer Intrusion and Cyber Stalking Investigation Against Tara Schmidt (dated 3/10/2014);
20. Federal Bureau of Investigation Interview of Alexander Grimes (conducted on 3/25/2014);
21. Federal Bureau of Investigation Interview of Alexander Grimes (conducted on 4/15/2014);
22. Federal Bureau of Investigation Interview of Margaret Grimes (conducted on 4/17/2014);
23. Audio Recording of Federal Bureau of Investigation Interview of Andrea Parks (conducted on 5/13/2014);

24. United States District Court for the District of North Carolina Application for Search Warrant for Information Associated with Taraschmidt@gmail.com Stored at Google Headquarters (dated 5/30/2014);
25. Federal Bureau of Investigation Interview of Wendy Smith (conducted on 1/6/2015);
26. Federal Bureau of Investigation Interview of Christian Jones (conducted on 1/9/2015);
27. United States District Court for the Western District of Arizona Application for Search Warrant for the Residence of Tara Schmidt (dated 1/29/2015);
28. Statement from "Wife of Victim #1" (dated 2/2/2015);
29. Statement from "Female Colleague of Victim #1 and Named Victim in the Investigation" (dated 2/2/2015); and
30. Statement from New York University School of Criminology Regarding Tara Schmidt (dated 2/2/2015).

To obtain information about Ms. Schmidt's offense history, online records of common pleas court docket sheets were also reviewed. Ms. Schmidt provided contact information for two collateral contacts: [1] her father, George Schmidt and [2] her mother, Karen Schmidt. Repeated attempts to contact George and Karen Schmidt were unsuccessful, however. Ms. Schmidt also provided names for two additional contacts: [3] her former roommate, Patrick Fields, and [4] her former coworker, Angela Hall. At the time this report was submitted, we were still seeking to contact these individuals and indicated to the court that an amended report would be submitted with their information if we were successful.

Relevant Background

Historical information was obtained from the collateral sources described above as well as from Ms. Schmidt. Whenever possible, we assessed the consistency of self-reported information with that obtained from collateral sources.

Family History Tara Schmidt was born in 1988 in Hamburg, Germany. The area where she lived in Germany was "very nice, almost like a resort town." Her family moved to North Carolina in 1992 after her father obtained a job. The family has lived in North Carolina since that time. Her father was a librarian and her mother primarily worked as a teacher, but both are now retired. When asked about her family's strengths, Ms. Schmidt said her parents are "very supportive" and that her mother is "brilliant" while her father "has great work ethic." Regarding family challenges, she reported her father was occasionally out of work when she was growing up. She never experienced any physical, emotional, or sexual abuse during his childhood, and she was not aware of anyone in her family having been involved in the criminal justice system (her current circumstances excepted).

Educational History Ms. Schmidt reported that she attended international school in Hamburg and began kindergarten upon her arrival in the United States. She described her attendance and academic performance as "good" throughout elementary, middle, and high school. In regard to undergraduate education, Ms. Schmidt reported that she auditioned for music schools but "got the best offer" from Arizona State University. She stated that she graduated summa cum laude from Arizona State University's honors college in 2010 with degrees in philosophy and violin performance. Ms. Schmidt reported that she majored in philosophy because she was interested in applying to graduate school in criminology, and she took the GREs twice in pursuit of this goal. She stated that she applied to 20 graduate schools with high GRE scores and an undergraduate GPA of 3.99, which she believed "should have been sufficient to get in." According to Ms. Schmidt, the only graduate school from which she was rejected was New York University (NYU) School of Criminology. She reported that she accepted an admission offer from the University of Arizona (UA) because the school offered her a full scholarship. Ms. Schmidt stated that she began graduate school in the fall of 2012 and that her initial semester at UA was "tough" as she "adjusted" to her new schedule. However, Ms. Schmidt stated, she enrolled in more writing-focused seminars the following semester and earned better grades, and she currently has a "respectable" A- average. Ms. Schmidt reported that she was placed on academic probation in August 2013 after she "lightened the font" on her transcript so that her C+ grade and her overall GPA would not be visible unless the transcript was printed. She described this manipulation of her transcript as a "one-time deal," adding that she has had no other disciplinary incidents at UA or any other schools. At the time of Ms. Schmidt's arrest for the current charges, she was in her third year of graduate school.

Employment History Since Ms. Schmidt had been enrolled in school for most of her life, her opportunities for employment have been limited to part-time and summer positions. She worked as a file clerk for a Law Firm, which she described as "very boring." Ms. Schmidt remains committed to becoming a criminologist. Much of her discussion of her current legal circumstances reflected her graduate training. For example, she stated that she has given her attorney a "white paper" arguing that "the statute I'm charged under is unconstitutional."

Substance Abuse Ms. Schmidt drinks alcohol occasionally and described her alcohol consumption as "a merlot or beer here and there, or a whiskey at a nice event." When asked if her alcohol use has ever influenced her behavior, she stated, "It may have altered my judgment a little bit and made me more careless." Ms. Schmidt denied use of any other substances.

Medical and Mental Health History Ms. Schmidt did not report any medical concerns or chronic illnesses. Ms. Schmidt likewise did not describe any history of mental health treatment (medications, therapy, or hospitalization). Ms. Schmidt reported that she was unaware of any family history of medical or mental health problems.

Offense History By her own self-report and online records of common pleas court docket sheets, Ms. Schmidt has no history of criminal offenses. Regarding the present charges, Ms. Schmidt said that she was interviewed by the alleged victim as part the application process for NYU School of Criminology in February 2012. The interview took place in a Starbucks in New York City, she indicated. According to emails that the alleged victim wrote to NYU, Ms. Schmidt was "rude and uncooperative" throughout the interview and was "unwilling to explain her interest in studying criminology, attending graduate school, NYU, or any other material aspects." The alleged victim wrote that Ms. Schmidt "would be a poor fit" at the graduate school, and Ms. Schmidt was not offered admission.

According to the search warrant application for Ms. Schmidt's residence, the alleged victim in this case became aware of "multiple Twitter, LinkedIn accounts, and blog postings in his name" in June 2013. These accounts "made false representations concerning [the alleged victim] and the Ku Klux Klan, spousal abuse, [and] molestation of children." In July 2013, the alleged victim received multiple pizza deliveries that he did not order that were payable upon delivery. Around this time, the alleged victim's contact information was posted on a website advertising escort services, and he subsequently received many telephone calls requesting these services. In October 2013, the alleged victim's contact information was included in multiple Craigslist postings soliciting sex from other Craigslist users, and on three occasions individuals came to the alleged victim's house in response to these postings. Postings were also made on multiple Internet forums in October 2013 stating the writer had been sexually assaulted by the alleged victim. It is alleged that the accounts and postings described above were made by Ms. Schmidt.

Behavioral Observations and Mental Status

Ms. Schmidt presented as a white female of above average height and medium build who appeared her stated age. She was dressed in prison garb and appeared well-groomed. Ms. Schmidt was generally cooperative during the evaluation session, and her speech was clear, coherent, and relevant. Her range of expressed emotion was somewhat limited throughout the evaluation, although she became visibly agitated when discussing situations in which she believed she was treated unfairly (e.g., the search of her apartment, her alumni interview, her current charges). Ms. Schmidt reported no history of head injury or loss of consciousness. She indicated she is fluent in English and German, speaks French and Spanish at a conversational level, and she is learning Cantonese while incarcerated. She wears glasses for nearsightedness, and she denied any auditory or motor problems. Ms. Schmidt has no tattoos, scars, or piercings. She worked consistently on all tasks during the evaluation and seemed to put forth full effort. It would appear, therefore, that this evaluation provides a valid reflection of Ms. Schmidt's functioning at the time of assessment.

Summary of Test Results

Ms. Schmidt was administered the MMPI-2 to measure her current psychological and personality functioning. Her responses yielded a valid profile that is indicative of frankness and openness (Welsh Code: 9″' + −80,625/74 13: F-/LK:). Ms. Schmidt had a high-point clinical scale score on the Hypomania (Ma) subscale (T = 85). Individuals with such profiles typically report experiencing emotional lability, erratic behavior, and poor judgment. They may engage in risky or impulsive behavior (e.g., risky sexual behavior, aggression, excessive alcohol or drug use) as part of a general pattern of disorganization. Individuals with such profiles may also present as very self-confident and possibly self-centered, and may be unrealistically convinced of their own importance. Such individuals may become distracted and frustrated easily, and may respond to minor provocation with hostility. Ms. Schmidt endorsed items suggesting she feels resentful of societal standards of conduct and holds some antisocial beliefs. Finally, her elevated scores indicate that she often feels alienated from others and has cynical views about life.

Ms. Schmidt completed two versions of a 53-item standard screening inventory of symptoms of mental and emotional disorders, the Brief Symptom Inventory (BSI). The first concerns her present functioning (described here), and the second describes her thoughts and feelings at the time that her apartment was searched (described below). Ms. Schmidt reported being "extremely" distressed at present by two items on the BSI: [1] other people not giving her proper credit for her achievements, and [2] feeling that people will take advantage of her if she lets them. She endorsed ten items as "quite a bit" distressing. She attributed most of her symptoms to the experience of being incarcerated, but she noted that people not giving her credit for her achievements is "always big for me generally." The BSI includes nine syndrome scales and three scales designed to measure general psychopathology and psychological distress. Scores of 63 or greater on these scales indicate an area of clinical concern relative to the norms for the comparison population. Compared to a non-patient sample, Ms. Schmidt's scores ranged from 64–80 on the syndrome scales and therefore reached the level of clinical concern across all scales. Her scores were also clinically elevated on all three general psychopathology scales. However, Ms. Schmidt's responses were only elevated on scales for Phobic Anxiety (PHOB) and Paranoia (PAR) when compared to an outpatient mental health treatment sample.

On the BSI assessing her functioning when her apartment was searched in 2017, Ms. Schmidt endorsed 26 items as "extremely" distressing: [1] nervousness or shakiness inside; [2] feeling afraid in open spaces or on the street; [3] feeling that most people could be trusted; [4] poor appetite; [5] suddenly scared for no reason; [6] feeling lonely even when she was with people; [7] feeling blocked in getting things done; [8] feeling lonely; [9] feeling blue; [10] feeling fearful; [11] feeling that people were unfriendly or disliked her; [12] trouble falling asleep; [13] difficulty making decisions; [14] feeling afraid to travel on buses, subways, or trains; [15] having to avoid certain things, places, or activities because they frightened her; [16] feeling hopeless about the future; [17] trouble concentrating; [18] feeling tense or keyed up;

[19] feeling very self-conscious with others; [20] feeling uneasy in crowds; [21] never feeling close to another person; [22] spells of terror or panic; [23] feeling nervous when she was left alone; [24] other people not giving her proper credit for her achievements; [25] feeling so restless that she could not sit still; and [26] feeling that people would take advantage of her if she let them. She reported being "quite a bit" distressed by two items. Ms. Schmidt attributed all of her distress to the unexpected search of her apartment. Compared to a non-patient sample, Ms. Schmidt's scores ranged from 40–80 on the syndrome scales, with all scales except for the Hostility (HOS) scale reaching the level of clinical concern. Her scores were clinically elevated on all three general psychopathology scales. Ms. Schmidt's performance on the Phobic Anxiety, Paranoia, Anxiety (ANX), Global Severity Index (GSI), and Positive Symptom Distress Index (PSDI) scales remained elevated when compared to an outpatient mental health treatment sample.

Diagnostic Conclusions

No specific diagnoses were made as part of this evaluation.

Summary of Data Relevant to Psycho-Legal Opinion

Specialized Risk Tool Ms. Schmidt was administered the Level of Service/ Case Management Inventory (LS/CMI), a measure of risk and need factors for adult offenders. On the LS/CMI, respondents are evaluated for their risk level in eight domains, which results in an overall risk level score. Ms. Schmidt's overall score of 7 on the LS/CMI indicates a low risk for reoffending. She did not score in the high-risk range in any domains. Her scores indicated that she was at medium risk in the domain for pro-criminal attitudes (she reported a commitment to a life without crime, but she also stated she has been "shocked" by the "incompetence of the [legal] system" and finds the conditions of her current jail placement to be unsatisfactory). Ms. Schmidt scored in the low risk range in the following domains: family (she reported close relationships with her parents); companions (she reported that apart from the individuals she has met with in jail, none of her acquaintances are involved in crime); alcohol and drug problems (she reported no history of abusing alcohol and drugs); criminal history (she has no prior arrests); recreation habits (she reported involvement in academic organizations in graduate school and engagement in rewarding hobbies such as playing the violin); education/employment (she reported that she obtained good grades throughout her education and was in her third year of graduate school at the time of her arrest); and antisocial behavior.

Mental State Surrounding the Alleged Offense When asked about her interactions with the alleged victim, she described him as "condescending about gender," "unprofessional," and "arrogant" during her graduate school interview. For example, she reported that the alleged victim told him that "NYU doesn't want foreign women" and asked whether Ms. Schmidt was proficient in English. Ms. Schmidt also stated that the alleged victim "got touchy-feely and started stroking my leg," and that he "suggested there would be consequences if I told." She completed her interview with the alleged victim because "I was taught to be polite." When asked why she did not report her concerns about her interviewer to the NYU School of Criminology, Ms. Schmidt replied, "Even if I was admitted, they didn't really want me there. I don't have time for that; I have my life and I needed to move on." She believes she was rejected from NYU because of cultural bias.

Ms. Schmidt was also asked about the online accounts and postings made in the alleged victim's name and the postings containing the alleged victim's contact information. She stated that the postings were "a parody" that "would be funny." Although she reported that she "didn't think anything would come out of [the postings]" apart from "being funny," she also stated "maybe future interviewees would be prepared" for interactions with the alleged victim after viewing the postings. Because the accounts and postings in the alleged victim's name were (according to Ms. Schmidt) "stories and not statements of fact," she believed they should be protected under the First Amendment. And, because the alleged victim was "not physically injured" by the postings, they "seemed reasonable" to her. When asked about the potential consequences of making online accounts in another person's name, Ms. Schmidt responded, "So what if it's someone else's real name? There's probably someone named Christian Grey; does he get to sue for emotional damages?" She also stated that "if anyone suffered a criminal injury, I would feel bad because that wasn't my intent. If that's how it's perceived, then they have my deepest sympathies."

Clinical Forensic Opinion

It is clear from a review of the evidence that the harassment of the alleged victim in this matter was extensive, conducted over a period of time and using multiple means. While Ms. Schmidt felt insulted and disrespected by the behavior of the interviewer, she also minimized this anger in some respects ("I don't have time for (reporting such conduct)…I have my own life…I have to move on"). Both her responses during the interview and her MMPI-2 profile suggested she has, as the oldest child in her family, received much treatment consistent with the view that she is very important. This is realistic and commensurate with her significant accomplishments in some respects. She appeared realistic in her perception that she has faced discrimination growing up.

Several aspects of her functioning may have contributed to her behavior in the present case. Ms. Schmidt does not easily relate to other people, finding it hard to imagine interacting with a romantic partner (for example) beyond areas of shared interest. She did not describe a good understanding that other people might be emotionally harmed by her behavior, and in some respects did not appreciate how angry she was as a consequence of this interview and subsequent rejection by NYU. It is very important to her that her achievements be recognized and valued. None of these characteristics have kept Ms. Schmidt from achieving in multiple, noteworthy areas (music, languages, graduate study in criminology). They do not combine to clearly indicate that she suffers from a personality disorder, an autistic spectrum disorder, or a mood disorder. Possible symptoms of all three are described at present and around the time her apartment was raided, although the influences of incarceration and arrest may account for many of her reactions.

Based on all of the above, it is our opinion that Ms. Schmidt had the capacity to exercise the power of reason and conform her conduct to the law.

Recommendations

Ms. Schmidt has mental health symptoms that could be addressed in the areas of depression, trauma, and limited empathy. If Ms. Schmidt continues to experience symptoms of depression, trauma, or maladaptive interpersonal functioning following disposition of charges, she would be an appropriate candidate for therapy or counseling.

Ms. Schmidt is knowledgeable about certain aspects of the law, and she may be correct that she has a first amendment claim for some of her acts. Yet a therapy intervention in these areas would help her consider the larger context, including potential harm to a variety of parties with certain kinds of behavior—and the alternatives to such behavior that would hopefully provide fair outcomes while not invoking the risk of harm through behavior that is minimized as a "parody."

As such, she would benefit from:

1. Continued assessment to determine the most appropriate diagnosis and treatment for these symptoms; and
2. Therapeutic interventions focused on decision-making, empathy, prosocial relationships, and communication skills

How Did Social Media Impact This Case?

In this case, it was alleged that Ms. Schmidt had used social media in an attempt to harm the victim. She did not deny doing so, but minimized the seriousness of the harm. (In addressing this minimization, it was important to be able to show her copies of the social media posts). She also questioned whether his conduct was criminal, framing it as a free speech matter.

The meaning of the social media in contributing to her risk and rehabilitation needs appraisal was complex. One cannot conduct a meaningful risk assessment without documentation of prior instances of threats or physical aggression. In this case, Ms. Schmidt had a virtual absence of both in her history, but the social media documentation made the scope of the alleged harmful behavior clearer than any verbal description could have. Accordingly, it played an important role in the risk appraisal that was part of this federal sentencing evaluation.

References

American Psychological Association (2013). Specialty guidelines for forensic psychology. Retrieved 12-18-2018 from https://www.apa.org/practice/guidelines/forensic-psychology.aspx, 7, 19, 68

American Psychological Association (2017). Ethical principles of psychology and code of conduct. Retrieved 12-18-2018 from https://www.apa.org/ethics/code/

Glancy, G. D., Ash, P., Bath, E. P., Buchanan, A., Fedoroff, P., Frierson, R. L., et al. (2015). AAPL practice guideline for the forensic assessment. *Journal of the American Academy of Psychiatry and the Law, 43*, S3–S53.

Heilbrun, K. (2009). *Evaluation for risk of violence in adults*. New York: Oxford University Press.

Heilbrun, K., Douglas, K., & Yasuhara, K. (2009a). Violence risk assessment: Core controversies. In J. Skeem, K. Douglas, & S. Lilienfeld (Eds.), *Psychological science in the courtroom: Controversies and consensus* (pp. 333–357). New York: Guilford.

Heilbrun, K., Grisso, T., & Goldstein, A. (2009b). *Foundations of forensic mental health assessment*. Oxford: New York.

Heilbrun, K., DeMatteo, D., Brooks-Holliday, S., & LaDuke, C. (Eds.). (2014). *Forensic mental health assessment: A casebook* (2nd ed.). New York: Oxford University Press.

Melton, G., Petrila, J., Poythress, N., Slobogin, C., Otto, R., Mossman, D., & Condie, L. (2018). *Psychological evaluations for the courts: A handbook for mental health professionals and lawyers* (4th ed.). New York: Guilford.

Metzner, J. L., & Ash, P. (2010). Commentary: The mental status examination in the age of the internet. Challenges and opportunities. *Journal of the American Academy of Psychiatry and the Law, 38*, 27–31.

Monahan, J. (2008). Structured risk assessment of violence. In R. Simon & K. Tardiff (Eds.), *Textbook of violence assessment and management* (pp. 17–33). Washington, DC: American Psychiatric Publishing.

Monahan, J., & Steadman, H. (Eds.). (1994). *Violence and mental disorder: Developments in risk assessment*. Chicago: University of Chicago Press.

Neimark, G., Hurford, M. O., & DiGiacomo, J. (2006). The internet as collateral informant. *American Journal of Psychiatry, 163*, 1842. https://doi.org/10.1176/ajp.2006.163.10.1842.

Otto, R., & Douglas, K. (2009). *Handbook of violence risk assessment*. New York: Routledge.

Pirelli, G., Hartigan, S., & Zapf, P. A. (2018). Using the internet for collateral information in forensic mental health evaluations. *Behavioral Sciences & the Law*. Advanced online publication. https://doi.org/10.1002/bsl.2334, 157, 169, 36

Recupero, P. R. (2008). Forensic evaluation of problematic internet use. *Journal of the American Academy of Psychiatry and the Law, 36*, 505–514.

Recupero, P. R. (2010). The mental status examination in the age of the internet. *Journal of the American Academy of Psychiatry and the Law, 38*, 15–26.

Chapter 5
Sexually Problematic Behaviors

Emily D. Gottfried, Abby L. Mulay, and R. Gregg Dwyer

With the enactment of Sexually Violent Predator/Sexually Dangerous Persons (SVP/SDP) Acts beginning in 1990, the number of referrals for forensic mental health practitioners to conduct evaluations of future sexual dangerousness has increased dramatically. Twenty U.S. states, the District of Columbia, and the United States federal government have enacted some version of an SVP/SDP act. Typically these Acts call for the civil commitment of individuals who have been convicted of a sexually violent offense, are reaching the end of his/her[1] criminal sentence, and are opined to be at risk of committing a new sexually violent offense due to a mental or personality disorder or anomaly which affects his/her volitional capacity (Janus 1997; Prentky et al. 2006). SVP/SDP Acts have been criticized because of low base rates of sexually reoffending and poor predictive validity of the measures used to assess sexual dangerousness (e.g., Lave and Zimring 2018). This chapter describes the empirical literature related to the assessment of sexual dangerousness and then provides a framework for conducting such evaluations, with an emphasis on the use of technology and social media. It should be noted that this chapter is not restricted to SVP/SDP evaluations; rather, it focuses on the assessment of problematic sexual behaviors and the risk associated with these behaviors, as a whole. The chapter concludes with two case examples, which include aggregate data from evaluations conducted by the authors.

[1] Although individuals committed under these Acts are primarily male.

E. D. Gottfried (✉) · A. L. Mulay · R. G. Dwyer
Department of Psychiatry and Behavioral Sciences, Community and Public Safety Psychiatry Division, Medical University of South Carolina, Charleston, SC, USA
e-mail: gottfrem@musc.edu

A. B. Batastini, M. J. Vitacco (eds.), *Forensic Mental Health Evaluations in the Digital Age*, https://doi.org/10.1007/978-3-030-33908-1_5

5.1 The Basics of SVP/SDP and Other Evaluations of Sexually Problematic Behaviors

5.1.1 *Base Rates and Predictions of Sexual Offending*

Base rates are an important part of predicting how often (or infrequently) a behavior will occur. A non-peer-reviewed article published in *Psychology Today* in 1986 erroneously indicated up to 80% of untreated sexual offenders would go on to commit new sex offenses after release (Freeman-Longo and Wall 1986). Even more unfortunate, this same figure was cited by Supreme Court Justice Kennedy when he authored the majority opinion and cited that the rate of sexual recidivism was "frightening and high" as support for a ruling that it was not a violation of the Fifth Amendment privilege against self-incrimination to require sex offenders to admit to their offenses as a term of treatment (*McKune v. Lile* 2002). Studies examining the recidivism rate for new sex offenses reports this figure to be much lower. For example, a meta-analysis of 29,450 individuals convicted of sexual offenses across 82 studies reported that the recidivism rate for new sex offenses was 13.7% over five to six years of follow-up (Hanson and Morton-Bourgon 2005). However, an important caveat should be noted: sex offenses are the least likely type of offense to be reported to the authorities so any reported recidivism rate is for *detected* offenses, as only approximately 30% of all sex crimes are reported (Finkelhor 2009; see also Scurich and John's [controversial[2]] 2019 paper about how the actual sexual recidivism rate may be significantly greater than those reported in the literature based on reported recidivism cases). Taken together, the true base rate of sexual reoffending is unknown, and the detected rate of sexual recidivism is approximately 14% within a five-year period following release from prison. Next, we discuss factors that have been shown to differentiate sexual reoffenders from those who were identified as not reoffending sexually.

5.1.2 *Risk Factors for Recidivism*

An assessment of risk factors is an important component of a comprehensive evaluation of sexual behavior (Association for the Treatment of Sexual Abusers 2014; Mann et al. 2010). Two major types of risk factors include static factors, which are not amenable to treatment (e.g., age, number of previous convictions, male victims), and dynamic factors, which are typically changeable (e.g., substance use, negative peer associations; Hanson 1998). Dynamic risk factors can be further divided into stable and acute risk factors. Stable factors are those that can be changed but normally persist for longer periods of time such as paraphilic sexual interests or

[2] This paper is viewed by some as controversial because it uses mathematical models to predict risk.

substance abuse (Hanson 1998). On the other hand, acute factors represent states, which frequently change, such as intoxication (Hanson 1998).

Hanson and Bussière 1998 and later updated by Hanson and Morton-Bourgon (2005), reported that the factors predicting sexual reoffending are different from those that predict general, non-sexual reoffending. Risk factors which have been shown to be specific to sexual reoffending include prior sexual offenses, stranger victims, extrafamilial (i.e., outside of the family) victims, young age at first sexual offense, male victims, diverse sexual crimes, and sexual 'deviancy' (i.e., abusive or nonconsensual; Hanson and Bussière 1998). Across 61 studies, sexual deviancy, specifically having a sexual interest in children, was the strongest predictor of sexual reoffending ($r = .32$; Hanson and Bussière 1998). The more recent Hanson and Morton-Bourgon (2005) meta-analysis yielded similar findings in that the strongest predictor of sexual reoffending was the presence of a deviant sexual interest and antisocial characteristics (Hanson and Morton-Bourgon 2005).

More recently, Mann and colleagues (2010) examined the literature and identified the following psychologically meaningful risk factors that were reported as being predictive of recidivism in at least three studies and had "more than trivial" effect sizes[3] (i.e., averaged $d > .15$; p. 196). The risk factors included emotional congruence with children; sexual preoccupation; general problems in self-regulation, including impulsivity, recklessness, and employment instability; conflicts in intimate relationships; never married; any 'deviant' sexual interest, including sexual preference for children as assessed by penile plethysmography, sexualized violence, and multiple 'paraphilias (which by current DSM-5 definition would likely be paraphilic disorders);' trouble following the rules and supervision conditions, including youth behavioral problems, not complying with terms of supervision, and violation of conditional release; having negative social influences; offense-supportive attitudes; poor cognitive problem solving; and grievance and hostility. The following factors were shown to be unrelated to sexual recidivism: depression; poor victim empathy; poor social skills; and lack of motivation for treatment during intake.

5.1.3 Assessing Sexual Offender Risk

The Association for the Treatment of Sexual Abusers (ATSA) published their latest Practice Guidelines for assessing and treating male sexual abusers in 2014. These guidelines stress the importance of adhering to ethical practices, using multiple data points, and consulting empirically-supported methods in conducting evaluations with individuals convicted or charged with sex offenses. Although these guidelines are helpful, it must be noted that no universally-accepted standards of practice exist specifically for the evaluation of individuals undergoing evaluations pursuant to an SVP/SDP statute for the prediction of sexual offender recidivism.

[3] Cohen's d is an effect size used to indicate the standardized difference between two means, with $d = 0.8$ being a large mean effect size, $d = 0.5$ being medium, and $d = 0.2$ representing a small effect size.

5.2 Sex Offenses and the Internet

The Internet has not just made life easier and more convenient for purchasing goods and social networking; it has also made accessing would-be victims easier and more convenient. This is true for both hands-on offenses, in which an individual may use social media sites to find and lure victims, and for hands-off offenses, in which trading child pornography has never been easier. Additionally, the dark web (i.e., part of the Internet that is only accessible by using software that makes the user anonymous and untraceable), live streaming applications, and encrypted applications can all be used to engage in both hands-on and hands-off offenses in ways that are more difficult to track. Although beyond the scope of our expertise and of this chapter, to follow is a list of mechanisms (e.g., routers, browsers, websites, applications) that although not necessarily designed or used primarily for such a purpose, can be used to perpetrate or facilitate sex offenses. Note that this is in no way an exhaustive list as similar mechanisms are routinely developed.

1. Accessing sites through the dark web or using The Onion Router (Tor) Browser (e.g., software that allows people to browse on the dark web and makes their browsing history untraceable by using onion routing [i.e., a technique for anonymous communication in which messages are encapsulated in layers of encryption; Goldschlag et al. 1999]).
2. It has been reported that child pornography is 'hidden' within the blockchains of Bitcoin (e.g., digital currency independent of a central bank; Matzutt et al. 2018[4]).
3. Peer to Peer (P2P) Networks are used to directly share files without a central network and can be used to share illegal content. Examples include Kazaa, LimeWire, and Skype.
4. Social networking sites, such as Facebook, Instagram, and Twitter all have direct-message functions in which a sender can send 'private messages' to people outside their own social network. Snapchat can be used to send messages that 'disappear' and are irretrievable. Additionally, there is ease in creating fake accounts to use for untoward purposes.
5. Instant/messaging apps (e.g., Wickr, WhatsApp, Pryvate, Telegram, FireChat, Stealth Messenger) have encrypted messages in which the content 'expires.' Additionally some apps allow for anonymous text/'feedback' posts and images (e.g., After School, Sarahah, Sayat.me).
6. Live video streaming apps (e.g., live.ly, Livestream, Yubo) and group video chatting apps (e.g., Houseparty).
7. 'Video walkie-talkie' apps (e.g., Marco Polo).
8. Apps to encrypt multimedia and text files (e.g., KYMS [Keep your media safe], Secret Calculator, Private Photo Vault, Best Secret Folder).
9. Web cameras and cellphone cameras have been used by people with voyeuristic disorder.

[4] It should be noted that this is not a peer-reviewed source.

The companies' attempts to prevent the use of the apps in illegal activity have largely been unsuccessful. For example, the parent company that owns WhatsApp banned hundreds of thousands of accounts that were identified by the group names that used titles that suggested they could contain child pornography. However, because the content on WhatsApp is completely encrypted, even the company cannot view information contained in the messages (Abboud et al. 2018). Additionally, the popular video-sharing website, YouTube has attempted to disable the 'comments' feature on videos that contain children under the age of 14 and restricts comments on some videos containing teenagers under the age of 18. This was reportedly done after it was discovered that viewers were commenting on videos and leaving timestamps and additional details describing when the children were in suggestive poses or in various states of undress (Mac 2019).

5.2.1 Online Interactions by Child Sex Offenders

Current media reports indicate that individuals have been arrested for using the dark web to distribute child pornography. For example, in Florida, Homeland Security agents searched a man's home and found 4000 images and 43 videos of him sexually abusing his 1-year-old child. He had posted a four-video series of the abuse and uploaded them to the dark web. In 2019, he was sentenced to 70 years in prison after pleading guilty to charges of producing, distributing, and possessing child pornography (Lapin 2019). A study examined 200 cases that included chat logs, emails, and social network posts from offenses involving the online solicitation of children who were actually undercover officers (DeHart et al. 2017). Four types of offenders were identified: cybersex offenders, schedulers, cybersex/scheduler offenders, and buyers. It was further noted that online interactions between children and sexual offenders may escalate rapidly (e.g., the offenders exchanged sexual images or arranged a meeting in less than 10 minutes; DeHart et al. 2017). A 2010 study reported that of the approximately 7010 arrests for internet-related sex crimes against minors in the United States in 2006, 33% (approximately 2322) of those cases involved social networking sites in some way (Mitchell et al. 2010). Seven percent of all cases involved an identifiable victim and of the cases that involved social networking sites, 22% also had an identifiable victim. It was reported that these sites were used in the following ways:

1. Initiating a relationship
2. Communicating with victim(s)
3. Distribution of information/pictures of victim(s)
4. Getting information about victim(s)
5. Contacting friends of victim(s)

Despite these statistics, which may sound frightening on their face, the authors noted that social networking sites were not the most common place that children met offenders; rather, 61% of the offenders met their victims on other internet sites, with chat rooms being frequently cited (Mitchell et al. 2010). Individuals who were on the sex offender registry in North Carolina were previously restricted from accessing websites in which minors were known to have accounts or frequent. Interestingly a Supreme Court case (*Packingham v. North Carolina* 2017) held that this restriction was a violation of the First Amendment. In a unanimous decision, Justice Kennedy wrote the majority opinion, noting, "Even convicted criminals-and in some instances especially convicted criminals-might receive legitimate benefits from these means [i.e., the Internet] for access to the world of ideas, particularly if they seek to reform and to pursue lawful and rewarding lives" (p. 2).

Taken together, the internet has provided new avenues for individuals who commit sex offenses. For example, the access to victims is increased, the chat functions and applications can be used for encrypted sexual chats, sex trafficking has increased, and child pornography rates have exploded (Adams and Flynn 2017). These types of data can be used in evaluations of sexual behavior in several ways. First, internet chat logs can be used to assess offense behaviors and sexual (and/or paraphilic) interests. Social media websites can be examined to determine if the age of the victim was readily apparent and to examine the nature of the relationship, if any, between the victim and the examinee before, during, and after the offense(s). Additionally, having information on the content of child pornography materials can provide data about potential pedophilic and other paraphilic interests.

There are practical, ethical, and legal considerations unique to the use of online collateral data in determining an examinee's risk for engaging in future acts of sexual violence or otherwise inappropriate sexual behavior. For example, even if the data were provided by law enforcement, it is not possible to determine who actually authored the post/chat/message. Additionally, should examiners ever conduct their own social media searches of examinees? Currently, it is unknown how juries perceive these data. It is possible that juries may place more weight on actual materials rather than something reported only by the victim. Other considerations include the potentially traumatic aspects of the evaluator viewing child pornography materials and causing them to have a negative bias against the examinee. Further, in the United States, viewing or possessing these materials, even for the purpose of conducting a court-ordered evaluation, is a federal offense. Thus, this would represent a practical limitation. In South Carolina, where we practice, if it becomes necessary to view these materials for the evaluation, we must travel to the prosecuting attorney or Attorney General's office so that we are not committing a federal offense.

5.3 Integrating Internet and SNS Data in Sexual Risk Assessment Instruments

Standard risk assessment instruments for assessing sexual behavior typically take the form of actuarial or some form of structured clinical judgment. It is important to note that actuarial measures do not predict risk at the individual level; no tool has that ability. At best, these measures match an individual to a group with similar characteristics, but it is unknown if the grouping was correct or if the individual's risk would be higher or lower than the comparison group. An exhaustive review of risk assessment tools and instruments used in these types of cases is beyond the scope of this chapter; however, a brief review of the most common actuarial instruments and considerations for how Internet data may be used to complete them is provided next.

Of note, in addition to measures of risk, evaluations of sexual behavior almost always include other types of assessment instruments including but not limited to, viewing time measures (i.e., psychophysiological measures that unobtrusively measure the amount of time an examinee looks at stimuli, see: Abel et al. 1998; Abel et al. 2001; Fischer and Smith 1999; Schmidt et al. 2017; Seto 2018); self-report measures of sexual behavior (e.g., Multiphasic Sex Inventory-II [MSI-II]; Nichols and Molinder 2005; see: Tong 2007); polygraph examinations (see: Fabian 2005; Iacono 2008; Iacono and Ben-Shakhar 2018); penile plethysmography (PPG; see: Chivers et al. 2010; Fedoroff et al. 2009; Gaither and Plaud 1997; Hanson and Bussière 1998; Laws et al. 2000; Letourneau 2002; Marshall 2014; Marshall and Fernandez 2001; McPhail et al. 2019; Murphy et al. 2015a; Murphy et al. 2015b; O'Shaughnessy 2015; Plaud 2019); tests of neurocognitive and intellectual functioning; objective personality tests; as well as specific measures of psychopathy (see: Gottfried et al. In press; Murrie et al. 2012; Porter et al. 2009; Woodworth et al. 2013); substance use; and impulsivity.

Static-99R (Phenix et al. 2016). Most evaluators use the Static-99R, which is a 10-item actuarial risk assessment tool used for adult men that assesses static factors shown to be associated with recidivism risk. It is the most widely researched measure of sexual risk/recidivism (Chevalier et al. 2015; Jackson and Hess 2007; Neal and Grisso 2014), and the authors of the instrument caution against using it as the sole data point in making decisions about risk (Phenix et al. 2016).

Despite its wide use, there are data to suggest that it is not always a reliable indicator of risk. The study with the largest sample known to date assessed the validity of the Static-99R in 34,687 sex offenders in Texas scored on the Static 99R and who had not been committed to the SVP treatment program (Boccaccini et al. 2017). Findings from this study indicated the Static-99R scores were medium-sized predictors of sexual reoffending (Area Under the Curves ranged from .62 to .65), but that they may overestimate risk for offenders with scores ranging from 1 (Low risk category) to 5 (Moderate-High risk category; Boccaccini et al. 2017). Additionally, a study assessing a sample of 21,983 sex offenders in Texas reported that the instrument had good interrater agreement between raters but that the reliability decreased as the Static score increased (Rice et al. 2014). Additional studies have suggested the Static-99R may not be useful in predicting sexual recidivism (e.g., Buttars et al. 2015; Reeves et al. 2018).

Sexual Violence Risk-20 (SVR-20; Boer et al. 1997). The SVR-20 is a structured clinical checklist used to assess risk for sexual violence. Rather than being a psychometric measure, it is a tool of structured professional judgment. It contains 20 total items that are divided into domains of psychosocial adjustment, sexual offenses, and future plans. Additionally, clinicians can code 'other considerations' for case-specific risk factors not accounted into the 20 items. The final risk judgment is rated as low, moderate, or high for a specific time period and setting. As it is not a psychometric instrument, the validity of the guidelines is primarily a function of the accuracy and completeness of the systemic research review on which they were based (Hart, personal communication, February 26, 2019). Further reading on the SVR-20 can be accomplished by referring to studies by de Vogel et al. (2004) and Rettenberger et al. (2011). A second version of the SVR-20 has also been published (Boer et al. 2018), but it has not yet been the subject of empirical study.

Sex Offender Risk Assessment Guide (SORAG; Quinesy et al. 2006). The SORAG is an actuarial risk assessment tool containing 14 items. Based on the SORAG total score, the examinee is placed into one of nine risk bins, which range from 1 (lowest risk) to 9 (highest risk). It has been shown to have excellent interrater reliability and good predictive validity (e.g., Rettenberger et al. 2017; Quinsey et al. 2006).

The Minnesota Sex Offender Screening Tool-Revised (MnSOST-R; Epperson et al. 1998). The MnSOST-R contains 12 historical/static factors and four dynamic factors. A meta-analysis indicated that the MnSOST-R is a moderate to strong predictor of sexual recidivism (Hanson and Morton-Bourgon 2009). In contrast to this finding, Boccaccini et al. 2009) found that the MnSOST-R was no better than chance at predicting sexually violent recidivism. Thus, the MnSOST-R has limited utility and its use in SVP evaluations is cautioned.

Violence Risk Scale-Sexual Offender Version (VRS-SO; Wong et al. 2003). The VRS-SO uses seven static factors and 17 dynamic factors to assess risk of sexual violence, particularly for examinees being released to the community after treatment and uses the examinee's stage of change and change level to do so. The risk levels were updated in 2018 and the VRS-SO has been shown to demonstrate moderate to high predictive validity for sexual recidivism after five and ten years (Olver et al. 2018). As an examiner is unlikely to know which stage of change the examinee was in prior to entering treatment, the VRS-SO has limited utility in SVP/SDP pre-commitment (i.e., initial evaluation prior to an individual being adjudicated as an SVP) or release evaluations (i.e., evaluation to determine readiness for release from an SVP treatment program).

Integrating Internet data. The use of Internet data can be used with caution in conjunction with the aforementioned measures of sexual recidivism risk. For example, when scoring the Static-99R, an evaluator can look at social media accounts for data supporting or contradicting whether the examinee has lived with a lover for at least two years. The evaluator may also confirm that a victim was not a stranger, if the examinee claims they were friends on social media. When scoring the SVR-20 or the MnSOST-R, an evaluator may examine social media accounts for data supporting or contradicting whether the examinee has experienced employment problems. Additionally, the evaluator may conduct a review of online communications between the examinee and victim to determine the use of threats and check on the examinee's level of minimization or denial of offense, and to assess if the examinee's future plans are realistic. For the SORAG, an evaluator can look at social media accounts for data supporting or contradicting whether the examinee lived with a biological parent up to age 16, history of alcohol problems by assessing social media posts/pictures that involve alcohol, marriage history, and possibly symptoms of personality pathology. Finally, regarding the VRS-SO, use of Internet data can be used with caution in conjunction with other data for scoring the static and dynamic factors of the measure.

Assessing paraphilic sexual interests. According to the *Diagnostic and Statistical Manual of Mental Disorder*, Fifth Edition (DSM-5; American Psychiatric Association [APA], 2013), a paraphilia is an enduring sexual interest in something other than sexual activity with an adult consenting partner, while a paraphilic disorder is a paraphilia that causes distress or impairment to the individual, or results in harm to self and/or others. Examples of paraphilic disorder diagnoses include pedophilic disorder (sexual arousal to prepubescent children), sexual sadism disorder (sexual arousal to hurting or humiliating someone else), and exhibitionistic disorder (sexual arousal to exposing one's genitals to an unsuspecting person; APA 2013). Based on prior literature, it would seem that those who offended due to a paraphilic interest would be at high risk for re-offense (e.g., Hanson and Bussière 1998; McPhail et al. 2019). Thus, an assessment of paraphilic disorders is a necessary component of evaluations of sexual offender risk for recidivism. As there are no standardized structured diagnostic assessments of paraphilic interests, the best way to assess these disorders is to assess for all paraphilias and paraphilic disorders that have the potential for victimization by asking about fantasies and behaviors during the clinical interview. At this point, it is unclear if social media data (e.g., Facebook, Instagram) could be helpful in the diagnosis of paraphilic disorders, unless individuals share their fantasies or behaviors on these websites. However, an examination of data obtained by law enforcement from the dark web may provide further evidence to suggest paraphilic disorders, based upon the individual's history of sharing pictures or communications with others.

Etiology. Determining the etiology of the offense behaviors is a necessary component of conducting evaluations of sexual violence risk. Individuals may commit sexual offenses secondary to paraphilic sexual interests (e.g., interest in/arousal to abusive or nonconsenting stimuli), antisocial practices, another medical condition, intellectual disability, symptoms of severe mental illness (e.g., mania), and in rare cases, due to effects of medication (e.g., dopaminomimetic treatment for Parkinson's disease; Solla et al. 2015). Use of SNS data may help to inform the evaluator of the aforementioned factors; for example, an individual may post about medical conditions or antisocial behaviors (e.g., "thrill seeking" behaviors), which may help to inform diagnosis.

5.4 Putting It All Together

Evaluations of sexual behavior typically contain a wealth of data points that do not always converge. As indicated in previous sections of this chapter, sexual recidivism is a low base rate condition typically involving examinees that are motivated to not be forthcoming. These are also typically high-stakes evaluations, with dire consequences on both sides (e.g., loss of freedom v. the potential of new victims). Additionally, the interrater reliability between different evaluators assessing the same individual for potential civil commitment under the SVP act has been shown to be poor (Kappa = .54) and the agreement between the evaluators on an individual's paraphilic disorder diagnosis ranged from poor to fair (Kappas ranging from .30 for sexual sadism disorder to .65 for pedophilic disorder; Levenson 2004). SNS data may enrich the sexual behavior evaluation, as it offers the opportunity to examine postings made directly by the individual, outside of the context of the evaluation; as such, the data may represent a more "pure" form of the individual's thoughts, feelings, behaviors and/or experiences, which may help to reduce the overall effect of social desirability during the evaluation.

5.5 What Do Other Forensic Practitioners Do?

Only two studies to our knowledge have explored forensic practitioners' practices for conducting evaluations pursuant to SVP/SDP Acts, and given the age of these studies, the use of SNS data were not discussed. Jackson and Hess (2007) surveyed 41 forensic mental health practitioners on their practices for conducting civil commitment evaluations with individuals convicted of sexual offenses. Results indicated that most respondents viewed the use of collateral records as being 'essential' or 'recommended.' The majority of their sample (80.5%) indicated they 'always' assessed for paraphilias (now termed paraphilic interests or disorders), substance use disorders (70.7%), personality disorders (65.9%), other mental illnesses (56.1%), psychopathy (51.2%), and developmental or cognitive disorders (34.1%). Over three-quarters of the participants reported 'always' using an actuarial risk assessment measure and the Static-99 was the most widely used. The majority (70.7%) of the sample indicated they 'never' used the PPG in their evaluations. The methods used for determining the presence of volitional impairment were most frequently assessing for the presence of a personality disorder coupled with a history of sexual offending (65.9%) followed by the presence or absence of paraphilic interests (63.4%).

Levenson and Morin (2006) examined the evaluations of 450 individuals who had been convicted of sexually violent offenses and were under consideration for civil commitment under the Florida SVP Act. The Static-99 and MnSOST-R were significantly correlated with being recommended for civil commitment. Additionally, psychopathy; a paraphilic disorder diagnosis, especially pedophilic disorder or one that was 'not otherwise specified' (NOS); antisocial personality disorder; committing a variety of sexual offenses; a history of failing on probation; violence or sex acts during incarceration; number of victims; the age of victim; the examinee's statement that he was going to commit a new sex offense upon release; and violence or weapon use during the sex offense were all correlated with the recommendation of civil commitment.

5.6 Conclusion

In sum, it is important to consider base rates when conducting evaluations of sexual recidivism risk. The base rate differs between studies based on the definition of recidivism that was used, sample characteristics, and the period of time that elapsed. Risk factors consistently cited in the literature include sexual 'deviancy' (i.e., abusive or nonconsensual interests), antisocial characteristics, and younger (adult) age at time of evaluation and young age at first sex offense. Risk instruments do not predict an individual's level of risk, rather they provide predictions for groups of individuals with similar characteristics. Despite the imperfect science of risk prediction, all evaluations should incorporate empirically-supported risk instruments. Multiple data points should be used to make risk predictions about an individual, but this is increasingly difficult when data points do not converge and when examining individuals who may be motivated to not be forthcoming. Practitioners should note the limitations of the data collected and of their risk predictions. Importantly, the rise of the Internet has arguably made certain types of sex offending easier, especially due to the advent of data encrypted software, applications, and file-sharing tools. Given changes in the online landscape, social media data can be helpful in SVP/SDP evaluations, but they have their own limitations, and it is currently unknown how these types of data are perceived by judges and juries. Practical applications of SNS data include the assessment of an examinee's psychosocial history and stressors, online relationships, communication between the examinee and the victim, and the examinee's static/dynamic risk factors for reoffending.

What follows are two case summaries in which social media data were used to help inform questions involving deviant sexual behavior and risk of sexual offending. Please be advised that these types of evaluations are typically quite extensive and often involve significant amounts of records review, interviewing, and test administration. For other examples of case reports and writing these reports, readers are directed elsewhere (e.g., Melton et al. 2018; Witt and Conroy 2009). The case examples in this chapter have been deidentified and truncated to focus more directly on contextual content and the information obtained from social media postings.

Case Profile 1

Type of Evaluation

The following evaluation was a Sexual Behaviors Consultation Evaluation to determine if Mr. James Klein met the definition of a "sexually violent predator" according to the state Sexually Violent Predator Act. The evaluation assessed for the presence of a mental abnormality and/or personality disorder that made him likely to engage in acts of sexual violence, which in turn required an assessment of (1) mental health, (2) risk of sexual offending recidivism, and (3) treatment needs, if any.

Case Context

The examinee in this case, 45-year-old Mr. Klein, was evaluated on three occasions, for approximately 15 h. He had been previously convicted of three sex offenses involving minors and was nearing the end of his confinement. The examinee was pending a hearing for return to the community or confinement. The evaluation was conducted at a facility housing a sexual behaviors clinic and laboratory with one of its mission functions being sexual behavior evaluations for the courts. The examinee was in custody and transported for the evaluation appointments to the laboratory site, which has security features in place for in-custody examinees to be evaluated.

Sources of Information

For brevity, the specific sources of information are not listed but included the police and court discovery documents for each case, the examinee's criminal history report, screenshots from cellphones, copies of direct messages from Facebook and Instagram, copies of the examinee's Facebook page, Department of Corrections records, clinical interview of examinee, and assessment measures administered for the current evaluation.

Confidentiality

On each day of the evaluation, Mr. Klein was advised that he was being evaluated at the request of the office of the State's Attorney General (AG). Mr. Klein was advised that information provided and obtained during his evaluation would not be confidential and that information provided to the AG would no longer be under the control of the laboratory. Mr. Klein signed a consent form indicating his understanding and approval of the purpose of the evaluation, his participation in the evaluation, and the limits of confidentiality.

Relevant Background

Mr. Klein was raised by his biological parents along with three younger siblings. He reported never being the victim of physical, sexual, or emotional abuse, and he did not witness domestic violence in the home. Mr. Klein did not endorse any significant youth conduct problems. Regarding academic functioning, he was retained in the fourth and seventh grades because he "couldn't stay in my seat, wasn't doing the work, just wanted to move." He was subsequently prescribed stimulant medication by a family physician to help manage these symptoms, but he discontinued the medication in high school. He also reported being suspended from school a few times per year, beginning in high school, for "not listening." He left school in the tenth grade to work, and at the time of the evaluation, had not obtained his General Education Development (GED). Mr. Klein reported a history of employment at a car wash, in fast food restaurants, in retail stores, and at an amusement park. He was fired from several jobs for "not showing up." He did not report any significant health issues, but he endorsed being rendered unconscious "a few times" secondary to physical altercations. He did not report any history of outpatient or inpatient psychiatric treatment. Regarding substance use, he described a history of alcohol use between the ages of 14 and 21. He stopped consuming alcohol at age 21 following a conviction of Driving under the Influence. He also endorsed a history of cannabis use, as well as disciplinary infractions during his incarceration related to cannabis.

Mr. Klein reported he had never been married and has no children. He stated he identified as heterosexual and had been in three committed relationships during high school. He reported he had never been in a romantic relationship as an adult. Regarding his sexual history, Mr. Klein began puberty at the age of 12, and he began masturbating at the age of 13. He started having sexual fantasies about girls in his class sometime around the age of 12 or 13. Mr. Klein was first sexually active with a consenting partner when he was 17 years old, though they did not engage in sexual intercourse. He said that his friends hired a female prostitute for him on his 18th birthday and that was his first and last sexual experience with a consenting partner. When asked about current sexual fantasies or thoughts, Mr. Klein said, "Just of normal stuff…whatever's normal," and he did not provide further information. Mr. Klein said that, as an adult, he masturbated "about weekly" and experienced an orgasm every time he masturbated. Aside from the DUI conviction and his sexual offenses (described below), Mr. Klein had no additional legal history.

Behavioral Observations and Mental Status

During the evaluation, Mr. Klein was dressed in standard-issued correctional attire, and he did not present with issues related to hygiene or grooming. His eye contact ranged from appropriate to avoidant, and he frequently stared straight ahead of him. His speech was of normal rate and volume. There was no indication that he was responding to internal stimuli or expressing delusional beliefs. His thoughts appeared to be logical and linear. Initially, Mr. Klein appeared to be cooperative with the evaluation process. When his sexual offenses and test results were discussed with him, however, he became guarded and somewhat defensive. He described his current mood as "distressed" about the potential of being committed as a sexually violent predator. He was oriented to person, place, time, and situation, and his attention and concentration were within normal limits. He demonstrated adequate judgment when presented with a hypothetical situation, and his abstract reasoning abilities appeared intact.

Summary of Test Results

Mr. Klein was administered the Conners Continuous Performance Test 3 (CPT 3), the Substance Abuse Subtle Screening Inventory (SASSI-4), the Personality Assessment Inventory (PAI), and a Penile Plethysmograph (PPG). Further, he was scored on the Static-99R and SVR-20. A summary of results follows.

The CPT 3 did not have indication of attention problems or impulsivity. Results from the SASSI-4 indicated that he approached the test in a consistent manner. There was no evidence of a defensive-style of responding. Mr. Klein's responses suggested a high probability that he had a substance use disorder at the time of the evaluation or had one in the past.

Regarding the PAI, Mr. Klein did not omit any items and appeared to answer the items in a consistent manner. There was no indication Mr. Klein was attempting to present himself in an unfavorable light. Results indicated that he may have been attempting to present himself in an overly-favorable manner and to minimize problems he may have been experiencing. In light of this response style, results were interpreted with caution. Overall, Mr. Klein did not endorse any significant problems or symptoms. His self-concept likely involved being withdrawn and introverted. Mr. Klein would likely report having little interest in socializing with others and not making an effort to appear friendly. His perceived level of social support was probably lower than that of the average adult. Mr. Klein would likely describe his temper as being normal and well-controlled.

Mr. Klein was administered a PPG using two stimuli sets. The Marshall set includes auditory stimuli that depicts various sexual and neutral scenarios read in a monotone male voice; Mr. Klein was given the female victim set, which features only female children and adolescents and compares the responses to consensual scenarios featuring adult women. The Real Child Voices (RCV) set includes auditory and visual stimuli that uses voices of male and female children, adolescents, and adults and compares the responses to consensual scenarios featuring adult men and women. Both sets met the minimum requirement for interpretation, including arousal indicated by at least one trial of at least a five-millimeter (mm) increase. The confidence level was high for both sets based on at least one trial with at least a 10-mm or greater increase on each set. Mr. Klein's maximum arousal for both sets was to scenarios depicting persuasion of a female prepubescent child. At the individual trial level, both sets showed clinically significant arousal (i.e., ≥5-mm increase) to persuasion of a female prepubescent child (three trials on the Marshall set and two on the RCV set) and the RCV set additionally showed clinically significant arousal to one trial depicting persuasion of a male child. For the Marshall set, the calculated female prepubescent (pedophilic), female prepubescent (pedophilic) rape, female pubescent, and female pubescent rape indices indicated the presence of "deviant" (abusive) sexual arousal for Mr. Klein. For the RCV set, the calculated female prepubescent (pedophilic) and male prepubescent (pedophilic) indices indicated the presence of "deviant" (abusive) sexual arousal for Mr. Klein. His arousal to the scenarios featuring prepubescent female children was more than two standard deviations greater on the RCV set and more than 3.5 standard deviations greater on the Marshall set than his arousal to consensual sex with an adult woman. This suggests that he demonstrated a preference for the scenarios featuring prepubescent girls over the adult consenting scenarios. These results are statistically robust evidence of a clear preference for prepubescent girls over appropriate consensual sexual behavior.

Using record information and data collected during the evaluation, Mr. Klein's Static-99R score was five (5), which placed him in the Above Average Risk category for being charged or convicted of another sexual offense. Using the 2016 Static -99R Evaluator's Workbook, in the routine sample with this same score, the 5-year sexual recidivism rate was 15.2 with a 95% confidence interval of 13.8 to 16.6. On average, offenders with a Static-99R score of 5 have a sexual recidivism rate that is 2.70 times the rate (the same rate) of offenders in the middle of the risk range (defined as a median score of 2). These values are based on routine, defined as relatively unselected, correctional samples.

For the psychosocial adjustment risk factors on the SVR-20, it was noted that Mr. Klein had a history of problems with sexual deviation (relatively stable pattern of sexual arousal to prepubescent female children), substance use problems (continued cannabis use while incarcerated despite sanctions), relationship problems (lack of relationships and poor interpersonal skills), and employment problems (problems maintaining employment). For the sexual offending risk factors, it was noted that Mr. Klein had a history of problems with chronic sexual offending (offended against several victims despite sanctions), psychological coercion in sexual offending (grooming behaviors), and extreme minimization or denial of sexual offending (coded as 'possibly/partially' as Mr. Klein had minimized his offenses but also pled guilty to his offenses). For the future plans risk factors, it was noted that Mr. Klein lacked realistic plans (no realistic plans upon release). SVR-20, Version 2, Conclusory Opinions indicated that Mr. Klein's Summary Risk Rating was in the High range as a high level of effort/intervention would be required to prevent further sexual violence. In terms of risk for serious physical harm, Mr. Klein was at low risk as there were no data to suggest that future sexual violence would result in life-threatening physical harm. The need for immediate action was rated as moderate as Mr. Klein did not pose any imminent risks at the time of assessment due to incarceration, but he would likely pose a risk at release. There were no other risks indicated.

Diagnostic Conclusions

Mr. Klein met diagnostic criteria for pedophilic disorder, exclusive type, sexually attracted to female children. According to the DSM-5 (2013), the diagnostic criteria for pedophilic disorder are "over a period of at least six months, recurrent, intense sexually arousing fantasies, sexual urges, or behaviors involving sexual activity with a prepubescent child or children; the individual has acted on these sexual urges, or the sexual urges or fantasies cause marked distress or interpersonal difficulty; the individual is at least age 16 and at least five years older than the child" (p. 697). A review of available records indicated that Mr. Klein pled guilty to sexually offending against girls aged approximately 5–10 years old. Offense behaviors included performing oral sex on the victims and digital penetration. Additionally, he groomed (i.e., process by which an offender draws a victim into a sexual relationship and maintains that relationship in secrecy) his victims by engaging in nail painting, discussing their interests, buying them things, and taking them horseback riding. Although Mr. Klein said he did not engage in these behaviors and was not sexually aroused by prepubescent female children, available data indicated that Mr. Klein pled guilty to these offenses and continued to contact his victims via social media while serving time for these offenses. Additionally, physiological data collected during the current evaluation suggested that he was sexually aroused by prepubescent girls. Specifically, results of the PPG indicated that Mr. Klein demonstrated a preference for prepubescent girls over consenting adult women. The specifier of 'exclusive type' was indicated for Mr. Klein, as he appeared to never have a sexual relationship with an adult woman, he was not sexually interested in adult women, and he was exclusively sexually aroused by prepubescent female children. The specifier 'sexually attracted to female children' indicated that he appeared to be sexually aroused by prepubescent girls and not boys.

Mr. Klein also met diagnostic criteria for a mild cannabis use disorder.

Summary of Data Relevant to Psycho-Legal Question

Officially Reported Information for Offense 1 According to records, Mr. Klein was arrested and charged with Lewd Act Against a Child and Criminal Sexual Conduct Against a Minor in the Second Degree. The victim in the case was Mr. Klein's 14-year-old female cousin, Rachel Watson, who said that Mr. Klein sexually abused her from the time she was 5 years old until she was 10. She said that Mr. Klein would paint her nails and allow her to paint his nails when she was 4 years old, would give her back rubs, and eventually began placing his hand and fingers inside of her underwear when she was 5 years old. He would frequently sleep over her house and she would wake up to find Mr. Klein "licking my private." She said he was about 16 years old when this started and continued until he was 21. She reported it to her sister about four years later and it was reported to the authorities when Mr. Klein was 25 years old. A review of Mr. Klein's computer at arrest indicated that Mr. Klein had frequently been "chatting" online with girls in a chat forum, "All 4 Ponies." Police attempted to contact the girls he had been "chatting" with but were not able to do so or to ascertain their ages. Mr. Klein was arrested and pled guilty to Criminal Sexual Conduct Against a Minor in the Third Degree. He was sentenced to 10 years in prison and served eight years before he was released on parole. He was mandated to sex-offender specific treatment and community supervision. It is unknown if he complied with the supervision terms.

Examinee's Report of Offense 1 Mr. Klein said that he was "curious" about his cousin when he was a teenager but said that he did not assault her. When asked to elaborate on how he was "curious," he said, "Just curious about ladies and all that stuff." He did not provide further information when asked to do so. He said that he did not know why his cousin say these things about him and said that he was not sexually aroused by her. When asked why he pled guilty to this offense, he said, "I knew that going to prison would be better than having to deal with my brother's wrath and her [the victim's] mother. I just said I did it, so they would leave me alone." He refused to provide additional information when the case discovery was discussed with him.

Officially Reported Information for Offense 2 According to records, Mr. Klein was arrested when he was 35 and charged with Criminal Sexual Conduct Against a Minor in the First Degree. Incident Reports from the Police Department indicated that the complainant called the police to report that her 8-year-old daughter, Annie White,[5] had just informed her that Coach Klein had sexually assaulted her. Witness/Victim statements indicated that Annie was contacted via her Facebook page by a boy she thought was 12 years old. The "boy," who was really Mr. Klein, had written her messages through the Facebook Direct Messenger Application on a near-daily basis for five months. A review of the provided Facebook messages indicated that initially Mr. Klein presented himself as being a 12-year-old boy from Annie's school but eventually told her that he was a 24-year-old man (although he was actually in his thirties). They discussed swimming, soccer, and horses, and Mr. Klein told her he was an equestrian coach and would give her private lessons. Mr. Klein picked Annie up at her school on three occasions and took her to ride horses and bought her cheeseburgers and frozen yogurt. After that, Mr. Klein picked her up and took her to his house. Mr. Klein engaged in oral sex on the victim and digitally penetrated her on multiple occasions before the assaults were reported. Mr. Klein met the victim's mother and she allowed Annie to spend time with Mr. Klein as Annie "really seemed to like him, he was like a father/brother figure" and he would take her to ride horses. When Annie reported the abuse to her mother, she showed her mother "love notes" from Mr. Klein on Facebook in which he told her that he loved her and described wanting to marry her. Mr. Klein pled guilty to Criminal Sexual Conduct Against a Minor in the Second Degree and was sentenced to 10 years in prison.

Examinee's Report of Offense 2 Mr. Klein initially said that he did not sexually assault Annie, and that she was a neighbor and he would babysit her to help her mother out. He said that she made false allegations against him because she had been sexually abused by someone else and Mr. Klein was an "easy target" because her family knew that he was registered sex offender. After the social media screenshots were discussed, Mr. Klein said that he authored the messages but that Annie had "started it" after discovering their mutual love of horses. He said that he per-

[5] The names of minor victims or alleged victims should never be included in an actual report; however, de-identified names are included here for ease of reading.

formed oral sex on her on one occasion because she "begged" him to and did not digitally penetrate or attempt vaginal intercourse with her because he would "never do that." He said that although he authored messages about wanting to marry her, this was all a "fantasy" that he would never actually engage in. He said that he was not sexually interested in her and was not aroused during the sex act.

Officially Reported Information for Offense 3 According to records, when Mr. Klein was serving his third year of his prison sentence for Case 2, a woman in another state contacted the police to report that a man was engaging in "vulgar" conversations with her 11-year-old daughter through the Instagram Direct Message function. She reported that the man told her daughter that they went to school together, but she suspected that it was an adult contacting her daughter. After an investigation, the police determined that the messages were being sent from Mr. Klein and prison officials in the state in which he was incarcerated were contacted. It was determined that Mr. Klein was accessing the Internet from a contraband cellphone from within the prison and was engaging in sexually explicit conversations about "licking pussy" with an 11-year-old girl. A search of Mr. Klein's cell/housing unit uncovered the cellphone and Mr. Klein had also been contacting victims from Cases 1 and 2, asking them for pictures of themselves and expressing his sorrow for what he had done to them. A review of the discovery documents indicated that Mr. Klein had messaged the 11-year-old girl 37 times and engaged in both sexually explicit and non-sexual conversations. Mr. Klein obtained an attorney and accepted a plea deal in which he pled guilty to Criminal Solicitation of a Minor in the Second Degree and was sentenced to five years in prison to be served concurrently with his current sentence.

Examinee's Report of Offense 3 During the current evaluation, Mr. Klein denied committing this offense. He said that the cellphone belonged to his cellmate, who was also serving time for a sexual offense against a minor, and that he pled guilty because his attorney said that he would lose the case if he took it to trial and would be sentenced to "serious time." He further said that he did not contact the victims in his two previous cases, but rather, it was his cellmate who was posing as him. Attempts to discuss the messages in detail with Mr. Klein were met with guardedness and Mr. Klein indicated he did not wish to answer any more questions about the incident.

Clinical Forensic Opinion

Mental Health Diagnosis There are multiple etiologies for inappropriate sexual behavior, to include sexually-abusive behavior. Mr. Klein met criteria for a diagnosis of pedophilic disorder, exclusive type, sexually attracted to female children, which is a type of paraphilic disorder.

Sexual Recidivism Risk Mr. Klein's Static-99R score was 5, which placed him in the Above Average Risk category for being charged or convicted of another sexual offence. Actuarial instruments only indicate the likelihood that a person belongs in a particular group. The results do not identify the risk for that specific person. The presence of "deviant" (unhealthy; abusive) sexual arousal correlates with sexual reoffending.

Identifying sexual arousal is done by self-report, documented behaviors, and physiological examinations such as penile plethysmography (PPG). In terms of self-report, Mr. Klein pled guilty to the sex offenses involving minor female children but denied that he was sexually aroused by them. Regarding officially reported behaviors, data suggest that Mr. Klein sought-out prepubescent children, groomed them, and digitally penetrated and performed oral sex on two of the victims. Physiological assessment of sexual arousal during the evaluation indicated that Mr. Klein was sexually aroused to sexual scenarios involving prepubescent girls and demonstrated a preference for prepubescent girls over consenting adults.

Mr. Klein did not have realistic plans to avoid acts of sexual re-offending. Mr. Klein said that a future prison sentence would be a deterrent for him against committing a new sexual offense. However, prior to his current prison sentence, Mr. Klein served a separate prison sentence for a sexual offense and committed another sexual offense during his current incarceration and those prison sentences were not a deterrent at those times. He estimated that his level of risk was nonexistent at the time of the assessment, which was unrealistic given that no one is at a zero risk for committing an offense. Additionally, Mr. Klein continued to contact his victims from prison and sought out a new victim while incarcerated, suggesting an active sexual interest in children and an inability to control himself. Mr. Klein minimized his sexual interest, sexual behaviors, and sexual thoughts and fantasies during the evaluation. Sexual suppression and avoidance are not realistic to prevent sexually re-offending. He also demonstrated poor insight into his need for treatment for pedophilic disorder and for his risk of future offending.

"Sexually Violent Predator" Criteria Based upon state statue, it was the opinion of the evaluator that Mr. Klein was a "sexual predator." He had been convicted of a sexually violent offense based on the statutory definition, and he had a "mental abnormality" or "personality disorder" that put him at risk of engaging in sexual violence if not confined.

Recommendations

Based on published scientific data, (although debated) there is the potential for medication and psychotherapy combination resulting in remission or even a cure for paraphilic disorders, though there are no current universally accepted cures for pedophilic disorder. However, like other chronic medical illnesses, this disorder can be successfully managed with professional intervention provided the client is willing to participate in the treatment process. Treatment for pedophilic disorder has been successful for some who have actively participated and responded to educational attempts, psychotherapy, and in some cases, pharmacological interventions with a holistic approach to managing the illness.

Records reviewed indicated Mr. Klein had not received treatment specific to his pedophilic disorder. In light of this, it was recommended that treatment be provided by a licensed mental health professional with specific training and experience in managing the type of difficulties Mr. Klein has exhibited. Management would likely be a lifelong commitment given the current lack of a definitive and universally accepted cure but living in the community could become an option with treatment. Given that he had engaged in sexual offending behaviors consistent with his diagnosis of pedophilic disorder that if acted on again would result in the abuse of another person, it was recommended that his treatment be conducted in a secure setting for public and his own safety.

How Did Social Media Impact This Case?

Social media was a large part of this case as Mr. Klein found two of his three victims via social media. Thousands of pages of screenshots of the communications that Mr. Klein had with the victims were provided for review and detailed Mr. Klein's offense behaviors and supported the diagnosis of pedophilic disorder as he expressed his love and sexual attraction for the children. These data were important as many cases only include victim statements and these messages detailed how Mr. Klein was grooming his victims and provided support for the diagnosis and ultimate opinion.

Case Study 2

Type of Evaluation

The following evaluation was a Sexual Behaviors Consultation Evaluation requested by a defense attorney who was representing a client who was charged with Criminal Solicitation of a Minor, Dissemination of Obscene Material to a Person under 18, and Attempted Sexual Exploitation of a Minor. The specific request was to determine if the client was "a pedophile [*sic*]," at "risk to children," and treatment needs, if any.

Case Context

The examinee in this case, 28-year-old Byron Hoffman, was evaluated on one occasion for approximately 7.5 hours in response to a request from his defense attorney. It was alleged that he had contacted a 15-year-old female teenager, sent pictures of his genitals, and requested that she send him nude pictures of herself. The examinee was on bond and transported himself to the evaluation.

Sources of Information

For brevity, the sources of information are not listed but included the police and court discovery documents for each case, the examinee's criminal history report, screenshots from cellphones, copies of direct messages from Facebook and Instagram, copies of the examinee's Facebook page, detention center and community mental health records, clinical interview of examinee, and assessment measures administered for the current evaluation.

Confidentiality

Mr. Hoffman was advised that he was being evaluated at the request of his attorney. Additionally, he was advised that information provided and obtained during his evaluation would not be confidential and that information provided to his attorney would no longer be under the control of the laboratory. Mr. Hoffman. signed a consent from indicating his understanding and approval of the purpose of the evaluation, his participation in the evaluation, and the limits of confidentiality.

Relevant Background

Mr. Hoffman was raised by his biological mother. He said he met his biological father, but they did not have much contact during his youth. He reported seven siblings on his father's side but was raised as an only child by his mother. Mr. Hoffman said he was never the victim of physical, sexual, or emotional abuse, nor did he witness domestic violence in the home. Regarding academic functioning, he did not report any history of placement in special education classes, suspensions, or expulsions. Following his high school graduation, Mr. Hoffman attended college and obtained a Bachelor of Science degree in Engineering. He obtained employment at an engineering firm, where he remained for six years. Mr. Hoffman did not report any significant health issues. He experienced a loss of consciousness several times in high school secondary to playing sports and sustained two concussions. Mr. Hoffman's first contact with a mental health professional occurred during his recent detention, at which point he said he was very depressed and was prescribed antidepressant medication. After being released on bond, he sought services from the local community mental center. Regarding substance use, Mr. Hoffman endorsed previous use of alcohol, cannabis, and cocaine, and he did not report any problems or negative consequences associated with his use of substances.

Mr. Hoffman has never been married and has no children. He reported being in two committed relationships and frequently dates when he is not in a relationship. Regarding his sexual history, Mr. Hoffman began puberty at the age of 12, and he began masturbating at the age of 13. He started having sexual fantasies sometime around the age of 12 or 13. He said his fantasies consisted of "things I wanted to do; like oral sex." Mr. Hoffman was first sexually active with a consenting partner when he was 15 years old. He reported approximately 15 consensual partners in total, all of whom have been women, and he identified as heterosexual. When asked about current sexual fantasies or thoughts at the time of the evaluation, Mr. Hoffman said, "Usually I think about previous sexual experiences I've had; the really exciting ones," and he stated he masturbates "about weekly" and experiences an orgasm every time he masturbates. Regarding his legal history, Mr. Hoffman was arrested once at the age of 14 for shoplifting. He was placed on juvenile probation, which he successfully completed. The current charge represents his first contact with the legal system as an adult.

Behavioral Observations and Mental Status

Mr. Hoffman was dressed appropriately for the weather and evaluation situation. There were no problems observed in his hygiene or grooming. His eye contact ranged from appropriate to evasive. In discussing his sexual offense history, he appeared to be extremely embarrassed and was tearful at times. His speech was of normal rate and volume. There was no indication that he was responding to internal stimuli or expressing delusional beliefs. His thoughts appeared to be logical and linear. Mr. Hoffman appeared to be cooperative with the evaluation process. He described his current mood as "depressed." He was oriented to person, place, time, and situation, and his attention and concentration were within normal limits. He demonstrated adequate judgment when presented with a hypothetical situation, and his abstract reasoning abilities appeared intact.

Summary of Test Results

Mr. Hoffman was administered the Minnesota Multiphasic Personality Inventory-2-Restructured Form (MMPI-2-RF). He did not omit any items, and there was no evidence of inconsistent responding or over-reporting of symptoms or problems.

There was possible under-reporting as indicated by Mr. Hoffman presenting himself as being well-adjusted. The absence of scale elevations should be interpreted with caution, given the evidence of minimization. Mr. Hoffman's MMPI-2-RF results were completely unremarkable. He did not report experiencing any problems or symptoms.

Mr. Hoffman was also administered the PPG using the Marshall and RCV sets (described in the previous case study of this chapter). His results for the Marshall set did not met the minimum requirements for interpretation, so no further analysis was conducted. There are multiple potential reasons for such an examination result to include: anxiety, effects of medications, effects of use of substances, erectile dysfunction due to a general medical diagnosis, lack of stimuli that is arousing for the examinee, purposeful manipulation, and being one of a low percentage of men who do not sexually respond during a PPG examination. During the follow-up interview, Mr. Hoffman reported being somewhat nervous during the PPG examination. He said that he did not notice sexual side effects from Prozac, had not used any substances, had never experienced erectile dysfunction, and was not trying to purposefully manipulate the results. A review of the respiratory and movement data did not suggest he was attempting to manipulate the results.

In contrast, the RCV set met the minimum requirements for interpretation, including arousal indicated by at least one trial of at least a five-millimeter (mm) increase. The confidence level was medium for the RCV set based on at least one trial with at least a five-mm increase but none at or greater than 10-mm increase. For the RCV set, the individual trial results indicated clinically significant arousal to two trials depicting a consenting adult woman and one featuring persuasion of a female adolescent/teenager. For the RCV set, the calculated female prepubescent (pedophilic), calculated female prepubescent (pedophilic) rape, male prepubescent (pedophilic), male prepubescent (pedophilic) rape, female pubescent, female pubescent rape, male pubescent, male pubescent rape, female adult rape, and rape of an adult man indices did not indicate the presence of "deviant" (abusive) sexual arousal for Mr. Hoffman. The calculated indices suggested a preference for appropriate consensual sexual behavior over any of the "deviant" stimuli.

Using record information and data collected during this evaluation, Mr. Hoffman's Static-99R score was three (3), which placed him in the Average Risk category for being charged or convicted of another sexual offense. This score was based on the following data: relative young age at release and having an unrelated and stranger alleged victim. On average, offenders with a Static-99R score of 3 have a sexual recidivism rate that is 1.39 times the rate (the same rate) of offenders in the middle of the risk range (defined as a median score of 2). These values are based on routine, defined as relatively unselected, correctional samples.

Diagnostic Conclusions

As the consult question was related to Mr. Hoffman's potential for dangerousness to children and if he is a "pedophile [*sic*]," a diagnosis of pedophilic disorder was considered and ultimately ruled-out. Mr. Hoffman did not report being sexually aroused by prepubescent children and there were no objective data to suggest the contrary. Specifically, Mr. Hoffman had not been accused of offending against a prepubescent child, the physiological data did not detect the presence of sexual arousal to prepubescent children, and there were no data that suggested he was sexually aroused or interested in prepubescent children. Regarding an arousal to pubescent (adolescent/teenage) children, Mr. Hoffman's PPG data indicated that he had sexual arousal to a scenario featuring a female adolescent/teenager and he was accused of offenses against a teenaged girl. Sexual arousal to teenagers is not a mental illness, although acting on the arousal may be illegal, depending on the age of the teenager and the state in which it occurs. Mr. Hoffman denied being sexually interested in teenagers.

Summary of Data Relevant to Psycho-Legal Question

Officially Reported Information According to records, the complainant, who was the mother of Holly Sullivan, a 15-year-old female teenager, contacted the police to report that a man had been contacting her daughter via Facebook. The mother had been monitoring her daughter's social media accounts and came across messages of a sexual nature from an adult man, Mr. Hoffman. A review of the messages indicated that Mr. Hoffman had contacted Holly approximately a month before the offense was reported and told her that she was "really beautiful." They chatted via the Facebook Direct Messenger Application over the course of the month and discussed the local sports team and their shared love for the beach and tequila. Mr. Hoffman repeatedly attempted to arrange in-person meetings with Holly but she listed reasons for why she was unable to meet at those times. Many of the messages had sexual content and Mr. Hoffman would initiate this talk. He sent one picture of his penis, and he asked the victim to send him nude pictures on multiple occasions. The victim statement indicated that Holly reported being "flattered" by Mr. Hoffman's initial message and liked the attention he was giving her. When the conversations turned sexual, she became "nervous" and was afraid that if she met him in person he would "rape" her. She did not tell her parents about this due to concerns about getting herself in trouble. A review of the victim's Facebook page revealed that Holly mostly posted pictures of "selfies" of being around town or reposted inspirational quotes. She did not make posts containing text describing her day or anything going on with her and the only text posts that she made were about the local sports team. The "about" section on her Facebook page indicated her city of residence but no information about her school or anything else.

Examinee's Report of Case Mr. Hoffman reported that he came across Holly's profile after she commented on one of his college friend's photos. He said that he clicked on her profile and thought she was "really beautiful." He said that he could not resist messaging her and telling her this and that she responded immediately, and they began messaging each other on a very frequent basis for about a month.

He said that this started off "slow" as they were "getting to know each other." He said that she seemed "really interested" in him so he invited her to a baseball game, but she said she could not go. Mr. Hoffman said that he was "very excited" about Holly because she seemed like "just my type" and that he had been single for nearly a year and was excited about meeting someone new. Mr. Hoffman said that he initiated the sexual conversations and told her "things I would love to do to her" and she seemed receptive to this. He said that he sent her a photo of his penis. When asked the reason for doing so, he said, "This is so embarrassing; I don't know… to show her what she was working with." He also said that he asked Holly to reciprocate by sending him nude photos of herself, specifically "topless shots," but she did not. Mr. Hoffman said that he first learned of Holly's age when he was arrested and was "shocked." When this was questioned, he stated that, since she was friends with his friend from college, he thought she was at "least 20."

Clinical Forensic Opinion

Mental Health Diagnosis It was the opinion of the evaluator that Mr. Hoffman did not meet diagnostic criteria for a mental illness. There were no objective data suggesting that he was sexually attracted to prepubescent children; thus, he did not meet diagnostic criteria for pedophilic disorder. Although he had some depressive symptoms, these appeared to be in proportion to his current stressors. Thus, he did not meet diagnostic criteria for a mood disorder.

Sexual Recidivism Risk Mr. Hoffman's Static-99R score was 3, which placed him in the Average Risk category for being charged or convicted of another sexual offence. Additionally, the Static-99R score may have been an overestimate for Mr. Hoffman. Specifically, he was never previously charged with an offense, sexual or otherwise; had stable employment; had appropriate relationships with others; did not abuse substances; and engaged in prosocial behaviors.

The presence of "deviant" (unhealthy; abusive) sexual arousal correlates with sexual reoffending. Identifying sexual arousal is done by self-report, documented behaviors, and physiological examinations such as penile plethysmography (PPG). None of these are definitive, but the more data points indicating the same result, the stronger the support for an opinion. In terms of self-report, Mr. Hoffman reported that he was not aware that the victim was 15 years old and that he thought she was "at least 20 [years old]." There were no objective data indicating that he was aware of her age. Regardless, sexual arousal to teenage girls is not "deviant"; although acting on this arousal may be illegal. Additionally, physiological data indicated a preference for adult consenting scenarios over the "deviant" stimuli.

Opinions Regarding the Consultation Questions It was the opinion of the evaluator that Mr. Hoffman did not have pedophilic disorder. Additionally, there were no objective data to support that he was "at risk to children." He did not meet diagnostic criteria for a mental illness, so no specific treatment recommendations were provided. He was in therapy at the time of the evaluation and was prescribed antidepressant medication for his low mood related to the stress of his case and he appeared to be benefiting from treatment. Thus, it was recommended that Mr. Hoffman continue to receive this treatment.

Recommendations

No specific recommendations were offered as part of this evaluation.

How Did Social Media Impact This Case?

In Mr. Hoffman's case, social media helped corroborate his report of the offense. Specifically, review of the victim's Facebook page and their messages to each other indicated that there was no mention of the victim's age. If her page described where she went to school or had other posts that suggested she was underage, this would be important information. The absence of this information corroborated Mr. Hoffman's report. However, it was unknown if he truly did not know she was underage. Regardless, as described in this case study, having sexual attraction to teenagers is not a mental illness.

References

Abboud, L., Kuchler, H., & Srivastava, M. (2018, December 20). WhatsApp fails to curb sharing of child sex abuse videos. *Financial Times*. Retrieved from https://www.ft.com.

Abel, G. G., Huffman, J., Warber, B., & Holland, C. L. (1998). Visual reaction time and plethysmography as measures of sexual interest in child molesters. *Sexual Abuse: A Journal of Research and Treatment, 10*, 81–95.

Abel, G. G., Jordan, A., Hand, C. G., Holland, L. A., & Phipps, A. (2001). Classification models of child molesters utilizing the Abel Assessment for sexual interest. *Child Abuse & Neglect, 25*(5), 703–718.

Adams, W. & Flynn, A. (2017). Federal Prosecution of commercial sexual exploitation of children cases, 2004–2013. NCJ 250746, U.S. Department of Justice, Office of Justice Programs, Bureau of Justice Statistics.

American Psychiatric Association. (2013). *Diagnostic and statistical manual of mental disorders, 5th Edition: DSM-5*. Washington, DC: Author.

Association for the Treatment of Sexual Abusers. (2014). *Practice guidelines. for the assessment, treatment, and management of male adult sexual abusers*. Beaverton: Author.

Boccaccini, M. T., Murrie, D. C., Caperton, J. D., & Hawes, S. W. (2009). Field validity of the Static-99 and MnSost-R among sex offenders evaluated for civil commitment as sexually violent predators. *Psychology, Public Policy, and Law, 15*(4), 278–314.

Boccaccini, M. T., Rice, A. K., Helmus, L. M., Murrie, D. C., & Harris, P. B. (2017). Field validity of Static-99/R scores in a statewide sample of 34,687 convicted sex offenders. *Psychological Assessment, 29*(6), 611–623.

Boer, D. P., Hart, S. D., Kropp, P. R., & Webster, C. D. (1997). *Manual for the sexual violence risk-20. Professional guidelines for assessing risk of sexual violence*. Vancouver: Institute Against Family Violence.

Boer, D. P., Hart, S. D., Kropp, P. R., & Webster, C. D. (2018). *Manual for the sexual violence Risk-20, Version 2. Professional guidelines for assessing risk of sexual violence*. Vancouver: Institute Against Family Violence.

Buttars, A., Huss, M. T., & Brack, C. (2015). Sex offender risk assessment: A reexamination of the coffee can study. *International Journal of Law and Psychiatry, 42–43*, 31–36.

Chevalier, C. S., Boccaccini, M. T., Murrie, D. C., & Varela, J. G. (2015). Static-99R reporting practices in sexually violent predator cases: Does norm selection reflect adversarial allegiance? *Law and Human Behavior, 39*, 209–218.

Chivers, M. L., Seto, M. C., Lalumiere, M. L., Laan, E., & Grimbos, T. (2010). Agreement of self-reported and genial measures of sexual arousal in men and women: A meta-analysis. *Archives of Sexual Behavior, 39*, 5–56.

de Vogel, V., de Ruiter, C., van Beek, D., & Mead, G. (2004). Predictive validity of the SVR-20 and Static-99 in a Dutch sample of treated sex offenders. *Law and Human Behavior, 28*(3), 235–251.

DeHart, D., Dwyer, R. G., Seto, M. C., Moran, R., Letourneau, E., & Schwarz-Watts, D. (2017). Internet sexual solicitation of children: A proposed typology of offenders based on their chats, e-mails, and social network posts. *Journal of Sexual Aggression, 23*(1), 77–89.

Epperson, D. L., Kaul, J. D., Huot, S. J., Hesselton, D., Alexander, W., & Goldman, R. (1998). *Minnesota sex offender screening tool-revised (MnSost-R)*. St. Paul: Minnesota Department of Corrections.

Fabian, J. M. (2005). The risky business of conducting risk assessments for those already civilly committed as sexually violent predators. *William Mitchell Law Review, 32*, 81–159.

Fedoroff, J. P., Kuban, M., & Bradford, J. M. (2009). Laboratory measurement of penile response in the assessment of sexual interests. In F. M. Saleh, A. J. Grudzinskas, J. M. Bradford, & D. J. Brodsky (Eds.), *Sex offenders: Identification, risk assessment, treatment and legal issues* (pp. 89–100). New York: Oxford University Press.

Finkelhor, D. (2009). The prevention of childhood sexual abuse. *Future of Children, 19*(2), 169–194.

Fischer, L., & Smith, G. (1999). Statistical adequacy of the Abel assessment of interest in paraphilias. *Sexual Abuse: A Journal of Research and Treatment, 11*, 195–205.

Freeman-Longo, R. E., & Wall, R. V. (1986). Changing a lifetime of sexual crime: Can sex offenders ever alter their ways? Special treatment programs provide some hope. *Psychology Today, 20*(3), 58–65.

Gaither, G. A., & Plaud, J. J. (1997). The effects of secondary stimulus characteristics on men's sexual arousal. *The Journal of Sex Research, 34*(3), 231–236.

Goldschlag, D., Reed, M., & Syverson, P. (1999). Onion routing for anonymous and private internet connections. *Communications of the ACM, 42*(2), 39–41.

Gottfried, E.D., Vitacco, M.J., Rogers, R., & Gay, J.G. (In press). The assessment of psychopathy and response styles in sex offenders. In Saleh, F.M., Grudzinskas, A.J., Bradford, J.M., & Brodsky, D.J. (Eds.) *Sex offenders: Identification, risk assessment, treatment, and legal issues*. New York: Oxford University Press.

Hanson, R. K. (1998). What do we know about sex offender risk assessment? *Psychology, Public. Policy, and Law, 4*(1/2), 50–72.

Hanson, R. K., & Bussière, M. T. (1998). Predicting relapse: A meta-analysis of sexual offender recidivism studies. *Journal of Consulting and Clinical Psychology, 66*(2), 348–362.

Hanson, R. K., & Morton-Bourgon, K. E. (2005). The characteristics of persistent sexual offenders: A meta-analysis of recidivism studies. *Journal of Consulting and Clinical Psychology, 73*(6), 1154–1163.

Hanson, R. K., & Morton-Bourgon, K. E. (2009). The accuracy of recidivism risk assessments for sexual offenders: A meta-analysis of 118 prediction studies. *Psychological Assessment, 21*(1), 1–21.

Iacono, W. G. (2008). Effective policing: Understanding how polygraph tests work and are used. *Criminal Justice and Behavior, 35*(10), 1295–1308.

Iacono, W.G., & Ben-Shakhar, G. (2018; OnlineFirst Edition). Current status of forensic lie detection with the comparison questions technique: An update of the 2003 National Academy of Sciences report on polygraph testing. *Law and Human Behavior.*

Jackson, R. L., & Hess, D. T. (2007). Evaluation for civil commitment of sex offenders: A survey of experts. *Sexual Abuse, 19*, 425–448.

Janus, E. S. (1997). The use of social science and medicine in sex offender commitment. *Criminal and Civil Confinement, 23*, 347–386.

Lapin, T. (2019, July 14). Florida man who raped baby daughter, posted footage to web gets 70 years. *New York post.* Retrieved from https://nypost.com/2019/07/14/florida-man-who-raped-baby-daughter-posted-footage-to-web-gets-70-years/.

Lave, T. R., & Zimring, F. (2018). Assessing the real risk of sexually violent predators: Doctor Padilla's dangerous data. *American Criminal Law Review, 55*, 705–787.

Laws, D. R., Hanson, K., Osborn, C. A., & Greenbaum, P. E. (2000). Classification of child molesters by plethysmographic assessment of sexual arousal and a self-report measure of sexual preference. *Journal of Interpersonal Violence, 15*, 1297–1312.

Letourneau, E. (2002). A comparison of objective measures of sexual arousal and interest: Visual reaction time and penile plethysmography. *Sexual Abuse: A Journal of Research and Treatment, 14*(3), 207–223.

Levenson, J. S. (2004). Reliability of sexually violent predator civil commitment criteria in Florida. *Law and Human Behavior, 28*(4), 357–368.

Levenson, J. S., & Morin, J. W. (2006). Factors predicting selection of sexually violent Predators for civil commitment. *International Journal of Offender Therapy and Comparative Criminology, 50*(6), 609–629.

Mac, R. (2019, February 28). YouTube has disabled comments on almost all videos featuring children. *BuzzFeed News*. Retrieved from https://www.buzzfeednews.com.

Mann, R. E., Hanson, R. K., & Thornton, D. (2010). Assessing risk for sexual recidivism: Some proposals on the nature of psychologically meaningful risk factors. *Sexual Abuse: A Journal for Research and Treatment, 22*(2), 191–217.

Marshall, W. L. (2014). Phallometric assessments of sexual interests: An update. *Curr Psychiatry Rep, 16*, 428.

Marshall, W. L., & Fernandez, Y. M. (2001). Phallometry in forensic practice. *Journal of Forensic Psychology Practice, 1*(2), 77–87.

Matzutt, R., Hiller, J., Henze, M., Ziegeldorf, J.H., Mullmann, D., Hohlfeld, O., & Wehrle, K. (2018). *A quantitative analysis of the impact of arbitrary blockchain content on bitcoin.* Abstract for the 22nd International Conference on Financial Cryptography and Data Security.

McKune v. Lile, (2002). 536 US 24-Supreme Court.

McPhail, I. V., Hermann, C. A., Fernane, S., Fernandez, Y. M., Nunes, K. L., & Cantor, J. M. (2019). Validity in phallometric testing for sexual interests in children: A meta-analytic review. *Assessment, 26*(3), 535–551.

Melton, G. B., Petrila, J., Poythress, N. G., Slobogin, C., Otto, R. K., Mossman, D., & Condie, L. O. (2018). *Psychological evaluations for the courts, Fourth Edition: A handbook for mental health professionals and lawyers*. New York: The Guilford Press.

Mitchell, K. J., Finkelhor, D., Jones, L. M., & Wolak, J. (2010). Use of social networking sites in online sex crimes against minors: An examination of national incidence and means of utilization. *Journal of Adolescent Health, 47*, 183–190.

Murphy, L., Ranger, R., Fedoroff, J. P., Dwyer, R. G., & Burke, W. (2015a). Standardization of penile plethysmography testing in assessment of problematic sexual interests. *Journal of Sexual Medicine, 12*, 1853–1861.

Murphy, L., Ranger, R., Stewart, H., Dwyer, R. G., & Fedoroff, J. P. (2015b). Assessment of problematic sexual interests with the penile plethysmograph: An overview of assessment laboratories. *Current Psychiatry Reports, 17*, 29.

Murrie, D. C., Boccaccini, M. T., Caperton, J., & Rufino, K. (2012). Field validity of the psychopathy checklist-revised in sex offender risk assessment. *Psychological Assessment, 24*(2), 524–529.

Neal, T. M. S., & Grisso, T. (2014). Assessment practices and expert judgement methods in forensic psychology and psychiatry: An international snapshot. *Criminal Justice and Behavior, 41*, 1406–1421.

Nichols, H.R. & Molinder, I. 2005. *Multiphasic sex inventory II: Adult male form*, Nichols & Molinder Assessments, Inc.

O'Shaughnessy, R. (2015). Commentary: Phallometry in court—Problems outweigh benefits. *Journal of the American Academy of Psychiatry and the Law Online, 43*(2), 154–158.

Olver, M. E., Mundt, J. C., Thornton, D., Begss Christofferson, S. M., Kingston, D. A., Sowden, J. N., Nicholaichuk, T. P., & Gordon, A. (2018). Using the violence risk scale-sexual offense version in sexual violence risk assessments: Updated risk categories and recidivism estimates from a multisite sample of treated sexual offenders. *Psychological Assessment, 30*(7), 941–955.

Packingham v. North Carolina, 528 US _ (2017).

Phenix, A., Fernandez, Y., Harris, A.J.R., Helmus, M., Hanson, R.K., & Thornton, D. (2016). *Static-99R coding rules revised.*

Plaud, J. J. (2019). The use of penile plethysmography in SVP assessment and treatment decision-making. In W. T. O'Donohue & D. S. Bromberg (Eds.), *Sexually violent predators: A clinical science handbook* (pp. 243–254). Cham: Springer.

Porter, S., ten Brinke, L., & Wilson, K. (2009). Crime profiles and conditional release performance of psychopathic and non-psychopathic sexual offenders. *Legal and Criminological Psychology, 14*, 109–118.

Prentky, R. A., Janus, E., Barbaree, H., Schwartz, B. K., & Kafka, M. P. (2006). Sexually violent predators in the courtroom: Science on trial. *Psychology, Public Policy and Law, 12*(4), 357–393.

Quinesy, V. L., Harris, G. T., Rice, M. E., & Cormier, C. A. (2006). *Violent offenders* (second ed.). Washington, DC, American Psychological Association Press.

Reeves, S. G., Ogloff, J. R. P., & Simmons, M. (2018). The predictive validity of the Static-99, Static-99R, and Static-2002/R: Which one to use? *Sexual Abuse: A Journal of Research and Treatment, 30*(8), 887–907.

Rettenberger, M., Boer, D. P., & Eher, R. (2011). The predictive accuracy of risk factors in the Sexual Violence Risk-20 (SVR-20). *Criminal Justice and Behavior, 38*(10), 1009–1027.

Rettenberger, M., Rice, M. E., Harris, G. T., & Eher, R. (2017). Actuarial risk assessment of sexual offenders: The psychometric properties of the Sex Offender Risk Appraisal Guide (SORAG). *Psychological Assessment, 29*(6), 624–638.

Rice, A. K., Boccaccini, M. T., Harris, P. B., & Hawes, S. W. (2014). Does field reliability for Static-99 scores decrease as scores increase? *Psychological Assessment, 26*(4), 1085–1094.

Schmidt, A. F., Babchishin, K. M., & Lehmann, R. J. B. (2017). A meta-analysis of viewing time measures of sexual interest in children. *Archives of Sexual Behavior, 46*(1), 287–300.

Scurich, N. & John, R.S. (2019). The dark figure of sexual recidivism. *University of California at Irvine School of Law Legal Studies Research Paper Series Number 2019–09*, 1–32.

Seto, M.C. (2018). *Pedophilia and Sexual Offending Against Children: Theory, Assessment, and Intervention, Second Edition.* Washington, DC: American Psychological Association Press.

Solla, P., Bortolato, M., Cannas, A., Mulas, C. S., & Marrosu, F. (2015). Paraphilias and paraphilic disorders in Parkinson's disease: A systematic review of the literature. *Mov Disord., 30*(5), 604–613.

Tong, D. (2007). The penile plethysmograph, Abel Assessment for Sexual Interest, and MSI-II: Are they speaking the same language? *The American Journal of Family Therapy, 35*(3), 187–202.

Witt, P. H., & Conroy, M. A. (2009). *Best practices in forensic mental health assessment: Evaluation of sexually violent predators*. New York: Oxford University Press.

Wong, S., Olver, M. E., Nicholaichuk, T. P., & Gordon, A. (2003). *The violence risk scale-sexual offender version (VRS-SO)*. Saskatoon: Regional Psychiatric Centre and University of Saskatchewan.

Woodworth, M., Freimuth, T., Hutton, E. L., Carpenter, T., Agar, A. D., & Logan, M. (2013). High-risk sexual offenders: An examination of sexual fantasy, sexual paraphilia, psychopathy, and offence characteristics. *International Journal of Law and Psychiatry, 36*, 144–156.

Chapter 6
Child Custody Litigation and Parental Fitness

Sean B. Knuth

Psychologists are often called upon to offer expert opinions in matters of child custody. The purpose of this chapter is to address how data from social networking sites (SNS) can assist in conducting psychological evaluations ordered as part of child custody litigation. Though evaluators are at times retained to conduct evaluations *ex parte*, this chapter will focus on their function when an evaluator is appointed as a court's expert witness, and when the evaluation is crafted for the purpose of offering professional opinions to assist the Court in making decisions related to child custody proceedings.

First, a brief overview of evaluations commonly ordered within the context of child custody litigation will be provided. Second, a discussion regarding the scope of such evaluations will be presented. Finally, suggested approaches for both collecting SNS data and how it might be considered and interpreted are offered.

There are several professional documents that should guide evaluations conducted within the context of child custody litigation. The Specialty Guidelines for Forensic Psychology (American Psychological Association 2013) and the Guidelines for Child Custody Evaluations in Family Law Proceedings (American Psychological Association 2010), both published by the American Psychological Association, should be heavily relied upon by psychologists conducting such evaluations. Also of substantial importance within this field are the Model Standards of Practice for Child Custody Evaluation (Martindale et al. 2006), published by the Association of Family and Conciliation Courts, hereafter AFCC Model Standards; and the Child Custody Evaluation Standards (American Academy of Matrimonial Lawyers 2011),[1] published by the Academy of Matrimonial Lawyers. Throughout this

[1] The AAML's Child Custody Evaluation Standards "utilize and rely upon major portions of [the AFCC's] Model Standards of Practice for Child Custody Evaluations" (pg. 8). This chapter will primarily refer to the AFCC document when providing references for best practices.

S. B. Knuth (✉)
Private Practice, Charlotte, NC, USA
e-mail: sbknuth@sbkphd.com

A. B. Batastini, M. J. Vitacco (eds.), *Forensic Mental Health Evaluations in the Digital Age*, https://doi.org/10.1007/978-3-030-33908-1_6

chapter, reference will be made to these documents, as they currently set the standard of practice of evaluations conducted within the context of child custody litigation.

6.1 Evaluations Ordered as Part of Child Custody

There are several theoretical frameworks that courts employ or have employed to guide decision-making within child custody litigation. A current prevailing framework in most child custody litigation is based upon the Best Interests of the Child (BIC) standard; that is, the decisions made by the court in child custody litigation are primarily guided by a desire to serve the best interest of the minor children (for review, see Stahl 2013; Weiner and Otto 2013; Gould and Martindale 2009). Even with this standard in mind, the scope of evaluations ordered within child custody litigation can vary markedly from case to case and order to order.

The widest-ranging, most complex evaluation typically ordered within a child custody litigation context requires an evaluation of each party, as well as all of the minor children, and is crafted to permit the evaluator to offer reliable, probative opinions on a wide range of issues, up to and sometimes including the ultimate issue; that of child custody schedule recommendations (i.e., whom the children live with and when). These evaluations are most commonly referred to as a child custody evaluation (CCE),[2] though some courts refer to them by other names (e.g., parental responsibilities evaluations, social studies).[3] These evaluations are sometimes limited or defined differently in various jurisdictions and by various professional organizations, but in its most broadly defined form, a CCE is an evaluation to investigate and help determine the needs of one or more named minor children, to describe the parenting strengths and weaknesses of two (or more) potential parenting figures as they relate to the named minor children, to identify specific areas of concern related to the well-being of the named minor child(ren), and to provide the ordering court with professional opinions on the goodness of fit between each parent and each minor child.

CCEs are some of the most time-consuming and complex evaluations conducted by psychologists. For each party evaluated, the psychologist conducts multiple lengthy interviews covering a wide array of topics, administers appropriate psychological testing, reviews records, and interviews third parties Additionally, best

---

[2] Of note, both courts hearing child custody matters and courts hearing Abuse/Neglect/Dependency matters order evaluations that they, and research, refer to as parental fitness evaluations or parenting capacity evaluation. Though both of these courts are seeking expert opinion on a parent's ability to parent specific children, the focus of these two evaluations can be substantively different (e.g., see Budd 2001).

[3] A brief survey of professionals on a listserv that discusses such evaluations returned the following names for CCEs, some designated by statue, some by tradition: Custody Evaluations, Parenting Plan Evaluations, Social Investigations, Parental Responsibilities Evaluations, Social Study Evaluations, Social Studies, Home Studies, Psychological Evaluations, Forensic Evaluations.

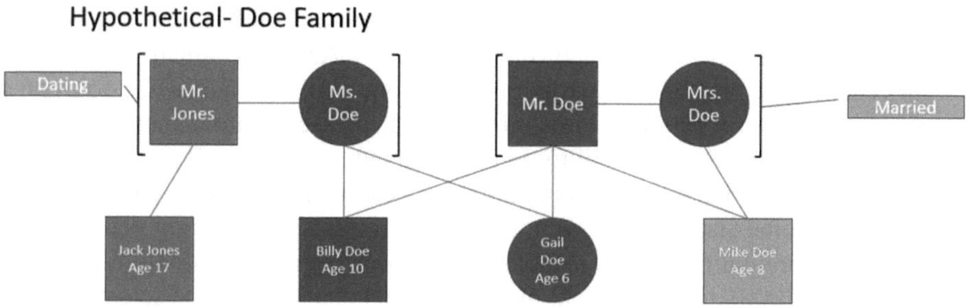

Fig. 6.1 Hypothetical- Doe Family

practices state that an evaluator must observe parenting interactions between each parent and all evaluated children (Association of Family and Conciliation Courts 2007).

To visualize the complexity of a child custody evaluation, consider the hypothetical Doe family. Mr. Doe and Ms. Doe have two children together, a ten-year-old boy named Billy and a six-year old-girl named Gail. They have divorced, and Mr. Doe has remarried. His current family unit thus also includes Mrs. Doe and her eight-year-old son (Mike) from a prior relationship, whom Mr. Doe has adopted. While Ms. Doe has not remarried, she is dating Mr. Jones, who has a seventeen-year-old son named Jack (Fig. 6.1).

If a full child custody evaluation were ordered in this hypothetical case, the evaluees would most likely be Billy Doe and Gail Doe, as well as Ms. Doe and Mr. Doe, as well as Mr. Doe's current wife. Mike Doe, Mrs. Doe's son, would not likely be named as an evaluee as Ms. Doe does not have any legal parenting responsibility of Mike Doe. Mr. Jones may or may not be named as an evaluee, as the extent to which Mr. Jones should be evaluated depends on his involvement with Ms. Doe and the evaluated minor children.

Another approach to conducting psychological evaluations that can be helpful to a court litigating a child custody matter is through a Brief Focused Assessment (BFA; for a review of BFA's see Association of Family and Conciliation Courts 2009). Within child custody litigation contexts, this term refers to a psychological evaluation that asks an evaluator to answer probative questions that require something less than an examination of an entire family system or a full child custody evaluation.

For example, sometimes evaluations are ordered that pertain only to a single parent and named minor children. Using the previous hypothetical family, a court might order an evaluation of Ms. Doe's parenting ability, as it pertains to Billy and Gail directly. Or, a court might desire an expert's opinion on Ms. Doe's parenting ability but wish to avoid exposing the minor children to additional psychological evaluation and so prohibit an evaluator from making direct contact with the children. While Mr. Doe is not an evaluee in either case, he would likely serve as an important collateral contact for the evaluator. In the latter case, the evaluator should advise the court that, because children have not been directly observed or evaluated, the evaluator is precluded from offering expert opinions on Ms. Doe's parenting ability as it might apply to Gail and Billy specifically. Another evaluation type commonly encountered in child custody litigation is one crafted to advise the court on a particular aspect of a parent's functioning (e.g., their use of intoxicants or pornography) might affect his or her ability to parent (again, in general, if the children are not evaluated), and what recommendations for treatment can be offered.

Although some states have begun to favor such terms as parenting plan, parenting time, or parental rights and responsibilities over the term 'custody' (American Law Institute 2000), the substantial majority of legal authorities and scientific publications still refer to custody when addressing the resolution of decision-making, caretaking, and access disputes. Within this chapter, any reference to an evaluation ordered or conducted within the context of child custody litigation will be referred to as a Child Custody Evaluation (CCE), though, as the preceding paragraphs suggest, some evaluations will be much narrower in scope than a traditional CCE.

The United States court system is based on the adversarial system; that is, two (or more) parties, or their advocates, represent their cases to an impartial party. This is true of child custody litigation as well. Most commonly, these parties represent their cases to a judge, though some jurisdictions allow for jury trials in child custody matters. From a forensic psychological evaluation standpoint, in the standard trial paradigm for criminal proceedings and even some civil proceedings, typically only one party is being evaluated. For example, if an evaluator is conducting a capacity to proceed evaluation, while they can be provided with records from both sides, these records will generally only be evaluated as they relate to a single party (i.e., the defendant). In a CCE, however, both parties can provide records and both parties are being evaluated. The records provided by Party A can be as informative in respects to Party A as they can in respects to Party B, regardless of Party A's intention in providing them. The implications of this arrangement will be discussed in depth further.

Generally speaking, most proceedings related to child custody feature only two parties to the litigation, each with a demonstrated interest and legal responsibility to parent one or more minor children. The typical paradigm is a biological mother and a biological father. Even if remarried, the step-parent does not represent a third party to the litigation, as they may not have any legal claim to parenting the minor child. Of note, however, is that step-parents, even if not legal guardians of the minor child(ren), still likely factor into an evaluation. The individuals a parent elects to bring around their children not only informs an assessment of a child's needs but also reflects on a parent's judgement; especially when the parent elects to formalize a relationship with the individual.

There can, however, be additional parties to the litigation. A commonly encountered additional party to child custody litigation is a court-appointed best-interest attorney or Guardian ad Litem. These individuals or teams of individuals are appointed to advocate for the best interest of the minor child or children, and are generally an excellent source of collateral information, including records. It is also possible, though not likely, that additional parenting figures might be party to litigation; usually grandparents or other individuals who hold some parenting responsibility for the minor child/children. The number of parties to a matter directly impacts the complexity of an evaluation conducted within the context of child custody litigation.

As one can see, evaluations conducted to advise triers of fact in child custody litigation can vary widely in scope, from tightly-focused inquiries into a single aspect of a parent's psychological functioning to a wide-ranging investigation into the general psychological functioning of members of more than one family unit. As described in the next section, the scope of these evaluations should be defined by the appointment order. It is the evaluator's responsibility to have a broad and deep enough understanding of child custody matters and basic principles of forensic psychological evaluation so that they can review a court order and determine if the scope of the evaluation, as proposed, is appropriate.

6.2 The Scope of Evaluations Ordered within a Child Custody Context

Whether the questions asked by a court necessitate a full-fledged child custody evaluation, a brief assessment of a parent's general cognitive functioning, or something in between, the scope of said evaluation is defined by the appointment order. An evaluation's scope, in turn, is defined through two sets of parameters: (1) the questions the evaluation is to answer by the court and (2) the data the evaluator is to consider.

For many applications of forensic psychology, the names of different types of psychological evaluations (e.g., fitness for duty, capacity to proceed, diminished capacity) are used as a shorthand for the specific referral question(s) needing to be addressed. An appropriately-qualified evaluator knows by these names what general questions the court wants answered. And a savvy evaluator will clarify and confirm these questions with the court before beginning his or her evaluation, if not before the appointment order itself is even crafted.

In the case of evaluations ordered through child custody litigation, however, the questions the court wants answered can vary substantially from situation to situation (see earlier discussion on BFA for example), and so it is especially important an evaluator clarifies with the court what questions their evaluation should attempt to answer. For this reason, best practice within the field is to have an appointment order specifically state the questions the evaluator is to answer. Table 6.1 provides several sample questions that might be asked as part of a full Child Custody Evaluation, an evaluation of only one party's parenting ability, and an evaluation specifically on an individual's substance use.

There are many complex issues associated with high-conflict child custody evaluations, including but not limited to substance use, relocation, parental alienation, and undisclosed or unknown special needs in children. A court might not be aware of the presence of these issues when an evaluation is ordered. For example, if an

Table 6.1 Sample questions for child custody evaluations and special cases

Sample questions for full child custody evaluation	Sample questions for evaluation of one party's fitness	Sample questions for evaluation of parental substance use
1. What are the strengths and weaknesses of each party as a custodian of the children?	1. Is Plaintiff suffering from any mental disorder or condition;	1. Describe Plaintiff's emotional and psychological health with a focus on Plaintiff's alcohol use.
2. What are the children's strengths, weaknesses, and needs?	2. How does the diagnosed condition or disorder manifest itself;	2. Allegations have been made that Plaintiff's alcohol use is problematic. Is Plaintiff's alcohol use problematic?
3. What are the mental and physical abilities of each part to provide custodial care for the children?	3. How does the condition or disorder affect Plaintiff generally;	3. If yes, what is the severity of her alcohol use?
4. If deficits are found in either party's parenting ability, ability to communicate or emotional stability, to what extent would each adult benefit from individual or group psychotherapy, parenting classes, family therapy or any other psychological or educational intervention?	4. How such mental health illness or condition may affect Plaintiff's ability to parent the minor children;	4. What psychological, social, and environmental factors, if any, impact how drinking alcohol affects Plaintiff's behavior?
5. What is the nature and quality of the relationship between the minor children and the Defendant?	5. Whether Plaintiff suffers from any physical illness or condition;	5. What are Plaintiff's risk factors, if any, for alcohol and/or substance use disorder(s)?
6. What is the nature and quality of the relationship between the minor children and the Plaintiff?	6. How such physical illness or condition may affect Plaintiff's ability to parent the minor children;	6. Does Plaintiff have an alcohol problem that requires treatment?
7. Have the children been alienated against either parent? What if any role has either party played in the alienation?	7. Plaintiff's level of cognitive/ psychological functioning; and	7. What treatment recommendations, if any, are recommended?
8. Has either party engaged in conduct which undermines the emotional stability of the minor children or the ability of the other party to parent the minor children? If the answer is yes, describe these behaviors and discuss the treatment prognosis as to each potential treatment option.	8. Whether any therapeutic intervention, treatment, or counseling is recommended for Plaintiff.	
9. What is the commitment of each adult to the minor children's emotional physical and educational needs?		

(continued)

Table 6.1 (continued)

Sample questions for full child custody evaluation	Sample questions for evaluation of one party's fitness	Sample questions for evaluation of parental substance use
10. Ho do each parent's beliefs and attitudes about the other parent and his or her lifestyle affect or influence the minor children?		
11. What custody and visitation recommendations are in the best psychological interests of the minor children?		
12. Has any physician previously diagnosed Mother or Father with a mental illness or deficiency, and if so is Mother and/ or Father receiving treatment for this diagnosis?		
13. Does either parent have a diagnosable DSM-V condition or disorder? If so:		
a. How does the diagnosed disorder manifest itself?		
b. What is the severity of the condition or disorder?		
c. How does the condition or disorder affect that parent generally?		
d. How does the condition or disorder affect that parent's ability to parent?		
e. hat is the recommended treatment and likelihood of success?		

evaluee gets engaged and then married during the course of an evaluation, an evaluator could reasonably desire to incorporate an evaluation of the new spouse into the custody evaluation. As such, an evaluator can potentially encounter problems if they are limited to only answering the questions outlined in the order. Such limitations might prevent them from offering full and useful professional opinions to the court. Permitting an evaluator to appropriately expand the scope of his or her evaluation to include data relevant to these or other special issues will likely result in a final product that is more useful for the individuals being evaluated and one that more clearly answers the court-ordered questions.

The restrictions or mandates on the data an evaluator is permitted to collect is thus the second factor defining the scope of a CCE. In an effort to produce the most useful evaluation, a good appointment order will have language in it similar to the following:

- The evaluator shall have access to the parties, the minor children and any other individuals for as many interviews, individual and in any combination, as the evaluator considers to be warranted. The evaluator shall utilize clinical interviews and whatever formal psychological tests he deems appropriate. Insofar as the evaluator considers it necessary to interview others, he shall have the privilege to do so, documenting information assembled in this regard.

- Each party shall authorize the release to the evaluator of all medical records and any other records the evaluator deems appropriate and necessary to complete his evaluation. Each party shall execute all releases necessary to obtain records, reports and the like, concerning that party or the child(ren), requested by the evaluator and being deemed necessary by the evaluator to perform his responsibilities as ordered herein, to include police records and the records of any child protective services agency.

This language compels cooperation by evaluees and empowers an evaluator to collect any data they may deem potentially relevant.

An appointment order can also sometimes specify data an evaluator is prohibited from considering/collecting. For example, sometimes evaluators are not permitted to contact a child's therapist. Such a limitation could conceivably be put into place to protect the therapeutic relationship between the minor children and their treatment providers. This limitation, however, would likely hamper an evaluator's ability to answer questions about the minor children, or even how parents are interacting with the therapists. If an evaluator is given an opportunity to consult on an appointment order they can inform the court early on if any limitations on data collection might impair an evaluator's ability to opine on questions to answer. If an evaluator is not permitted such an opportunity, they can attempt to address such concerns through conferences with counsel for each party. In other cases, an appointment order will require an evaluator to collect and consider specific data. This requirement most commonly takes the form of an appointment order designating one party as being responsible for providing an evaluator all pleadings and filings generated for the current case. As another example, the order may include a specific mandate that an evaluator be provided with hospital records for a medically fragile child.

The questions asked by a court, taken together with the data an evaluator is required to collect, permitted to collect, or prohibited from collecting, defines the scope of an evaluation.

6.3 Collecting SNS Data

Data collected as part of psychological evaluations generally come from one of four types of sources: direct interview, collateral interview, psychological testing, and review of records. Data from social networking sites (SNS) and the Internet in general are considered records, and best practices for record collection should be applied to data from SNS (see Chap. 9 for a discussion on recommendations specific to Internet-based data). The use of SNS data is becoming commonplace in CCEs. In fact, a survey of forensic evaluators (Coffey, Batastini, Vitacco, 2018) revealed that social media evidence was used most often in child custody evaluations compared to other common psycho-legal referrals (e.g., competency to process, criminal responsibility, disability, violence risk), with about 95% of respondents who conducted such evaluations having used SNS data at least once. In fact, a quick Google search will reveal numerous articles describing cases in which information posted online was used in child custody proceedings and blogs warning parents involved in custody or divorce disputes about the impact of their online activity on these decisions.

Records obtained during CCEs can be thought of as coming into an evaluator's possession in one of two ways: (1) they can be solicited by the evaluator directly or (2) they can be offered for consideration by an external source, either an evaluated party, by a collateral contact, or mandated to be provided by the appointment order. Evaluators should each establish their own processes for how they receive data. For example, each evaluator must decide whether documents can be submitted in paper format, electronically via USB drive or optical media, must be handed to the evaluator directly, can be dropped off with a secretary, or delivered to a post office box. Related to electronic documents in general, and SNS data in particular, it is recommended that evaluators consider the implications of obtaining records by visiting provided links (e.g., "www.facebook.com/ThisPostRightHereDoctor), or downloading documents from cloud services such as Dropbox, Google Drive, or Microsoft OneDrive, as such sources are not always secure, or the source documents might change over time (e.g., "oh, you downloaded that on the 3rd? That's an old version of the spreadsheet. I meant for you to download that on the 4th.")

In all cases, a psychologist should maintain and distribute records in accordance with local statutes and their governing licensing board. Some jurisdictions require that when an evaluee provides records to an evaluator, they are required to provide a copy of the records to opposing counsel contemporaneously. Sometimes court orders specify this practice is to be followed anyway, even in jurisdictions in which it is not required. It can save an evaluator a substantial amount of clerical work if they establish at the outset of an evaluation, preferably through language in their memorandum of understanding, that it is the responsibility of each party to ensure opposing counsel is provided with such duplicate records.

Best practices for maintaining records includes provisions that evaluators keep all records they consider as part of their evaluation. Doing so would be extremely difficult if documents are shown to you on an electronic device such as a cellphone or computer. In order to maintain proper records, an evaluator should only accept SNS records in a format they can maintain, such as printed out screen captures or saved electronic files with appropriate date and time stamps.

If an evaluee presents an exchange of chat messages, make sure you have the entire exchange. If, for example, an evaluee provides you with a series of messages between him or herself and another party (say, a conversation of 40 messages sent between 2:00 PM on a Friday and 10:00 AM the next day), it might be worth requesting the same message exchange from the second party. This would provide an evaluator with data that would allow them to determine if either party had provided less than the entire exchange, or possibly modified them in any way. If a party provided only select messages from the conversation, the evaluator would have an

Table 6.2 *List of common social media/networking sites to consult*

Site name	Useful for examining direct communication	Useful for examining indirect communication
Facebook	✓	✓
Instagram	✓	✓
LinkedIn	✓	✓
Twitter	✓	✓
Pinterest	✓	✓
YouTube		✓
KIK	✓	
WhatsApp	✓	✓
Snapchat	✓	✓
Reddit	✓	✓

opportunity to review which messages were selected for removal, and to follow up in interview as to why the selected messages were omitted.

When interviewing an evaluee, listen for how they describe their communication with others. Do they mention text messages? Do they mention emails? Do they talk about Facebook or Twitter? It can also be helpful to ask evaluees directly about particular SNS (see Table 6.2 for a list of SNS commonly in use at the time this chapter was originally authored, in Spring, 2019. This list was generated from the author's own experiences but, of course, will be ever-changing and evolving).

Evaluees might not think of all of these sites as social media, or as possible sources for corroborating information, so following up with questions such as the following might be helpful:

1. Do you (or does the opposing party) talk with people on-line?
2. Do you (or does the opposing party) have apps on your/their phone or tablet used to communicate with others?
3. Do you (or does the opposing party) read or post on any particular websites or message boards?

Depending on the scope of the evaluation and the details of a particular case, it might be worthwhile to search these sites independently to see what information, posted or shared by evaluees, might be publicly available; the extent to which an evaluator elects to do this should be made on a case-by-case basis, and careful consideration should be given to how they document and record such efforts for their records. Some evaluators might be curious about the implications of requiring from evaluees their user names and passwords to SNS. Though it is conceivable that usable information could be gained this way, this approach is strongly recommended against as there are some significant drawbacks. The main drawback is that this approach is similar to asking an evaluee to turn over their journals or diaries and is extremely invasive to an evaluee's privacy. Further, such access would allow an evaluator the ability to actually alter content (either accidentally or purposefully) under the guise of the evaluee. Evaluators arguably do not need this level of access, only enough to view the relevant content that has been posted by the individual. It is an evaluator's responsibility to appropriately limit the scope of their evaluation to only collect data that could reasonably be anticipated as being probative; it would not likely be any more reasonable to request carte blanche access to an evaluee's SNS account than it would be to request an evaluee hand over copies of every single one of their text messages or voicemails. Additionally, an evaluator would be responsible for downloading and archiving an entire evaluee's profile. If this is something an evaluator might want to do, it is recommended they disclose the hypothetical possibility in their memorandum of understanding.

6.4 Consideration and Interpretation of SNS Data

Four major areas of an individual's functioning as a parent can be informed through consideration of SNS data: (1) how they communicate with others and how they interpret communication from others, (2) whether they possess insight into how their actions potentially benefit or harm the relationship between the minor children and themselves or the opposite parent, (3) how well an evaluee understands social networking and technology, and (4) whether they effectively monitor and control a minor child's access to information in an appropriate manner.

For consideration of SNS data and how it can inform an evaluation, it is recommended data from SNS be considered as being classifiable into one of two categories: (1) direct communication and (2) indirect communication. Direct communication refers to communication directed from one individual to another individual or group of individuals, with a reasonable expectation of privacy, and would include site-specific chats like direct messages on Twitter, or messages sent through Facebook Messenger. Indirect communication would refer to SNS communication made to general audiences or communication with no reasonable expectation of privacy, such as unsecured posts to a personal Facebook wall or another's Facebook wall, tweets on Twitter, or Snapchat stories. Another example of indirect communication would be posts to groups within these SNS or to message boards (e.g., divorce support groups).

Direct communication in the SNS sense is equivalent to text messages or emails. Direct communication would likely come into an evaluator's possession the same way most other records do—provided directly by an individual; either the evaluee or a collateral interviewee. As the interview is being conducted, the evaluator should attend to statements made by the interviewee about SNS communication (as well as email and text communication), and should consider requesting copies of said communication. It is also recommended, when soliciting records, to remind an evaluee that direct communication can occur through SNS as well, like WhatsApp, Facebook, Twitter, KIK, Snapchat, etc., and that they could provide the evaluator with copies of conversations they think might corroborate their claims. Of note, the context within which a conversation takes place is also important. Therefore, it can be helpful to review time and date stamps on communication and relate that to other data that might have been gathered, from SNS or otherwise. Further, and as emphasized elsewhere in this book, it is also important to note that records of SNS communication can be fabricated. If one evaluee provides a copy of a SNS conversation between himself and a third party, it might be worthwhile to request the same conversation from the third party, and then compare the two provided records for consistency and completeness.

Similar to examining emails or text messages, examining communication that has taken place on SNS, direct or indirect, can illustrate how an individual communicates with others. In viewing SNS data in the context of CCE, it may be useful to keep the following questions in mind:

1. Are messages reported as antagonistic or patronizing but do not appear to be so?
2. Does the examinee maintain a rational and calm style of online communication in the face of clearly antagonistic behavior?
3. Are the content and tone of the examinee's messages with others consistent with how he or she represents during the interview?

All this data can tell an examiner several things. First of all, it can provide an example of the way the parties communicate, related to parenting or otherwise. Second, it can help examiners figure out if the parties are accurately interpreting communication from the other, or ascribing intent or emotion that does not appear to be present. From this data an evaluator could investigate a hypothesis that the accuracy with which a particular evaluee interprets communication from another individual in one modality (e.g., Facebook messenger or text message communication) is likely similar to how they would interpret communication from the same individual in another (e.g., emails or telephone conversation). For example, individual A might frequently send short, one- or two-word text messages. Irrespective of intent, such a response style might be interpreted by individual B as being antagonistic, gruff, or dismissive, and then carry that interpretation over to emails sent by individual A. Various combinations of each of these scenarios can potentially have significant implications for the parties' likelihood of engaging in effective communication around co-parenting.

Data from indirect communication, in particular, can inform hypotheses regarding how much insight the evaluee has into how they present themselves publicly. For example:

1. Does an evaluee post on Facebook "pray for me and the safety of my children?"
2. Does an evaluee join groups such as "co-parenting with a narcissist" and not take steps needed to keep such activities private?
3. Does an evaluee post messages to otherwise anonymous forums with information in them that make them easily identifiable?

Such an approach to communication could potentially cause several difficulties. For example, a minor child might be placed in a position where they feel they need to deny or confirm to others comments made by party A about party B. As another example, party A might make public information about party B, true or otherwise, that could hamper party B's ability to establish relationships with the parents of a minor child's friends, or that could discourage a minor child's friend's parents from supporting a relationship between their child and the minor child. If data is collected suggesting an evaluee does engage in indirect communication that might be problematic, a follow-up interview can be conducted to investigate how much insight they might have in this regard.

Though not directly related to data culled from SNS, the above-discussed lines of data gathering, and investigation relate closely to another potentially important aspect of parenting that could be relevant to a CCE: the extent to which a parent understands and is capable of monitoring and guiding a child's use of technology. A full discussion of technology and parenting would not be appropriate for this chapter's scope, but the following items are presented for possible inclusion in evaluations of an individual's parenting:

1. Does a minor child share/have uncontrolled access to devices used by the parent or other adults, or are these devices password-protected and is their use monitored? If the minor child does have access, do adults always log out of SNS when they are done using them or do they remain logged in? If not, a minor child has access to all of the communication, direct or indirect, that the parent has engaged in through that site.
2. Does a minor child have access to age-appropriate SNS? Do they have their own accounts? Does the parent have access to these accounts? Do they monitor them appropriately?
3. What are the parent's attitudes and beliefs regarding a minor child's access to SNS? Do they have a realistic understanding of how important SNS may be to a child's social development? Are they able to communicate an understanding of what type of use is appropriate and what is not?

Like data from any other source, data from SNS can help an evaluator generate hypotheses for investigation and can provide an evaluator with data that lends support or argues against particular opinions. And, like data from any other source, data from SNS is rarely in and of itself dispositive. Much like with email and text messaging before it, the proliferation of SNS use by individuals provides evaluators with yet another source of communication they can use to direct their evaluation.

6.5 Disclaimer Regarding Case Profiles

As detailed above, child custody litigation involves multiple parties, multiple informants, and multiple data sources. As such, these evaluations are quite complex and the reports generated from them are arguably far lengthier than any other that fall under the umbrella of forensic mental health assessment. Due to page limitations, the case profiles that follow represent more or less a summary of each assessment. Each profile contains a partial list of data, areas of investigations, conclusions, and opinions from this case that were believed to be relevant to the scope of this chapter.

Case Profile 1

Type of Evaluation

An evaluation was ordered to assess two parents (Ben and Shirley) and their ability to properly parent two minor children, ages four and fourteen years old. The younger child was a product of the marriage. The older child was from one of Shirley's prior relationships; while Ben did not have any legal rights to parent the older child, the court asked the evaluator to opine on aspects of Ben's relationship with the older child.

Case Context

The evaluation was ordered related to ongoing child custody litigation and the court was operating under a Best Interest paradigm. The evaluations were ordered under consent of both parents. Both parents were in their late 40s at the time of the evaluation. They were married 10 years prior to the evaluation, separated 2 years prior to the evaluation, and divorced 1 year prior to the evaluation.

Sources of Information

Various pleadings were provided and reviewed, for both criminal and civil matters. Each adult party was interviewed about similar initial topics (e.g., their family of origin, their work history, their mental health history, their perceived strengths and weaknesses) and select topics (e.g., substance use history, history of psychiatric hospitalization, history of abuse and neglect as a child) as they appeared to become relevant during the evaluation process. Records from multiple child protective services involvements were made available to review.

Over two dozen collateral interviews were conducted with family friends, friends of one party or the other, neighbors, parents of the parties, siblings of the parties, current mental health providers for each party and for the older child, past mental health providers for each party and the older child, and school personnel, as well as current and former significant others for each party.

Each adult party was administered an identical battery of psychological tests: the Minnesota Multiphasic Personality Inventory-2 (MMPI-2), the Personality Assessment Inventory (PAI), the State-Trait Anger Expression Inventory 2 (STAXI-2); the Stress Index for Adolescent Parents (SIPA) regarding the older child, the Parenting Stress Index, Fourth Edition (PSI-4) regarding the younger child; and age-appropriate version of the Behavior Assessment System for Children,

Third Edition (BASC-3) and BASC-3 Parenting Relationship Questionnaire (BASC-3 PRQ) regarding each child. The older child completed a BASC-3 self-report and an adolescent version of the PAI (PAI-A).

Relevant to the focus of this chapter, each party provided their own records for review, including printed-out emails, screen captures of text message conversations, screen captures of direct and indirect communication made on Facebook, video recordings, voicemail and other audio recordings, and various medical and mental health records.

Relevant Background

Relationship History The current relationship was the first marriage and second significant relationship for both parents. Both parents self-disclosed a history of trauma as children; Ben for sexual abuse and Shirley for physical abuse. Ben had an alleged history of engaging in sexually explicit conversation with adolescents, both in-person and over social media sites. Ben was also alleged to have been physically violent with Shirley and the older child and to have engaged in sexual abuse of the younger child (with no substantiated findings by child protective services and no charges pursued subsequent to law enforcement investigation).

Shirley had an alleged history of significant instability and volatility in intimate relationships and had made multiple allegations of sexual and domestic violence against past romantic partners, none of which had been substantiated or reported to law enforcement. Allegations and reports of sexual and physical abuse were also made by Shirley against Ben.

The older child was refusing contact with Ben; otherwise neither child was reported to display concerning behaviors or signs of maladjustment.

Clinical History for Ben Ben reported a family history significant for mental illness. Ben said his mother was diagnosed with dissociative identity disorder, but that her symptoms had largely abated due to treatment. Growing up, Ben reportedly witnessed his mother be verbally violent toward his father. His father also had problems with alcohol and would consume alcohol to the point where he would "pass out." Ben stated his father stopped drinking alcohol at age 45. Ben further reported his brother has a diagnosis of depression and substance use disorder. Ben described a history of sexual trauma. He stated he was sexually abused by a babysitter at around the age of five.

Clinical History for Shirley Shirley reported a history significant for multiple traumatic experiences. Both during interview and to prior therapists, Shirley described her biological mother as significantly abusive; Shirley's biological brother corroborated this assertion. Additionally, Shirley stated that the older child's father held a knife to her throat "when the older child was little." Shirley reported during interview that she was sexually assaulted in a mall parking garage parking lot 10 years prior, as well as other sexual assaults prior. Although there is ambiguity regarding some instances of sexual assault, the data collected supports an assertion that Shirley has experienced multiple traumatic events, some ongoing/complex, starting in early childhood.

Behavioral Observations and Mental Status

Both parents presented as unremarkable regarding mental status and cognitive functioning. While Ben did not require significant redirection or structuring during interview, Shirley required redirection, often going to significant lengths to focus conversation away from herself and onto Ben, particularly on what she viewed as his shortcomings.

Summary of Test Results

Of greatest significance from psychological testing was Ben and Shirley's response style. Ben's responses to testing did not result in elevations on validity scales of any type, including positive impression management, while Shirley's responses to testing resulted in substantial elevations on validity scales related to defensiveness and positive impression management. Such elevations, or lack of elevations, held even when profiles were interpreted using norms published for suggested use within child custody contexts. Also of note, despite her markedly defensive approach to testing on the MMPI-2 and PAI, Shirley's responses on these instruments resulted in significant elevations on scale 4 of the MMPI-2 (Hysteria), suggesting consideration of a hypothesis that she experiences or reports experiencing physical ailments or maladies to a much more significant extent than is typical, possibly unrelated to actual physical manifestation, and possibly at times in rigid avoidance of expressing hostility to others. Results also suggested Shirley might be resistant to making disclosures during therapy and resistant to therapeutic intervention in general. Results from the older child's testing were moderately defensive, and suggested some symptoms related to depression and interpersonal suspicion.

Diagnostic Conclusions

No specific diagnoses were made as part of this evaluation.

Summary of Data Relevant to Psycho-Legal Opinion

Of particular relevance, substantial records were provided by each party from social media sources (i.e., Facebook Messenger conversations and Facebook posts), as well as email conversations and text messages. All data was provided either in paper printout, as .pdfs, or as screen capture graphic files.

Some items of note include:

1. Messages from Shirley to family friends detailing reports Shirley had made of Ben to police and social services; particularly Ben's alleged history of engaging in sexually explicit conversation with minors and of soliciting sex from minors. A primary focus of the evaluation involving these posts was the reasonableness of Shirley's concerns regarding Ben's alleged behavior (i.e., was there good reason to be concerned and was the level of concern appropriate?). Another focus of the evaluation explored Shirley's insight into how making public posts could potentially disrupt Ben's relationship with the children, especially if no corroborating evidence is found.
2. Public messages posted on Ben's Facebook account stating Ben's Facebook account had been shut down by Facebook "pending criminal investigations." As part of this evaluation, allegations were made by several parties that Shirley gained access to Ben's Facebook account and posted these messages. Shirley denied the allegations. Several parties also alleged that Shirley created or gained access to multiple social networking profiles to engender jealousy in her past and current significant others. For example, she would create false profiles as other men (i.e., using pictures of males as profile pictures) and would then post flirtatious messages on her own profile or threatening messages on the profiles of her former boyfriends. A focus of this evaluation explored these allegations, especially as they might unnecessarily negatively impact Ben's quality of life and his ability to provide for the minor children.
3. Text message conversations between Shirley and third parties, some of whom consented to be interviewed as part of the evaluation, detailing Shirley's expressed interest in "ruining" Ben's reputation in several social circles. A focus of this evaluation explored these conversations, how they related to the above two items, and how all gathered information might inform decisions regarding Shirley's ability to foster Ben's relationship with the minor children.

Clinical Forensic Opinion

Two primary issues were considered in formulating an opinion about Ben and Shirley's parenting ability: Ben's alleged sexual abuse of their youngest child and Shirley's psychological functioning.

Allegations of Sexual Abuse of the Younger Child Data gathered as part of this evaluation suggested Ben, at least while married to Shirley, possibly engaged in concerning sexual or sexualized behavior. For example, a collateral source stated Ben told her he had sex with "many women" while married to Shirley. Shirley provided screenshots of sexually suggestive Facebook communication between Ben and at least twenty individuals, most of whom appear to be under the age of 18. Ben stated he no longer engages in this type of behavior. In all, these above behaviors, while certainly problematic within the context of a marriage, did not directly involve either child.

Shirley's Overall Psychological Functioning Though data collected as part of this evaluation did not give rise to substantial concerns that Shirley's current psychological functioning markedly affects her ability to parent the older child in the present, it would be reasonable to assume Shirley might have difficulty engaging in future co-parenting in the absence of effective therapeutic intervention.

Data collected as part of the evaluation also gave rise to a few areas of concern that *are consistent* with individuals experiencing maladaptive psychological difficulties often observed in individuals with long-term, untreated trauma. While these areas of concern in and of themselves would not preclude Shirley from parenting effectively, they did suggest Shirley would likely substantially benefit from structured, intensive therapeutic intervention, which would likely in-turn help her to more effectively parent over time as well as co-parent with Ben.

One area that raised concern regarding Shirley's psychological functioning was that of her chaotic employment history. For example, Shirley's self-reported work history was significantly sporadic and inconsistent, and her descriptions of her work history was not always consistent with third party information in regards to time and duration of employment, or reason for leaving a particular job. For example, Shirley stated she owned a sandwich shop at one point, but closed it down due to lack of support from Ben. A review of Internet review sites were full of complaints by customers of poor service and by vendors for lack of payment.

Another area of note is that, while Shirley expressed an understanding of the importance of therapy and a belief that she needed therapy, Shirley did not have a track record of meaningful participation in therapy. For example, she failed to complete a mental health assessment ordered by court proceedings related to child protective services and when interviewed about this could not provide a cogent reason as to why. As another example, Shirley provided records and collateral contact information for eight therapists she had seen over the past 12 years; the six that were still in practice reported Shirley attended only two or three appointments with each and had several no-call/no-shows.

Data collected as part of this evaluation further suggested Shirley experiences intense anger for which she sometimes has difficulty controlling, and later expresses regret. Examples of this response pattern generally relate to the loss of a relationship or a perceived impending loss of a relationship. For example:

1. Ben stated that Shirley was driving a Honda he had leased, and the vehicle was not turned in at the end of the lease period. When asked why she did not turn in the Honda lease on time, Shirley said, "basically I suck with paperwork. That was my first experience with a lease," and "I thought that I could turn it in later, thought I could pay a fine later for it." However, a third-party collateral provided a screenshot of a message sent to her from Shirley stating Shirley wanted to ruin Ben's reputation "at Honda," When asked about this, Shirley said she was "venting."
2. Ben's former fiancée (prior to his marriage to Shirley) stated she did not speak to Ben after terminating their engagement until "late 2007 when [Shirley] started semi-harassing" her. Ben's former fiancée stated that a "made up" profile on Facebook, with "a picture of a guy in the profile, with no friends…sent out a message to people saying I was a whore and had herpes." Ben's former fiancée reported she "started getting messages from [Ben] saying 'stop calling [Shirley],'" but Ben stated he never sent those messages. Ben's former fiancée also stated she filed a harassment complaint against Shirley. Shirley denied an awareness of this.
3. A friend of Shirley stated that on one occasion when Shirley separated from a former boyfriend, Shirley "started contacting his friends' wives. She would tell his friends' wives he was verbally abusive," and after they got back together Shirley "[became] very obsessed with Facebook. She's tracking who likes [her former boyfriend's] posts, how many are girls." A friend of Shirley also said that Shirley "makes fake Facebook accounts 'with guys' info, blocks the guys so they never can see that they've been duped, and then logs in as those guys to comment on pics of herself to get attention." Her former boyfriend stated he believes Shirley had made fake Facebook accounts for males "that had beef with me," who "started messaging me," that they were "going to take [Shirley] away from me, that I'm mean to her, abusive to her. But the whole time it was [Shirley]" sending the messages.
4. At or around the time she separated from Ben, Shirley sent the following Facebook message to an individual: "Sorry I have to delete you for now. NOTHING against you, just because of all the crap Ben is doing I have to delete people who know him for now until his crazy blows over and the Feds are done investigating his sex crimes," to which the individual replied, "Ok? I haven't heard from either of you two in years." When asked why she sent this unsolicited email, Shirley said she did not know who the individual was; she had sent that message because she was instructed by her attorney to send messages and to state that Ben was being investigated for sex crimes. When asked what the ramifications of sending such a message might be, Shirley said "I started seeing 'hey this is causing a lot of conflict and craziness and a mess.' I didn't like how doing that felt."
5. Ben stated he was terminated from a position of 8 years, "for breaking the code of conduct. I sent an email to a coworker commenting that I had liked her that day. [Shirley] found out about that email, reported to my company, my boss,"

and he was terminated as a result of the company's "zero strike policy." Ben said he was not in a relationship with the coworker, but "we were both in crappy marriages, we flirted." When asked about this, Shirley stated Ben was fired because he was "having an inappropriate relationship with a coworker," and "sexually soliciting clients." When asked how Ben's work learned he was having an 'inappropriate relationship,' Shirley said "I'm not sure. When I found out [about the relationship]...I spoke to [Ben] about it and told him 'hey I'm going to contact [the coworker's] supervisor.'" When asked why she was going to do that, Shirley said "at the time I was suing her for disrupting my home. I ended up not doing that. It was a... knee jerk reaction," but that "after calming down from that shock of such a horrible thing," Shirley stated that she realized the coworker "was not the problem." When asked how contacting the sales representative's employer caused problems for Ben, Shirley said, "Maybe she did the same" to Ben.

Recommendations

Though no diagnosis was made, treatment recommendations for Shirley included regular, consistent therapeutic intervention from a professional qualified to administer treatment appropriate for individuals displaying behaviors consistent with borderline personality disorder.

How Did Social Media Impact This Case?

Social media was helpful in this case as it provided a solid record of Shirley's historical conversations with friends and family, including documented inconsistencies between her messages/actions and her self-report during the interview. These conversations often included descriptions of actions Shirley had intended to take to harm Ben's relationship, a substantial portion of which were eventually carried out. Having access to SNS data in this case provided direct talking points for interviews with Shirly and collateral sources; without SNS data, the interviews would have been much less substantial. In addition, the data points that came from Shirley's public-facing social media posts allowed for discussions of insight to be less hypothetical and more grounded in actual behavior. Finally, transcripts of Ben's communication with allegedly underage individuals provided insight into Ben's current behaviors and provided credibility to some of Shirley's claims of Ben's past behaviors; this data supported an assertion that his behavior had, indeed, likely occurred, and, when taken into consideration with other data, did not support an assertion that the behavior was likely on-going.

Case Profile 2

Type of Evaluation

An evaluation was ordered to assess two parents (Craig and Vicki) and their ability to properly parent a minor child and to offer an opinion on possible negative and positive consequences of altering the minor child's overnight schedule.

Case Context

The evaluation was ordered related to ongoing child custody litigation and the court was operating under a Best Interest paradigm. The evaluations were ordered under consent of the parents. At the time of the evaluation, both parents were in their mid-20s and the minor child was 22 months old. Craig and Vicki were married approximately 2 years prior to the evaluation, separated 1 year prior to the evaluation, and divorced 1 month prior to the evaluation.

Sources of Information

Various pleadings were provided and reviewed. Each adult party was interviewed about similar initial topics and select topics (e.g., medical history, child's medical history, their knowledge of the child's medical history and their ability to articulate their roles in the care of the child) as they appeared to become relevant over the course of the evaluation. Ten collateral interviews were conducted with family friends, neighbors, parents of the parties, and child care workers.

Each adult was administered an identical battery of psychological tests, including the MMPI-2, the PAI, the STAXI, and the Child Abuse Potential Inventory (CAPI). In addition, both parents completed a PSI-4 and BASC-3 PRQ regarding the minor child.

Relevant to the focus of this chapter, each party provided their own records for review, including printed-out emails, screen captures of text message conversations, screen captures of direct and indirect communication made on Facebook, video recordings, and various medical and mental health records.

Relevant Background

The current relationship was the first marriage for Craig; Vicki had been married once prior, in her late teens, for less than a year. Vicki stated she was unable to provide her prior husband's contact information and so he was not interviewed as part of this evaluation. Craig's parents divorced and remarried when Craig was approximately 11; Vicki's parents divorced when Vicki was approximately 14 and neither had remarried. Neither party's history was significant for trauma, substance use, any other areas of concern.

Vicki alleged Craig was physically violent with Vicki and the minor child; however, no reports were made to child protective services. Neither parent had a relevant criminal history or a history of substance use.

The minor child was alleged to have displayed problematic behavior when in Vicki's care, such as poor sleep patterns, throwing food, and age-inappropriate toileting habits. The minor child was also medically fragile, as he was recovering from major organ surgery and had several prescription medications he was required to take.

Behavioral Observations and Mental Status

Both parents presented as unremarkable regarding mental status and cognitive functioning. While Craig did not require significant redirection or structuring during the interview, Vicki did. She went to significant lengths to focus the conversation on her perception of Craig's shortcomings and her resultant concerns about the minor child's safety and well-being.

Summary of Test Results

Test results for both parties resulted in substantial and significant elevations on validity scales indicating defensiveness, even when compared to normative data more directly related to child custody matters and including on the CAPI. Because such defensiveness was observed across the board, little weight was given to results from testing, and more effort was made to corroborate statements made by the evaluees through review of records and interview with third parties.

Diagnostic Conclusions

No specific diagnoses were made as part of this evaluation.

Summary of Data Relevant to Psycho-Legal Opinion

Of particular relevance to this chapter, substantial records were provided by each party from social media sources (i.e., Facebook Messenger conversations and Facebook posts), as well as email conversations and text messages. All data was provided either in paper printout, as PDFs, or as screen capture graphic files.

Some items of note include:

1. Facebook messages (as well as email and text messages) from Vicki to child care providers countermanding Craig's instructions for the minor child's care, including statements that allegedly included instruction directly from the minor child's pediatrician. For example, in one message, Vicki wrote that the minor child should, per the child's doctor's instruction, be given additional medication at 10:00 AM and 2:00 PM, as the minor child had a fever and was irritable. This message was sent shortly after a text message exchange between Craig and Vicki in which Craig asserted the minor child was appropriately rested and Vicki asserted that Craig was not able to accurately make such determinations.
2. Posts by Vicki to Instagram groups related to the minor child's disability that included statements showing insight into the standard of care for the minor child's condition.
3. Facebook messages from Craig to mutual friends refuting Vicki's claims of his maltreatment of the minor child or of Craig placing the minor child in danger through negligence. These messages to mutual friends also included photographs corroborating Craig's claim. For example, Vicki had previously messaged a mutual friend that Craig's car had broken tail lights; Craig sent a photograph showing otherwise.

Clinical Forensic Opinion

Part of the opinion provided to the court was that no data was collected suggesting either parent was directly parenting the child inappropriately or directly placing the child in danger. There was evidence, including social media data referenced above, however, to suggest the following concerns:

Data gathered from SNS, as well as other sources, including from medical providers refuting the veracity of Vicki's claims made to child care providers, gave rise to concern that the minor child was being placed in minor but not insignificant danger. When interviewed about the apparent lack of veracity of her claims about the minor child's medical provider's instruction for care, Vicki asserted memory of being given the instructions she was conveying, and that the minor child's condition, as she understood it at the time of her messages to child care providers, justified her instructions for additional medication.

Vicki's posts to Instagram that correctly represented what had been communicated to her by treating physicians was in contrast with what she had communicated to child care providers. This would suggest Vicki likely had the knowledge required to care for the minor child. It was also noted that Vicki's erroneous care instructions to child care worker was, at least on two occasions, based upon information regarding the child's status that Vicki received from Craig, which was presented ambiguously by Craig and interpreted by Vicki as being more concerning than was actually the case (e.g., Craig sent Vicki a message stating the minor child was feeling tired, which Vicki took to indicate that the child was concerningly lethargic).

Recommendations

Given Vicki's apparent misunderstanding of medical instruction, it was recommended that care instructions, from providers to both parents, are provided in written format to ensure accurate transmission of information. It was further recommended that both parents work with the minor child's medical providers to establish a format for reporting the minor child's condition that would minimize room for editorializing or offering concerns or criticisms of the opposite party.

How Did Social Media Impact This Case?

Social media was helpful in this case as it provided useful information regarding Vicki's actual understanding of the minor child's condition and requisite care; data suggested she had a robust understanding of the minor child's medical care needs but would appear otherwise in the presence of conflict between herself and the minor child's father. Without the information collected from Instagram it would have been much more difficult to assert that Vicki had longstanding requisite knowledge of the minor child's medical condition and care requirements.

Additionally, the time and date stamps of the messages from Vicki (and from Craig) to the child care workers allowed comparisons to be made of messages sent by Craig to messages sent by Vicki. For example, on one of the more contentious occasions, timestamps indicated Vicki sent messages to childcare providers during and immediately following an angry text message exchange with Craig. Comparing these messages to other data regarding each parent's understanding of the minor child's functioning helped establish where the breakdown in communication between parties occurred. Without the ease of communication that SNS provides, it is possible neither party, nor third parties, would have communicated to this extent about the minor child with each other, or that they would have communicated by telephone or in-person, which would have been much less reliable a data source given that these forms of communication are typically not documented or recorded. SNS data allowed for a more robust examination of the communication dynamic between parties and allowed for more precise recommendations, particularly as they relate to a recommendation that a parenting coordinator be appointed, and how that parenting coordinator might best assist the parties to structure (and limit) their communication.

References

American Academy of Matrimonial Lawyers. (2011). Child Custody Evaluation Standards. Retrieved from http://aaml.org/library/publications/child-custody-evaluation-standards-doc

American Law Institute. (2000). Principles of the law of family dissolution: Analysis and recommendations. Retrieved from https://scholarship.law.duke.edu/cgi/viewcontent.cgi?article=1038&context=djglp

American Psychological Association. (2010). Guidelines for child custody evaluations in family law proceedings. *American Psychologist, 65*(9), 863–867.

American Psychological Association. (2013). Specialty guidelines for forensic psychology. *The American Psychologist, 68*, 7–19. https://doi.org/10.1037/a0029889.

Association of Family and Conciliation Courts. (2007). Model standards of practice for child custody evaluation. *Family Court Review, 45*(1), 70–91. [Martindale, D. A., Reporter.].

Association of Family and Conciliation Courts. (2009). Guidelines for brief focused assessment. Association of Family and Conciliation Courts. Retrieved from https://www.afccnet.org/Portals/0/PublicDocuments/Guidelines/BFATF2009final.pdf

Budd, K. S. (2001). Assessing parenting competence in child protection cases: A clinical practice model. *Clinical Child and Family Psychology Review, 4*(1), 1–18.

Gould, J. W., & Martindale, D. A. (2009). *The art and science of child custody evaluations*. New York: The Guilford Press.

Martindale, D., Martin, L., Austin, W., Drozd, L., Gould-Saltman, D., Kirkpatrick, H. D., et al. (2006). Model standards of practice for child custody evaluation. *Family Court Review, 45*, 70–91. https://doi.org/10.1111/j.1744-1617.2007.129_3.x.

Stahl, P. M. (2013). *Conducting child custody and parenting evaluations*. Los Angeles: SAGE Publications.

Weiner, I. B., & Otto, R. K. (2013). *The Handbook of Forensic Psychology. 137–170*. Hoboken: Wiley.

[illegible]

Chapter 7
Pre-Employment and Fitness-for-Duty in the Law Enforcement Arena

Sepideh A. Souris

Over the past few years, law enforcement (LE) agencies have been confronted with many situations and incidents leading to the question of officers' judgments. These situations have not only drawn intense scrutiny but have also resulted in very negative reactions from the public. In several of these situations, especially as related to the questionable use of force, it has been revealed that the officers had demonstrated prior instances of "poor judgment." This has led to a rise in questions as to whether the LE agencies had taken appropriate steps prior to hiring applicants pursuing LE careers. Many have also speculated whether the LE agency had properly investigated these earlier occurrences of unbecoming conduct, and had tried to supervise, train and implement a corrective action plan as related to the officers' problematic behaviors.

When problematic issues with an officer's behavior occur, concerns focused on negligent hiring, training and supervision, and negligent retention inevitably are mentioned. It is understood that LE is a field where there is more scrutinized public contact than there is with almost any other job. Public interactions in LE are generally of a very personal nature and often grant the officer access to people's homes. This privilege is known as a "passkey" job. In these cases, the courts have found that the LE agencies have a higher duty of care to conduct a thorough background investigation of the applicants. For example, in *Reeves v. Town of Cottageville (*2014*)*, a federal court jury awarded a total of $97.5 million to the plaintiff for the police shooting death of the former mayor of Cottageville, South Carolina. Reportedly, the officer who shot the deceased had been employed by the police department even though he had been terminated previously by a number of other LE agencies for insubordination, dangerous use of firearms, and other infractions. In an earlier decision, the trial judge commented that evidence of the officer's departure from six other police departments in seven years was "obviously admissible" against him with respect to not only the claim for

S. A. Souris (✉)
Private Practice, Woodland Hills, CA, USA

A. B. Batastini, M. J. Vitacco (eds.), *Forensic Mental Health Evaluations in the Digital Age*, https://doi.org/10.1007/978-3-030-33908-1_7

municipal liability for violation of civil rights, but also the claim that the town and police department negligently hired, retained, and supervised the officer. This evidence, the court ruled, had an impact on whether the municipal defendants properly evaluated the officer's credentials before hiring him. Thus, negligent appointment or hiring is an area of liability involving the agency in two ways: (1) failing to safeguard against employing someone unfit for the position of peace officer and (2) falling short in adequately screening the individuals and hiring someone known to be unfit or unqualified. The existence of these types of claims have made it critical to uncover as much information as possible about a candidate and an employee, given that the burden falls on the LE executives to refute these claims, regardless of the type, by proving proper and effective management in the hiring and training process.

7.1 Rationale and Legal and Ethical Considerations for Peace Officer Pre-Employment Psychological Evaluations (PEPE)

The demands on LE personnel are, indeed, considerable and extensive. Peace officers must be capable of being law enforcers, first responders, mediators, negotiators, and public servants. This position requires them to have leadership and interpersonal skills, be able to take initiative, be truthful, persevere, be conscientious, utilize good judgment, and be adaptable and creative in obtaining a solution in critical situations. Their work conditions are frequently dangerous and stressful; the stakes are immensely high both personally and in terms of maintaining public safety. As peace officers, these individuals routinely come into contact with the more adverse aspects of human characteristics and should accomplish their job in an objective and non-emotional manner, while being governed by policy and laws (Dantzker 2005; Dantzker 2011). Additionally, peace officers face high rates of occupationally-related stress and injuries (Schlosser and McAleer 2018). In fact, according to a Federal Bureau of Investigation report, a total of 106 LE officers were killed in the line of duty in 2018.

The distinctive nature of policing, issue of police use of force, suicide and corruption among LE officers, and the fact that this is one of the most health threatening careers necessitate a selection and evaluation process to find individuals who have adequate interpersonal and emotional control skills to cope effectively in stressful and volatile situations (Beutler et al. 1988; Hargrave and Hiatt 1989; Cochrane et al. 2003). One manner of screening out unsuitable police and public safety candidates is through the Pre-Employment Psychological Evaluation (PEPE).

In fact, the pre-employment evaluation of LE candidates can date back to the first quarter of the century (Termin and Otis 1917). Most specifically, the President's Commission on Law Enforcement and administration of Justice (1967) strongly encouraged and emphasized the selection of peace officer candidates who are: well adjusted, have the ability to adapt to unusual demands and unique activities, possess adequate coping skills, are agreeable to be exposed to danger, are amenable to supervision, and can adapt to conflicting roles (Beutler et al. 1988; Craig 2005). Furthermore, the 1968 National Advisory Commission on Civil Disorders proposed and advocated that peace officer candidates should be examined by psychologists or psychiatrists, and the selection process should include administration of psychological tests to aid in determining job fitness (Davis and Rostow 2008). To that end, and in order to offer consistency in the police screening arena, the Police Psychological Services Section of the International Associations of Chiefs of Police (IACP) established its first set of guidelines in 1986 (Curran 1998), with the latest revision being approved in 2014.

There are strong indications that PEPE can help identify individuals who are less likely to succumb to stress, engage in deleterious or criminal behavior, and be terminated for cause. It is important to note that conducting PEPE should be done in adherence with and while considering applicable laws and regulations. In this regard, Federal Laws such as Civil Rights Act of 1964, Title VII which was amended in 1991, prevail. This Act, which is enforced by the Equal Employment Opportunity Commission (EEOC), prohibits hiring practices that have the effect of disproportionately excluding people in a covered class (i.e., race, color, religion, sex or national origin) unless justification is delineated. Another federal law which is enforced by EEOC and the states' Fair Employment Housing Act (FEHA) is the American with Disabilities Act (ADA), Title I. ADA prohibits discrimination against qualified persons with a disability and only permits medical examinations or inquiries under specific conditions. It requires that all candidates in a similar job class receive the same medical evaluation, and that the examination can only occur ***after*** a conditional offer of employment has been tendered. It further entails that applicants must be rejected on the basis of information that is job-related and consistent with business necessity. In addition, Genetic Information Nondiscrimination Act of 2008 (GINA, Title II) prohibits the acquisition and use of genetic information in hiring and employment process; thus, data about the manifestation of disorder in family members cannot be gathered and play a role in hiring decisions.

Since the pre-screening process for LE positions have been in existence for over 75 years, there have been ample opportunities for LE agencies to incorporate these laws and regulations and comply with them. Distinctively, there are 38 states that have established pre-employment or precertification requirements for the mental or psychological health, functionality or suitability of peace officers; at least 20 states specifically mandate a psychological assessment separate from the general medical evaluation.

Thus, the PEPE is established as a specialized evaluation which is conducted prior to the individual starting to work; in order to discern whether a peace officer candidate meets the minimum requirements for psychological suitability mandated by jurisdictional statues and regulations, as well as any other criteria established by the hiring agency (IACP 2014). The candidate needs to be found free from any emotional, behavioral, personality characteristics, or psychological condition that might adversely affect the exercise of the powers of a peace officer; or, in other words, be able to withstand the psychological demands of the position demonstrating "adaptive efficiency" (per California Government Code §1031). To aid with that, the Peace Officer Standards of Training (POST) Regulations (1955) in California have authenticated ten psychological dimensions as the minimum standards for assessing statutory and regulatory criteria (11 California Code of Regulations §1955). These ten psychological dimensions, which are indeed utilized by the Board Certified Police and Public Safety psychologists in Arizona, Georgia, Colorado, New York, Oregon and Utah, to name a few state, are comprised of: (1) Emotional Regulation & Stress Tolerance, (2) Avoiding Damaging and Excessive Risk-Taking Behavior, (3) Impulse Control and Attention to Safety, (4) Assertiveness/Persuasiveness, (5) Social Competence, (6) Teamwork, (7) Decision Making & Judgment, (8) Adaptability and Flexibility, (9) Conscientiousness/Dependability, and (10) Integrity/Ethics. These dimensions are prominently aligned with the essential functions of a peace officer and have been applied in assessing the fitness-for-duty of the officers, as well (*Brown v. Sandy City Appeals Board* 2014). While the candidate has received a conditional offer and is referred for PEPE, it is critical for the LE agencies to ensure that the background investigation continues throughout this stage, and the candidate needs to be notified that they can still be disqualified at the background level as well, for misstatement, inaccuracy, or omission of critical information.

Furthermore, per the IACP, Psychological Services Section's Pre-employment Psychological Evaluation Guidelines, in addition to requiring the administration of psychological measures that are indicative of "normal" and "abnormal" traits; analysis and incorporation of other data sources such as a psychological history questionnaire, background investigation summary report, an in-person interview with the candidate, and in some cases treatment summaries from medical or psychological treatment sources, is necessitated. Specifically, under the Background Information, Criteria 10, it is stated that information regarding the applicant's relevant history such as education, occupation, interpersonal, family/developmental, legal, financial, substance use, and mental health should be collected and integrated with psychological test and interview data in a standardized manner. It further adds that, when available, relevant information from the background investigation and methods used for the detection of deceptions should be shared with the individual who is performing the PEPE. After conducting the interview, the data for each candidate needs to be analyzed and compared preferably (while in California it is mandatory) against the ten POST psychological dimensions. When there are substantive discrepancies between information obtained in the psychological evaluation and that gathered through other stages of the hiring process, it is required that this data be brought up and reviewed thoroughly with the hiring agency. Only then can the psychological evaluator make a recommendation of the candidate's psychological suitability before a final hiring decision is made.

7.1.1 The Introduction of Social Media in the Hiring Process

Among the sources of data to be considered by the psychologist, as well as the background investigator, social media posts have become critical. Since social media has become mainstream (Segal 2014), it is extremely simple to Google someone's name and discover information about them within seconds via their online "footprint" and behaviors. Individuals offer a great amount of information virtually about themselves which may be considered and deliberated upon by employers. Given the social desirability bias, there are times in which applicants may not present themselves in a forthright manner on their resume or during the interview. Hence, it becomes important to canvas their social media and other online outlets to discover whether the person behaves in the same ways as they were presenting during the interview and have the qualifications that they are claiming on their resumes (Cross-Tab 2010).

Increasingly, employers are searching the Internet for information on LE recruits and existing employees (Haefner 2009; Segal 2014). This assessment of the individual's suitability to hold a position using information found on the Internet has become known as Cybervetting (Mikkelson 2010). Most specifically, this practice entails viewing social networking sites (SNS) such as MySpace, Facebook, LinkedIn, blogs and microblogs like Twitter and using search engines such as Google and Yahoo! to attain information about job applicants or to monitor current employees. In fact, a recent research effort sponsored by the Microsoft Corporation discovered that approximately 70 percent of U.S. recruiters and human resource professionals have used online information as a basis for not hiring candidates. This information has included negative content related to the applicant's use of drugs and abuse of alcohol, bad mouthing previous employers, supervisors and co-workers, evidence of poor communication skills, and inappropriate pictures. Thus, in the event that this simple method of investigation is not utilized, and it comes to light that there was adequate information to demonstrate that the person is not qualified for the position of a peace officer, the LE agency has left itself wide open to negligent hiring claims, thereby increasing the agency's liability.

7.1.2 The Role of Cybervetting in PEPE: Uses, Cautions, and Accessibility

Cybervetting poses its own problems to PEPE which will be reviewed. However, there are issues inherent in the use of posts to make hiring decisions. For instance, there is a likelihood that job applicants may not represent themselves honestly and may purposefully create false identities/profiles to represent themselves online. Therefore, even if SNS data can corroborate behavior or statements made during an interview, it remains possible that such SNS data is simply corroborating a fabrication. Additionally, their profiles may be "contaminated" with the behaviors of others. For example, other people may post information that appears within the social media content of an applicant, thus, contaminating it (Landers and Schmidt 2016). To further exemplify how contamination can occur, a "friend" may post additional pictures of a social gathering the candidate attended depicting underage individuals and the candidate holding drinks in their hands with "hukkahs" and "joints" captured in the background of the pictures, then posts inappropriate comments accompanying the images about how "blasted" the candidate appeared.

In a similar vein, it should also be considered that SNS platforms bring with them online cultural norms and standards that influence user behavior. When social media postings are observed by those making hiring decisions, they are viewing a person-situation interaction. Thus, judgments cannot be overgeneralized without considering contextual issues (Tett and Burnett 2003). That is, the way someone conducts themselves as an employee may not be accurately reflected in or predicted by their SNS content. Someone may be an excellent employee but behave more recklessly online in a way that does not relate to their job performance or skills, or vice versa.

Many of the concerns with utilization of SNS posts in selection and hiring decisions revolve around using the information in an inconsistent manner across applicants and gathering data that are not job related (Chambers and Winter 2017). It is also significant to keep in mind that, even if the information is useful, it may not be legal to consult it. Although information posted on the Internet is generally believed to be public, many regulatory systems and acts, such as invasion of privacy and Fair Credit Reporting Act, bar the consultation of particular types of information by those making recommendations and hiring decisions since it may lead to discrimination, as well as violations of consent and privacy (Society for Human Resource Management 2015). For example, the postings may contain information about the applicant's race, religion, skin color, national origin, sex, and pregnancy that may intentionally or unintentionally influence hiring decisions even before other information can be gathered (e.g., via a formal interview) which may be in violation of the Civil Rights Act-Title VII protections.

It needs to be emphasized that there are laws which pose certain restrictions on access of SNS posts. For example, in California, Labor Code section 980 prohibits employers from requesting or requiring individuals to give access to their private social media accounts, and potentially limits the information to what is available publicly. It should be noted that there are similar restrictions and case laws in other states, as well, and many companies have their own policies. Thus, most agencies likely have or need to have policies or guidance with regard to their cybervetting strategies, including the use of the information in investigations. Even if the information can be viewed in such a way that it is legal to do so, it may not be ethical (Landers and Schmidt 2016). Consider a candidate who did not provide his/her explicit consent for the hiring agency to view and/or review their SNS profile or other online information; despite this, the employer searches for information on the candidate and, after browsing it, decides to not hire the applicant.

Nevertheless, as with every other component of evaluating an applicant, certain considerations are necessary. Such considerations include having policies that inform applicants, candidates, and incumbents that an Internet search for relevant information will be conducted and the information collected will or may be used to make decisions on whether a conditional offer of employment will be made. As an extension of this and in line with informed consent, there should also be a policy addressing the type of SNS information that will be offered to the psychologist for the purpose of consideration in PEPE (Rose et al. 2010).

Through a brief discussion with a representative from each of three large scale LE agencies in California and an open-ended telephonic and unpublished survey conducted by this author, it appears typical for the background investigation process to also entail informing the applicant that a search of social media would be completed; however, this involves only accessing the information that can be garnered from public and/or "open" sources. After the information that has been gathered is discussed with the candidate, the background investigators assess it in terms of how it compares with other data, as well as the essential functions of the peace officer; ultimately withholding or passing the candidate at the background level. Relaying the social media post or including the findings from the SNS into the background investigation summary appears to be a judgment call made by the agency. Hence, it is not consistently pursued. Anecdotally, the common practice seems to be that if the information is considered by the investigator to be insignificant as related to the individual's job skills or duties, the investigator will indicate there are no relevant findings. However, if the applicant's social media post is important (but not significant to the degree of finding him/her unsuitable at the background stage), and the investigator believes it may relate to the psychological dimensions set forth by POST, it will be integrated into the summary of the background investigation and will be offered to the psychologist performing the pre-employment psychological evaluation. In the event that it is not considered in the background investigation, the evaluator will not have access to the data and posts that were viewed.

Additionally, 20 licensed psychologists in California (recruited through the POST Psychological Evaluators listserv)who conduct pre-employment psychological and second opinion evaluations were surveyed by this author via sending them a list of semi-structured and Likert scale statements and questions, for example, if they ever received information from the hiring agency or background investigation as related to candidates' posts on SNS and if the response is affirmative, on the scale of 0 (not at all) to 3 (a lot of importance), how much weight was given to the SNS information in consideration of the candidate's suitability during the pre-employment or second opinion evaluation process. The replies offered (unpublished data), revealed that based on their experiences, there has been a notable increase in receiving background investigation summaries that have included information about candidates' social media posts. Generally, all the psychologists who had received the information, stated that they viewed it as another source of information which they addressed directly with the candidate and integrated in to the interview component of the evaluation, if they perceived it was relevant to the peace officer's essential functions and the POST psychological dimensions. Indeed, in the event that the

SNS contained information (written or visual) that was of an egregious nature (viz., in violation of operationally defined POST Guidelines, and/or had derogatory statements and racial slurs), there was convergence of other data points, and the information had relevance to the job for which the person was seeking, then the post was weighed heavily in consideration of suitability by those psychologists who responded to this survey.

Thus, it can be surmised that when implemented within the framework of the law, cybervetting has numerous advantages and the potential to yield a number of benefits to law enforcement in that it can: (1) validate or refute the information offered by the candidate on his/her resume or application, (2) identify those who may have engaged in criminal offenses or been involved with hate/criminal groups, and (3) detect inappropriate behaviors that may pose a danger to self and/or others, or may be unbecoming and reflect poorly on peace officers (Rose et al. 2010). Usually, plaintiff's attorneys, who can also conduct their own search online, have used the negative information uncovered about the individual during the PEPE to demonstrate that the LE agency had access to the information yet chose to hire the "unsuitable" candidate; consequently, evoking allegations of negligent hiring.

The use of information gained from SNS in pre-employment psychological evaluation process is presented in Case Study 1 at the end of this chapter.

7.2 Psychological Fitness-for-Duty Evaluations (FFDE)

As noted initially, other claims threatening an employer are that of negligent training and supervision, as well as negligent retention. Negligent training occurs when the employer's training of the employee fails to prevent the employee from engaging in the acts that injure the person and others or when the employer fails to remediate a pattern of behavior which can lead to an injury. Negligent supervision is related to negligent training in that it entails the employer's failure to reasonably monitor or control the actions of the employee.

On the other hand, negligent retention occurs when the employers retain an employee despite knowing that he/she is not qualified to perform his/her essential functions satisfactorily or safely. Negligent retention also includes failure to remove an employee from a position of authority or responsibility even after the employers have become aware that the employee may be misusing his/her authority or responsibility in a way that poses a danger to others. Again, the criticality of this matter for LE executives is increased exponentially. Nevertheless, keeping in mind that there are layers of protection such as Peace Officer Bill of Rights (POBOR), and the fact that the person cannot be terminated without due process give rise to other courses of action, as well.

As research delineates, numerous physical illnesses and psychological sequelae have been associated with exposure to traumatic events in the work conducted by LE and other emergency responders. These include, but are not limited to, poor sleep (Neylan et al. 2002), higher prevalence of alcohol abuse and dependence,

Post-Traumatic Stress Disorder (PTSD) (Patterson 2001), depression, and other mental health problems (Perrin et al. 2007; Stellman et al. 2008). Consequently, when a peace officer begins to exhibit behaviors and/or symptoms, either physically or psychologically, that interfere with his/her ability to conduct the required job functions, the responsibility to ensure public safety and that the officers are capable of performing their assigned duties falls on the LE agency and the executive management (Corey 2011; Corey and Borum 2013). Given the fact that per Occupational Safety and Health Act of 1970 (OSHA), the employer "... shall furnish to each of his employees, employment and a place of employment which are free from recognized hazards that are causing or are likely to cause death or serious physical harm to his employees [Section 5(a)(1)]," From this language, it is implied that the LE executives have the right to mandate a psychological Fitness-for-Duty evaluation (FFDE) to determine the overall fitness of their officers as a means of ensuring a safe working environment. In fact, FFDEs serve to offer an avenue for agencies to comply with OSHA as well as other regulations and laws, such as American with Disabilities Act (ADA) and Fair Employment and Housing Act (FEHA). For example, an FFDE may help LE agencies sort out whether an employee's behavior is the result of a disability for which accommodations can be made, thus reducing the risk of inadvertently violating an employee's rights by terminating them on the basis of incomplete or inaccurate information. Consequently, when a FFDE is mandated by the LE agency, the examination must be conducted by a qualified and licensed psychologist and should be in adherence with commonly accepted guidelines for the process.

As defined by the IACP, FFDEs are a specialized and formal evaluation of an incumbent employee that is predicated on objective evidence that the employee may be unable to safely or effectively perform their job functions and a reasonable basis that the cause could be ascribed to a psychological impairment or condition. A significant objective of the FFDE is not only to protect the community and the officer, but also to lessen the liability of a LE agency as it relates to the behavior of an officer who may be psychologically unfit to handle the essential duties of the position and to assist in defending against negligent hiring and retention claims.

When FFDEs are requested on a LE officer, they are done under the authority of a police chief or executive of a security agency by a specifically qualified mental health professional. A distinguishing factor between PEPE and FFDE is that not all incumbent officers are evaluated. A FFDE generally has a narrower focus and scope, and entails administration of relevant psychological measures, as well as conducting a semi-structured in-depth clinical interview with a person who usually has not requested and did not volunteer for the evaluation (Decker 2006). In fact, the employer must have a reason to believe that the employee presents with some difficulty (safety or business necessity) in relation to the workplace as a result of some emotional or mental disorder. Generally, FFDEs may be initiated after a verified report of events or a specific incident to the executive or chain of command that an officer is exhibiting signs and symptoms of poor judgment, mental impairment or illness in the workplace or off-duty. Hence, only after observed behavioral issues have been noted, addressed, and appropriate corrective actions have not led to remittance of the problematic conduct, a FFDE is performed (Fischler 2001). At that point, the focus of FFDE is to discern the likelihood that the person presents a mentally or emotionally based danger to the employer or other persons by active misconduct, or what the officer may do that is potentially damaging (also known as positive risk); or the inability to perform the job (what the officer may neglect to do such as dereliction of duty) also known as negative risk (Corey 2011; Corey and Borum 2013).

While violence or excessive force accounts for 29% of FFDEs (Allen, Hibner, & Miller 2000), other conduct such as domestic violence, substance abuse, lack of alertness, and a myriad of counterproductive behaviors may lead to a request for an FFDE. Threats to self or others, psychiatric hospitalizations, suicide attempt(s), along with observable behaviors such as excessive suspiciousness, extreme irritability and frequent crying that may point to experience of a psychological condition are amongst the "red flags." In fact, any conspicuous or insidious negative change in an officer's performance of their duties or demeanor frequently precedes a request for consultation or evaluation about workplace performance (Fischler et al. 2011). A pattern of excessive use of absence, sexual inappropriateness, insubordination, interpersonal conflicts with co-workers or supervisors, high rate of mistakes, tactical errors, and information (written or visual content) posted on SNS may not automatically denote that the officer has a psychological problem, but it may offer "probable cause" for further investigation.

The employer must weigh the significance of public safety with the civil and constitutional rights of their officers before mandating a FFDE (Mayer and Corey 2016). In fact, many courts have upheld this position (*Maplewood and Law Enf. Labor Services* 1996; *McGreal v. Ostrov* 2004; *Merillat v. Mich. St. Univ.* 1994; *Watts v. Alfred* 1992). Each agency must determine a *threshold* that balances public safety, the rights of the employee, while adhering to existing employment laws, which are comprised of:

The EEOC, as aforementioned, dictates that when an individual commences employment and is on the job, the employee's ability to perform the functions can be measured by his/her actual performance on the job. Courts have held that punitive or retaliatory demands for psychological evaluation of an incumbent employee, predicated just on the will and not the reason of the public employer is an unlawful imposition (*Hill v. City of Winona* 1990). However, the courts have also granted wide authority to employers so they can mandate medical and/or psychological evaluation of their employees, specifically those engaged in safety-sensitive work, when the goal is to reduce the risk of injury to the employee or others.

Furthermore, ADA and its 2008 Amendments, 42 U.S.C. §§12012; 12101 et seq., is the Federal statute that has the furthermost authority over an employer's ability to require a medical evaluation of an employee. According to Title I of the ADA, an employer may "require a medical examination and/or inquire about the medical information of a current employee as long as the examination or inquiry is shown to be job related and consistent with business necessity…. Or that an individual (applicant or employee) not pose a direct threat to the health or safety of other individuals in the workplace." In other words, the "business necessity" standard requires existence of objective evidence of impaired performance, a reasonable basis for believing it may be due to a psychological condition; and a reasonable basis for believing that a condition may prevent the employee from *safely* and effectively performing the essential functions of their position. This is where the concept of direct threat is implied and would be illustrated in presentation of the second case profile. To reiterate, the EEOC's position is that the ADA's business necessity standard does not permit medical testing of an incumbent employee unless and until the employer has an individualized, reasonable suspicion of impairment or direct threat due to a medical condition.

Moreover, under the Family Medical Leave Act (FMLA), 29 C.F.R. Part 825, the employers are permitted to have a policy or practice that requires employees in similar job positions who take leave for similar health conditions (meaning the same occupation and same serious health condition) to provide a return to work certification from the employee's physician. At that point, the certification regarding the employee's "fitness" submitted by the treatment provider should be considered sufficient and an FFDE cannot be requested. Most courts have interpreted the FMLA as prohibiting an employer from forcing an employee returning from this type of leave to submit to an independent evaluation of his/her fitness for duty once the individual's own treatment provider has certified that they are ready to return to work although pre-leave or post-return behaviors may justify an FFDE. When an employer is able to establish that it would have ordered an FFDE had the employee not taken a leave, the courts have generally held such an examination to be permissible once the employee has been reinstated (*White v. County of Los Angeles,*2014). The second case profile at the end of this chapter will demonstrate the interplay of this regulation.

It is important to note that, as delineated by IACP, Police Psychological Services (2013) in the guidelines for FFDEs, the LE agency must provide the evaluator with all the collected information which are clearly related to job performance issues and/or suspected job impairing mental condition. These include but are not limited to:

1. A written description of the objective evidence giving rise to concerns about the employee's fitness for duty and any particular questions that the employer wishes the examiner to address.
2. Background and collateral information regarding the employee's past and recent performance, conduct and functioning, including:

    a. Job class specifications and/or job description
    b. Performance evaluations
    c. Previous remediation efforts
    d. Commendations and testimonials
    e. Internal affairs investigations
    f. Formal citizen/public complaints
    g. Use of force incidents
    h. Reports related to officer involved shootings
    i. Civil claims

j. Disciplinary actions
k. Incident reports related to any triggering events
l. Medical records and certifications that the Department may have, and
m. Prior psychological evaluation results, if any.

Therefore, information gained from the sources such as postings of the employee on SNS which may have raised concerns or strengthened the justification for requesting an FFDE is considered to be important data that should be offered to the evaluator.

As noted previously, social media provides a window into the life of the individual, including not only personal but also professional life when the person chooses to share those aspects with others on the social networking sites. With respect to peace officers, their posts on SNS often presents complex problems that challenges their constitutionally protected rights (i.e., freedom of speech and association and the necessitated limitations on certain expressions of those rights). The accessibility of SNS also serves as an opportunity for attorneys to use the content of the post, not only to impeach an officer's testimony but also be more successful in their claims of negligent retention of the peace officer. For example, a New York police officer's testimony was impeached when a defense attorney offered the officer's off-duty postings into evidence during the criminal trial of a suspect who was arrested by the officer. This influenced not only the outcome of the criminal trial, but it had an impact on pending criminal cases involving the same officer. It further diminished the value of that peace officer to the LE agency, since the individual could no longer testify credibly in court as part of the job (Rose et al. 2010). Nevertheless, it is significant to note that in our existing litigious milieu, it is not very difficult to envision an employee claiming a violation of the First Amendment, if their posts lead to an adverse action by the agency (including through the result of a FFDE), even though as elucidated by the two court cases outlined below, this argument has failed to be successful for public employees (Mikkelson 2010).

In *Curran v. Cousins* (2007), a corrections officer was fired by the LE agency for posting messages on the union's public discussion web board comparing the administrators to Nazis and urging other departmental employees to act in an insubordinate manner. Although the court held that a government entity, as an employer, has wider discretions to restrict speech, those restrictions must be directed at speech that has some potential to influence operations. In this instance, the court held that the posting was of public concern because Curran accused a public official of basing personnel actions on a political affiliation, and the posts encouraged defiance, which could jeopardize government operations. Given the status as a LE agency, the court held that Curran's First Amendment assertion was outweighed by the increased need for "harmony and order."

In *City of San Diego v. Roe* (2004), John Roe, who was a San Diego police officer, produced sexualized videos of himself while stripping off a police uniform and sold the videos on eBay. Upon discovering this information, the city terminated him. Mr. Roe proceeded to sue the city in federal district court and asserted that his termination was in violation of his First Amendment right. The Supreme Court ruled that Roe's termination was not in violation of the First Amendment, stating: "Government employers can limit their employees' speech in way that would ordinarily be unconstitutional. However, government employees are protected by the First Amendment when their speech pertains to matters of public concern." The court delineated that Roe's actions and speech were not in the pursuit of promoting more knowledge and information about government policies of interest to the public and did not "inform" the public about the policies and practices of the police department. Additionally, his behaviors were ascertained to be "detrimental to the police department," in that it brought disrespect to the "uniform" and led to reduction of the credibility of the peace officer and thereby the LE agency. Thus, the existence of these types of cases elucidate the utmost importance for the employer to inform its employees of the intention to monitor their online activities.

Furthermore, the National Labor Relations Act (NLRA) describes five unfair labor practices under which an employer can be held liable. Specifically, Section 8(a)(3) of the act prohibits discrimination as related to hiring, tenure of employment, or any term of conditions of employment for the purpose of encouraging or discouraging labor organization membership (Mikkelson 2010). According to NLRB, an employee's use of social media to share concerns about important terms and conditions of employment are concerted and considered to be protected activities (O'Shea 2012). For example, in *Konop v. Hawaiian Airlines,* a pilot maintained a personal and restricted website and expressed his critical views of his employer and labor concessions that he had sought from his union. The employer had allegedly accessed the website by utilizing other employee's login information and had placed the pilot on "medical suspension." The pilot claimed that this was in retaliation of his union activity. In this case, the court held that the development and maintenance of the website was considered a protected activity.

As it relates to the SNS posts and performance of FFDEs, in a brief survey performed by this author via sending a list of semi-structured and Likert scale statements and questions (unpublished data), to psychologists who conduct this type of assessment in California, respondents indicated an increase, over the previous years, whereby the LE agency has offered posts on SNS as contributing data for requesting a psychological FFDE. Survey responders unanimously stated that after they verify the manner in which the employer had obtained the information (i.e., through permissible and legal access which, for example, included instances in which the FFDE evaluee posted on their Facebook page and another employee brought the concerning post to the attention of his/her chain of command), they would consider and address it with the peace officer who is the subject of the FFDE. The psychologists also indicated that the SNS posts are taken into consideration and impact their decision making about the officer's fitness, especially when SNS information was aligned with other data and converged with personnel records, documentation of conduct and discipline, results of the administered psychological measures, the findings from the clinical interview and the review of the treatment records. An illustration of the decision-making process in an FFDE whereby SNS posts had been offered is presented in Case Profile #2.

7.3 Best Practices Related to Integration of SNS Data in PEPE and FFDE

For the psychologists who conduct pre-employment psychological evaluations, it is of critical significance to be intimately familiar with the agency's cybervetting policy and be offered a copy of the consent which was obtained by the LE agency. Furthermore, they should know whether the cybervetting occurred on all candidates or whether there was information which led to conducting a search of SNS on an individual they are evaluating. The material gained through SNS should be taken into consideration when making the suitability recommendation to the agency depending on the nature of the posts, its perceived relevance to the essential functions and its convergence and/or divergence with other important data that is considered as related to the POST psychological dimensions.

In the event that the psychologist is considering finding the candidate unsuitable for the job, largely due to the information gathered through SNS and its convergence with other data points, such as test findings and responses to the interview, it may be significant to discuss the matter with the LE agency to better understand and help improve the initial decision-making process utilized by the LE agency that failed to identify the individual as unsuitable prior to extending the conditional offer of employment.

Furthermore, it is well accepted and agreed upon that LE personnel should not post or disseminate any type of material which may discredit or reduce the reputation, integrity or efficiency of the LE agency by which they are employed. For example, depictions of themselves in uniform, showing their patches or badges or other logos that may identify the agency cannot occur without the LE executive's approval. For example, posts:

- Showing images or details of restricted areas within the facility or within its grounds;
- About details concerning official and sensitive activities and their locations;
- Related to materials or images obtained during the course of the officer's employment which may reflect proprietary or sensitive technologies used by their employing agency; and
- Comments about the conduct of chain of command, peers, or on the operations of agency that may negatively impact the public perception are not permitted and have been found by the courts to proceed beyond the First Amendment rights of the peace officer. Therefore, the individual can be held accountable for displaying them.

Consequently, in the event that the posts on SNS, in conjunction, with other actions of the peace officer have not resulted in their discharge, and the agency is proceeding with a psychological FFDE; then the psychologist should request to be provided with not only the information about the performance, but also data about the criminal or administrative investigations including photographs, videos or recordings, personal statements concerning use of force incident; or about current or pending prosecutions that have been posted without the prior LE executive's approval. At that point, the information that is offered should be taken into consideration when it falls within the scope of the FFDE and is relevant to the POST psychological dimensions and the ability of the officer to safely and reliably perform their duties. More general recommendations for accessing and integrating SNS and Internet-derived data are discussed in Chap. 9 of this book.

Case Profile 1

Type of Evaluation

Pre-employment Psychological Evaluation (PEPE) of Peace Officer candidate.

Case Context

The candidate in this case is 44-year-old Christopher Powers, who was evaluated for approximately 4 h as part of the pre-employment psychological evaluation for a peace officer position with a local LE agency.

Sources of Information

1. A clinical interview with Mr. Powers.
2. Administration of the following psychological measures:
   a. Minnesota Multiphasic Inventory- 2 Restructured Form (MMPI-2RF)
   b. California Psychological Inventory (CPI)
   c. Psychological History Questionnaire (PHQ)
3. Background Investigation Jacket including polygraph findings and summary of SNS posts

Relevant Background

Mr. Powers is a 44-year-old male who was born in Kansas City, Kansas and was raised in California. He stated that his parents were divorced when he was in the sixth grade and his father was continuously absent from his life after their separation. To this date he has no relationship with his father who was reportedly married and divorced more than five times. His mother is currently married to her third husband. Mr. Powers has one biological brother and sister and he estimated about five half siblings. He stated that his second step-father physically abused him; however, he denied any sexual abuse while growing up.

Mr. Powers graduated high school with a 2.0 grade point average. He reported being suspended for 3 days from high school for fighting. He denied receiving any special education, being diagnosed with any learning disabilities or Attention Deficit Disorder. The candidate obtained two bachelor's Degrees in Business Administration and Occupational Education. He also earned a Paralegal Certificate.

Moreover, Mr. Powers served in the U.S. Air Force from 1993–2000 and was part of security forces (military police). He joined the Air National Guard in 2001 and served full time for one and a half years followed by the same duration of time on a part-time basis. He re-enlisted in the U.S. Air Force Reserves in 2004 and remained an active reservist with the rank of Master Sergeant (E-7). Review of the documents related to his military service (as part of the background investigation jacket) resulted in the following findings:

1. He received a letter of reprimand for driving under the influence of alcohol on the Base.
2. He had an unacceptable rating on the Off/On duty conduct category. Comments noted outstanding traffic warrants, Driving Under the Influence (DUI) and letter of reprimand and an "unfavorable information."
3. An investigation had ensued after it was reported that Mr. Powers had been making false statements and filed false claim, indicating that he was providing financial support to his wife and child, in order to receive basic allowance in excess of his entitlement. He blamed filling out the documents incorrectly on what his superiors had told him. Although he had been ordered to repay the government, he did not take any actions to do so.
4. He was accused of excessive force; however, he stated he was exonerated.
5. His security clearance was revoked when he failed to respond to a financial inquiry from the military.

Apparently, after separation from the military, Mr. Powers started working as a security officer with a private company; however, soon afterwards, his employment was terminated due to a "safety violation." Mr. Powers is currently married to his third wife. He stated there was "domestic violence" with his first wife after they had an argument over infidelity and her use of illegal substances. Reportedly, since he was with military police at the time, he decided to detain her and as he was physically restraining her, she slapped him. He also admitted that when he was going over the divorce papers, his second wife "bit" him. Mr. Powers denied any instances of domestic violence in his relationship with his third wife; nevertheless, he admitted that a few years ago when he and his wife were arguing, his step-son became involved and swore at him. Mr. Powers had in turn slapped him. Although the police were called, no charges were filed. Mr. Powers has a 23-year-old child from his first marriage and two younger children ages 13 and 8, as well as a 22-year-old step-son.

Mr. Powers stated he was mandated to receive counseling after his DUI; however, he has not received any other type of mental health services, has never been psychiatrically hospitalized, and has never been prescribed any psychotropic medication.

Mr. Powers stated that he drinks socially and has never abused alcohol. After further exploration, he stated that he drinks alcohol about three times a week and has 1 or 2 beers each time. He stated that other than the DUI which he received years ago, there are no other instances when he has driven with a buzz or under the influence. He denied ever missing work due to a hangover or needing a drink in the morning to get going. He admitted he has used marijuana only once in the sixth grade. He denied use of any other illicit drugs or abuse of prescribed pain medication.

Mr. Powers stated that several of his accounts were turned over to collection when he was going through his second divorce because he had changed his address and had not received the statements. He denied any history of bankruptcy or foreclosures. He admitted to receiving citations for two moving violations which were "red light camera" tickets that occurred at the same intersection on both occasions. He has not been involved in any traffic accidents in the past five years. He admitted to driving without insurance on couple of instances and has also driven with a suspended license when he "didn't know" about the suspension.

Behavioral Observations and Mental Status

Mr. Powers arrived on time and was professionally dressed. He was well groomed and appeared his stated chronological age. He was cooperative, alert, and maintained appropriate eye contact throughout the interview process. Rapport was easily established. He was oriented in all spheres. There were no sensory, perceptual, or psychomotor abnormalities noted. His thought process was linear, and goal directed. There was no indication of distorted, delusional, or bizarre ideations. Speech was clear and of normal prosody, volume and tone.

Mr. Powers' mood was euthymic with congruent affect. He denied any symptoms of mania, anxiety and depression at the time of the evaluation. He did not report any difficulties with appetite, and fluctuating energy level. He stated he had slept well the night before and generally does not experience any symptoms of insomnia or intermittent awakening.

Mr. Powers exhibited adequate fund of general knowledge. His concentration, short- and long-term memory appeared intact. There were no discernible difficulties with abstractions and reasoning abilities. Nevertheless, his impulse control and judgment based on history seemed moderately impaired and/or questionable. The candidate's overall attitude towards the examiner emerged as acceptable for a valid interview process.

Summary of Test Results

The Minnesota Multiphasic Personality Inventory – 2- Restructured Form (MMPI-2RF) contains 338 true-false items. Specifically, MMPI-2-RF Police candidate interpretive report (PCIR) which is utilized by many psychologists who conduct pre-employment psychological and fitness-for-duty evaluations, has updated comparison group based on 2074 subjects from agencies throughout North America. PCIR features evidence-based information and all correlate-based interpretations are grounded on findings from peer reviewed research. This measure is more relevant and transparent, whereby the source of every interpretive statement in the report is identified, and all interpretive statements pertain to behaviors and performance domains that are meaningful in police work.

Mr. Powers' MMPI-2-RF profile was demonstrative of defensiveness, nevertheless interpretable. The Validity T-scores were L-r (Uncommon Virtues, T = 66) and K-r (Adjustment Validity, T = 62). His score on RC3 (Cynicism, T = 65) and AGG-r (Aggressiveness-Revised, T = 65) suggested that he is cynical and tends to use instrumental aggression as a primary method of interpersonal influence. Additionally, utilizing law enforcement norms, he obtained elevated scores on RC1 (Somatic Complaints, T = 56;98th percentile), NFC (Inefficacy, T = 48; 91st percentile), and FML (Family Problems, T = 53;96th percentile), indicating a greater sense of inefficacy, family issues, and somatic problems. Mr. Powers' T-score on Substance Abuse was elevated (SUB, T = 58) as well, raising more concern about substance abuse proclivities.

The California Psychological Inventory (CPI) contains 434 items which can be scored to yield 18 scales. The 18 scales are further grouped into four classes: (1) measures of poise, ascendancy, self-assurance, and interpersonal adequacy; (2) measures of socialization, responsibility, intrapersonal values, and character; (3) measures of achievement potential and intellectual efficiency; and (4) measures of intellectual modes and interest. The CPI Police and Public Safety Selection Report aids psychologists, who are involved in the examination of police and other public safety applicants and employees, to discern the psychological suitability and emotional stability of the candidates. This test is known to be effective in identifying the traits that may interfere with or enhance an applicant's effective performance of specific job functions.

Reviewing the CPI results, Mr. Powers' profile was considered to be interpretable even though, similar to MMPI-2-RF, he had a defensive response style. His Good Impression Scale, (Gi) was T = 59 based upon Incumbent norms. Based on these norms, his profile showed low scale scores on Empathy (T = 49). There were also indications of high risk for anger management problems and medium risk for substance abuse proclivity, integrity and job performance problems.

Diagnostic Conclusions

No specific diagnoses were made as part of this evaluation.

Summary of Data Relevant to PEPE

The background jacket information contained the following information: (1) pictures and excerpts of posts which showed Mr. Powers. in inappropriate poses with drinks in his hand taken at different times on multiple dates; one also depicted him rolling a joint; (2) multiple pictures of guns and rifles with magazines as well as knives and assault rifles; and (3) specific polygraph results to explore aggressive incidents and substance use after two polygraphs were inconclusive. The LE agency indicated that once exploration was conducted on the picture of rolling a joint, Mr. Powers said it was a joke and he was trying to be funny, because he did not know how to roll one. As related to inappropriate poses with drinks, he had cited that these were taken at special occasions. The background jacket did not contain information addressing the picture(s) that contained multiple weapons. The LE agency raised concern about impulsivity and substance abuse, as it relates to the essential functions of a peace officer and POST psychological dimensions.

Mr. Powers' Account as Related to the SNS Posts As the content of the posts and the pictures were explored during the clinical interview, Mr. Powers was consistent in his responses, and identical to his conveyance to the background investigator, he said he was "goofing off." When the fact that he had been disciplined in the military for a DUI was brought up, he shrugged and stated he did not have much to add other than he was joking and having a good time with his friends. He vehemently denied that he had used marijuana at the time the photo was taken and stated that he had rolled it as a dare by one of his friends. His explanation about multiple pictures of rifles and weapons was given in a matter of fact manner and he stated that his career has been in the military and he likes to show his "knowledge" and mastery. He denied existence of any obsessions and stated that, as related to weapons, he keeps up in his "trade."

Suitability Opinion and Recommendation

After all the components of findings were given appropriate weight, it was concluded that there were concerns about Mr. Powers in relation to the following CA POST psychological dimensions:

- **Emotional Regulation/Stress Tolerance**: ability to maintain even-tempered composure and demeanor in highly charged emotional events and other stressful situations. This also includes being able to accept criticism of one's personal limitations and mistakes, and not become excessively defensive when challenged or criticized.

- **Decision Making/Judgment**: being able to make sound decisions and size up situations quickly to determine what to do and take appropriate action. This includes having common sense and using practical judgment while also prioritizing competing demands.
- **Impulse Control/Attention to Safety:** taking proper precautions and avoiding impulsive or unnecessarily risky behavior to ensure the safety of oneself and others. It entails keeping one's "knee-jerk reactions" in check and instead behaving in conscious respect for the bigger situation at hand.

Thus, Mr. Powers did not meet the minimum standards for psychological qualification as a peace officer due to not being able to fulfill the aforementioned POST psychological dimensions.

How Did Social Media Impact This Case?

Social media posts by Mr. Powers were presented in the Summary section of the Background Investigation jacket. Even though the nature of the posts had not led to Mr. Powers' disqualification at the Background stage, it nevertheless had been forwarded to the psychologist for further exploration based on its relevance to the essential functions of a peace officer, as well as POST psychological dimensions. The candidate's SNS posts converged with some of the critical findings from results of the administered psychological measures and his background history. Founded on the coalescence of all the gathered information, it was opined that they were not in accordance with the above-mentioned psychological dimensions of POST and the psychologist could not certify that Mr. Powers was a suitable candidate.

Case Profile 2

Type of Evaluation

Psychological Fitness-For-Duty Evaluation of a Peace Officer.

Case Context

Harvey Reeves is a 42-year-old peace officer who was evaluated for approximately 6 h in response to the LE agency's request to determine whether he can safely perform the essential functions of a peace officer after he had exhibited unusual and inappropriate behaviors.

In April 2016, the Agency requested a consultation from this examiner by offering all personnel records, investigations as related to claims of discrimination that Mr. Reeves had alleged against the agency, his performance evaluations, medical certifications, and most notably the videos and information he had posted on different SNS. Based on a letter from Mr. Reeves' primary care provider alleging that additional time off following a work-related injury was required due to safety issues, the fact that Mr. Reeves was in a safety sensitive position, and that behaviors he was exhibiting off-duty called into question his ability to demonstrate adequate impulse control, judgment, emotional regulation and stress tolerance, and social competence, the agency was advised to seek a psychological FFDE prior to returning the employee to work.

In May of 2016, upon being released to full duty, the agency assigned Mr. Reeves to work from home and placed him on administrative leave with pay after holding an interactive process meeting (IPM) with him and requesting that he voluntarily submit to a FFDE. This decision was made due to the fact that a clearance by his physician only addressed the physical injuries and not the safety issues that had subsequently been raised. Initially, Mr. Reeves stated he would discuss the evaluation with his legal representative and would inform the agency at a later time whether he was willing to comply. However, despite the LE agency's efforts for a few months, Mr. Reeves did not consent to the evaluation.

While the LE agency was trying to pursue requesting an ordered FFDE, Mr. Reeves was placed off work by his psychiatrist, from December 2016 through March 2017, for treatment of issues related to alleged "harassment, discrimination, and retaliation." After his release date in March 2017, the LE agency continued its IPM with the employee and made an effort to again secure his consent for a FFDE. Nonetheless, despite numerous meetings and correspondence with Mr. Reeves and his representative, Mr. Reeves maintained that he has been released to work by his treatment providers and there is no need for another examination to occur. The agency took the position that because Mr. Reeves' psychiatrist had not directly addressed the safety issues involved and it was unclear whether this treatment provider had been aware of the off-duty conduct to include the videos and posts on the SNS and may not have offered an "informed clearance." the officer was compelled to attend and cooperate with the FFDE to discern whether he can safely perform his peace officer duties.

Sources of Information

1. Documents and collateral information from the LE agency regarding the employee's past and recent performance, conduct and functioning, including:

   a. Job description
   b. Performance evaluations for the past three years
   c. Commendations and testimonials

   d. Incident reports related to any triggering events
   e. Medical records and certifications, and
   f. SNS posts and videos on Youtube

2. A Clinical Interview with Mr. Reeves
3. Administration of the Following Psychological Measures: Millon Clinical Multiaxial Inventory-Third Edition (MCMI-III), and Personality Assessment Inventory (PAI), MMPI-2-RF, as well as PHQ
4. Mr. Reeves' pertinent treatment records

Relevant Background

Mr. Reeves was born and raised in Pomona, California to the intact union of his parents; he is the third out of four children with two older brothers and one younger sister. He stated he would work at his father's business after school and during summer and since his older brothers had moved away. Reportedly, his father was hoping that one day Mr. Reeves would take over running the business. However, Mr. Reeves had always wanted to be a peace officer and was excited when he was placed on the list, and successfully passed all stages of the process and became an officer in 1997. He stated that he was able to move into his apartment soon afterwards and was married to his high school sweetheart a year later. Their daughter was born about a year after the marriage and, at that time, they moved to a house they bought. He stated they began to have marital difficulties when their daughter started kindergarten and his wife appeared "jealous" of his interactions and perceived relationships with female officers. They were separated and divorced a year and a half later. His ex-wife and daughter moved to another state to live closer to his ex-wife's siblings.

Mr. Reeves married his second wife a couple of years after the divorce. She is a homemaker and they have two children, a 12-year-old daughter and a 10-year-old son. Mr. Reeves stated that a few years in to his second marriage, he started a business with one of his friends in swimming pools; however, after an injury, his friend left the business and Mr. Reeves was spending his time off trying to maintain the business. Following a few complaints to the Better Business Bureau and negative information posted on Yelp (an online business directory and crowd-sourced review forum) about his business, Mr. Reeves reported that "everything went downhill." Apparently, the decline of the housing market resulting in most homeowners not being able to invest in installing pools also contributed to lack of income in his personal business. Therefore, Mr. Reeves filed for bankruptcy.

Concurrently, Mr. Reeves was injured on duty and had been considered temporary totally disabled (TTD). He stated that a few months later, one of his close friends who was diagnosed with cancer, died by suicide by "eating his gun." Mr. Reeves was devastated and was trying to help his friend's widow with the arrangements and fund the funeral. At this time, he stated that he started feeling very alone and thought the LE agency he had "dedicated" his life to was not offering any assistance to him during his recovery. He stated that he would have disturbed sleep and no energy. He gained about 50 extra pounds and started drinking. Additionally, he was taking more pain medication to deal with the physical pain from the injury.

Behavioral Observations and Mental Status

Mr. Reeves arrived on time for the ordered psychological FFDE in June 2017. He was attired in long shorts and a plaid, short sleeved shirt that was not tucked in. He had his hair in a ponytail and had a long and bushy beard. He was wearing dark glasses and was resistant to taking them off due to his "light sensitivity." As he was working on the psychological measures, Mr. Reeves took the glasses off. Mr. Reeves was carrying a brief case and as soon as he sat down, he took out his tablet, some documents, and put his cell phone on the table with the recorder on. Then he sat back and crossed his arms. The fact that he had cell phone recorder application on was explored and he was informed that he is unable to record the evaluation. He replied that his attorney wanted him to do that. The reasons that the recording cannot occur was explained to him. He was presented with the consent form as well as authorization forms pertaining to the release of pertinent treatment records. Mr. Reeves leaned forward, read the documents, and stated that this was not explained to him by the LE agency and he still needed to discuss the recording of the evaluation with his attorney. The process for the FFDE, including the reasons for not allowing the recording and the need to obtain treatment records were discussed. He was informed that it was his option if he did not want to proceed with the evaluation, until such time that he had discussed the matters with his attorney. He stepped outside to make a call and returned within a few minutes stating that the attorney was unavailable, and he wanted to proceed. At that time, he reviewed the informed consent form and signed it. He understood the nature of the evaluation and understood the limits of confidentiality, and the fact that this evaluator is not his treating psychologist but is conducting a fitness for duty evaluation of him. Mr. Reeves was reminded that his cell phone should be turned off, he grinned and stated "so, you know, I recorded my conversation with the Chief without his knowledge. You know I did it because I knew they were coming after me and were planning to get me." Then he asked, "When was the last time that you checked this place for bugs?" Upon seeing the look of confusion on the evaluator's face, he stated that he was not sure that his agency or the evaluator were not recording the conversation. This evaluator assured Mr. Reeves that the evaluation was not being recorded and took this opportunity to discuss the process and procedure again.

At various times during the evaluation, Mr. Reeves seemed to be short of breath requiring pauses in his responses. He explained that his health has been compromised by the distress that he has experienced, and his only wish is to return to work at this time. Towards the middle of the evaluation, he appeared fatigued and his physical movements were slow. He said that he has been depressed, and "this whole situation has taken a toll on my health and my family."

Mr. Reeves stated he has gained a lot of weight (approximately 50 pounds) due to a "metabolic syndrome." He complained of having problems falling asleep and intermittent awakening as a result of nightmares he has in which "a couple of the guys that I used to work with are holding my head down and knocking my teeth out, then they are putting chemicals in my mouth." He added, "It is totally scary."

He stated that his workers' compensation case had been resolved since last February and it had been more than 6 months since he was released to full duty. Mr. Reeves explained that the LE agency played games with him and ordered him to be absent from work, which he reported only happened to 10 people in the entire law enforcement agency and that is a "top secret thing." He said he gets full pay but is restricted to his home by his employer from 8 AM to 5 PM with an hour for lunch. He said he feels like an inmate, given his home restriction, and that this is currently chiefly bothering him and making him very sad. Mr. Reeves cried at this time during the interview and stated that "instead of treating me like a hero because I came forward with a whole bunch of stuff and called out the corruption and am a whistle-blower, they're treating me like a villain." He stated that he has since received a letter of reprimand for the information and videos that he had posted on different SNS.

Mr. Reeves denied experiencing any memory problems or issues with focus and concentration. He believed that he is a "pretty good self-evaluator." He stated that as soon as he is returned to duty, he wants to be involved as a "mentor to others and give them a voice."

Mr. Reeves stated that he has thought about killing himself in the past although he denied any present suicidal ideation in the past several months. He denied any psychiatric hospitalization; he further disclosed that he has not entertained any past or current homicidal ideations, intent or plan.

Summary of Test Results

Mr. Reeves's results on the MMPI-2-RF were deemed to be valid and interpretable. The MMPI-2-RF validity scales T-scores were L-r = 52 & K-r = 72 indicating underreporting and Mr. Reeves' response style was to present himself as remarkably well-adjusted. No significant elevations were noted on the substantive scales. On the Item Level Information under Unscorable Responses Mr. Reeves left the statement *Someone is trying to rob me* blank. When reviewed, Mr. Reeves reported he did not realize he had skipped that statement and clarified he did not believe anyone is trying to rob him. On the Restructured Clinical Scales, Mr. Reeves' score on RCd (Demoralization, T = 68) and RC6 (Ideas of Persecution, T = 79) were elevated. The high score on RCd indicated he feels discouraged and generally distressed. He may be insecure and pessimistic and may have poor self-esteem. He may expect to fail or may believe he has failed in various areas of his life. Additionally, higher T-scores on RC6 are suggestive of the individual being characterized by paranoid thinking and reflect symptoms of delusional disorder or other disorders within the psychotic spectrum.

On the Internalizing Scales, Mr. Reeves' high score of T = 70 on the Anxiety (AXY) scale signified that he reports life as a strain on him much of the time and he is consistently feeling anxiety or distress about something or someone almost all the time. He worries quite a bit about possible misfortune, and he finds it difficult to keep his mind focused on tasks.

On the Somatic/Cognitive Scales, Mr. Reeves' high score on GIC (Gastrointestinal Complaints, T = 70) confirmed his complaints about his gastrointestinal symptoms that he had voiced during the interview. He is likely to be pre-occupied and report recurrences of stomach aches and related ailments.

The Millon Clinical Multiaxial Inventory – Third Edition (MCMI-III) is a 175 question, true/false psychological instrument utilized in clinical settings with individuals 18 years and older. This test's normative population is comprised of patients seen in individual practices, forensic settings, hospitals, mental health centers, and residential facilities. The MCMI-III uses "Base Rate" (BR) for scores for the purpose of interpretation and reporting. A BR score of 60 is representative of a median score which is similar to 50 T. The presence of a specific personality trait is generally reflected at BR75; whereas a BR85 and above suggests the full presence of a personality characteristic. The MCMI-III has 28 scales including 14 Personality Disorder Scales, 10 Clinical Syndrome Scales, 4 Response style/validity Scales.

As related to Mr. Reeves, on the MCMI-III, two Validity Scales (V = 0 and W = 0) met criteria for a valid and consistent protocol. The Modifying Indexes showed the following scores: Disclosure (BR = 47); Desirability (BR = 85); and Debasement (BR = 63). Mr. Reeves' responses suggested an effort to present a socially acceptable appearance with resistance to admitting personal shortcomings. Taken together, these scores may reflect either a broad-based concern about being appraised unfavorably by others or an active suspicion of the arcane motives of psychological inquiry.

The Clinical Syndromes and Severe Clinical Syndromes revealed two elevations on Anxiety (BR = 77) and Major Depression (BR = 89). These findings signaled that Mr. Reeves has many feelings associated with worthlessness, fatigue, inefficiency, and inability to concentrate. He may be withdrawn and is not inclined to exhibit emotions. Furthermore, Mr. Reeves had endorsed a number of items which indicated that he feels tense, agitated, suffers from chest palpitations, muscular pain, and may feel jumpy, weak and fatigued.

Although the Severe Personality Pathology section did not show any elevations that would have met the minimum criteria of the MCMI-III, the Clinical Personality Patterns of this test revealed three elevations on the Histrionic (BR = 67), Compulsive (BR = 90) and Narcissistic (BR = 67) scales. The Clinical Personality Patterns profile indicated Mr. Reeves tends to be somewhat overly dramatic with a strong need to be the center of attention. His profile also suggested that he may be behaviorally rigid, constricted, meticulous, polite, conscientious, over conforming, organized, and respectful. He may often be perfectionistic, moralistic, efficient and inflexible. Per the test publisher, these types of individuals are known to suppress the resentment and anger towards those whose approval they seek (usually authority figures). These individuals also tend to have a strong sense of duty and they strive to avoid criticism. They rely on achievement and accomplishment of personal goals to feel worthwhile, and expect others to consistently recognize, praise, and admire them for their special qualities. They feel excessively entitled and demand special favors simply on the basis of who they are. When they experience a narcissistic injury, they are prone to develop an affective disorder or even paranoia.

In addition, the Personality Assessment Inventory (PAI) was administered. PAI is an objective test of personality and a multiscale inventory that contains 344 items which comprise 22 non-overlapping scales: 4 validity scales, 11 clinical scales, 5 treatment scales, and 2 interpersonal scales. Like the MMPI-2-RF, PAI scales are expressed in T-scores that are based on sampling a reference group was mean score is 50 and standard deviation is 10. Mr. Reeves' validity scales where as follows: ICN (Inconsistency) T = 67, INF (Infrequency) and NIM (Negative Impression) were both T = 44, and PIM (Positive Impression) T = 54. Despite the elevation encountered on the Inconsistency scale, which suggested Mr. Reeves' may have not been forthright and may have tended to make himself appear to be free from any short comings, the protocol was within the normal range. The highest elevation of the Full-scale Profile was noted on the PAR or Paranoia scale which was at T = 72. Discerning the Paranoia scale is a difficult task because individuals who experience mistrust and suspiciousness are often very defensive and unwilling to disclose information that would describe them as paranoid. The paranoia scale measures vigilance in monitoring the environment for potential harm, and those who score higher on this scale tend to be resentful and hold grudges. Additionally, they may tend to feel that they are being treated unequally and others are involved in a concerted effort to undermine them. A review of the subscale profile also revealed a significant elevation on the Persecution dimension which was also T = 72. Individuals who score in this range believe others are attempting to obstruct or impede their efforts. Of the three subscales of the PAR scale, the persecution is most closely associated with manifestations of delusional disorder involving paranoia. Moreover, individuals who score in this range have working and social relationships that are likely to be very strained; despite many efforts made by others to demonstrate support and assistance.

Diagnostic Conclusions

No specific diagnoses were made as part of this evaluation.

Summary of Data Relevant to FFDE

Documents received from the LE agency indicated that prior to the denoted incidents, Mr. Reeves had minimal disciplinary and interpersonal problems. However, on or about March 2016, this employee began exhibiting behaviors that were of concern to the agency. Reportedly, while on medical leave due to an injury, Mr. Reeves. had presented himself at a commanding officer's work location unannounced, wearing sunglasses and a bandana. This manner of attire had been very different from his previous off-duty appearances, based on the information from those who had worked with him. Without waiting to be granted permission, he entered the office and ignored that the executive was involved in a private phone conversation; Mr. Reeves had closed the door behind him and had sat in front of the executive with crossed arms. After the executive concluded the phone conversation, Mr. Reeves started "ranting" and, per the commanding officer, he "was not making any sense." The executive considered these actions as "inappropriate and unusual behavior" by a subordinate and someone much lower in rank. Shortly thereafter, the agency had become cognizant that Mr. Reeves tape-recorded a conversation between himself and another high-ranking officer without the other individual's knowledge or consent and posted YouTube videos on the Internet of himself wearing his uniform or showing his badge, while acting in a "potentially irrational manner." Furthermore, Mr. Reeves contacted the agency's Employee Relations Unit and used profanity, was yelling, and then started crying. Despite the fact that he was on medical leave, the agency had consulted with the mental health professionals who were employed by the agency appropriately as related to these incidents, since this behavior concerned the agency as to the psychological well-being of their employee. On the same date as his contact with Employee Relations, the LE agency received information from a compliance officer who interviewed Mr. Reeves about a complaint of discrimination. The compliance officer had reported similar interactions with Mr. Reeves while reflecting the same consternation about Mr. Reeves' safety and well-being. After discussing the matter with the appropriate security and safety unit, the agency took steps to ensure the welfare of the employee by requesting assistance from another LE agency that had jurisdiction over the area where Mr. Reeves resided. A mental evaluation team was requested later and responded to Mr. Reeves residence. At the time they evaluated Mr. Reeves, it was determined that he did not meet the criteria to be put on a 72-hour involuntary psychiatric hold pursuant to California Welfare and Institution Code 5150.

However, a few days later, Mr. Reeves reportedly went to a nearby police station, while still being off duty and after identifying himself as an officer, he proceeded to yell and use profanity towards the watch commander. As a result of feeling threatened based on Mr. Reeves' "body language," behavior, and verbalization that he would return to the station later in the afternoon, the officers in the station were on alert and informed Mr. Reeves that his actions would be reported and he should "stand down" and leave immediately or they would take steps to detain him. Mr. Reeves did not in fact return later that day, but it was discovered by the LE agency that he had posted more videos of himself on Facebook and other social media accounts wearing army fatigues and hiding behind bushes, or jumping out from behind a non-descript building and stating that he knew he was being watched/followed by others due to his race. There were other videos showing him opening the door to his residence and having a frightened look on his face, peering outside, and then crying. At this time, the agency received a letter from Mr. Reeves' treatment provider, stating he needs to remain off work "for his safety and the safety of others." Thus, Mr. Reeves' medical leave due to the physical injury that he was claiming was extended for a longer period of time.

Review of Records Per his authorization, a large amount and myriad of documents and records was received from Mr. Reeves treatment providers. This also included the letters that these providers had offered for Mr. Reeves' workers compensation case, as well as the discrimination lawsuit.

The psychological treatment records entailed that Mr. Reeves had first sought treatment about non-work-related issues (suicide of his friend) in August 2014. He was deemed to have a psychological condition and was referred to his primary healthcare provider for medication management. After reporting a decrease in symptoms, psychotherapy had been terminated. It appeared Mr. Reeves had several phone conversations and had been in treatment with the clinician sporadically from February 2015 until September 2015. The records revealed that treatment resumed in March 2016, a few weeks prior to manifestations of Mr. Reeves concerning behaviors while he was off duty. The treatment provider's notes for the next 3 months indicated improvements of symptoms. Curiously, this is the time period when Mr. Reeves' psychiatrist placed him on medical leave. Additionally, there was a note provided to the agency by Mr. Reeves' psychologist dated a few months later indicating he was "fit for duty" and that the "best 'therapy' would be for Mr. Reeves to be released to active duty without restrictions." However, there was no mention of administration of psychological measures, knowledge or coordination of treatment with the psychiatrist, or any objective means of arriving at this conclusion.

The primary care physician's (PCP) notes from early 2016 indicated Mr. Reeves had various medical problems and physical injuries. Although some psychological symptoms were noted and pharmacotherapy was offered, the clearance that the PCP offered for Mr. Reeves to return to work mainly considered his physical ability and his limitations. There was also a notation clarifying that the letter sent to the LE agency approving Mr. Reeves' return to work was a result of the doctor's concern for Mr. Reeves' wellbeing. Specifically, the PCP concluded Mr. Reeves' "history of a brief psychological problem" should not be an obstacle for Mr. Reeves maintaining a full-time position. This notation was not indicative of whether there had been any consultation with Mr. Reeves's other treatment providers as related to the nature and intensity of the "psychological condition" and its brevity.

The treatment records from Mr. Reeves' psychiatrist stated Mr. Reeves was seen for psychopharmacological management purposes and had been placed on Temporary Total Disability (TTD) during the initial consultation visit for one month in 2016. Although there was indication that some psychological measures (most notably MMPI-2) were administered, the progress notes did not contain any results or interpretation of the testing that would provide more information or confirmation of the self-reported symptoms by Mr. Reeves, neither did it offer the purpose of the testing by the psychiatrist. Also, on the other self-report measures that were administered, Mr. Reeves endorsed items and/or intensity of experience that were not consistent with the data about symptomatology reflected in the psychiatrist's initial report. That is, Mr. Reeves had not endorsed experiencing guilt, sadness, lacking self-confidence, being discouraged about the future, whereas, the psychiatrist had laid out in his report that Mr. Reeves. experienced these feelings and perceptions. Nonetheless, Mr. Reeves was diagnosed with Post Traumatic Stress Disorder and Major Depressive Disorder, Recurrent, and had been prescribed a variety of medication to include Pristiq 100 mg, Seroquel XR 50 mg, Ambien CR; Actiq for pain; Abilify; Clonazepam; Testosterone; Vitamin D3; CoQ10; and Omega 3 fish oil.

Additional notes from the treating psychiatrist stated that Mr. Reeves's diagnosis had remained active and he was experiencing a myriad of symptoms. Yet, as noted previously, these were inconsistent with the psychologist's notes documented around the same time that conveyed improvement and ability to return to duty. In fact, it was not discernible whether Mr. Reeves was referred for further psychological treatment, and/or the treatment providers had ever conferred with each other about Mr. Reeves' treatment plan. Despite the use of the aforementioned medications, Mr. Reeves was noted to be very symptomatic and his prognosis was guarded. Further certification was offered by his psychiatrist of Mr. Reeves' need to be off work and remain on TTD until the end of January 2017. Finally, a few months later there was notation from the same provider releasing Mr. Reeves to unrestricted duty.

Despite the fact that Mr. Reeves denied any psychiatric hospitalizations during this evaluation, he gave authorization to obtain hospital records. The review of the records revealed that in late 2016, Mr. Reeves had been brought in by the police after driving very slowly with the "loudspeakers blasting." When peace officers had approached him after being stopped, they found him to be confused and unable to make eye contact. He told police he had been driving around town for a couple hours. Then he had started to laugh uncontrollably. He was not able to provide any valid identification but declared himself to be a peace officer while continuing to laugh. He also disclosed that he was going through a divorce. When he had arrived at the emergency room accompanied by the officers, Mr. Reeves was noted to have been in "great distress," yet continued to laugh as questions were posed to him. Upon evaluation, he had questioned the credentials of the attending psychiatrist and then started to laugh uncontrollably again, per admission notes. He reported taking Ativan and Klonopin before but preferred Klonopin. He also stated that he was prescribed "Nuvigil" for his depression. According to admission notes, he stated he had "not slept for more than one year." As he had continued to laugh, he had also related that he had read the manifesto of Chris Doner and realized why he wanted to kill people. At that point, Mr. Reeves had started crying.

Following these observations, the attending psychiatrist had placed Mr. Reeves on a 72-hour involuntary psychiatric hold for danger to others and grave disability. At the time of hospitalization, Mr. Reeves received an initial injection of Haldol and Ativan. Benadryl had also been administered to him. Later in the day, was found pulling the fire alarm, destroying property, and unable to be redirected verbally or with gentle physical redirection. He was put into seclusion and restraints and had received another Haldol injection. The next day while the hospital attending psychiatrist had talked to him, he could not be convinced to take any medication and just wanted to be transferred to a different hospital. On the third day he was released to his mother's care. Over the three days Mr. Reeves spent in the hospital, he had attended two groups, but remained symptomatic, not exhibiting a logical thought process, and had shown a range of behaviors suggestive of impulsive dyscontrol.

Interestingly, there was no mention of this hospitalization anywhere in his outpatient treating psychiatrist records.

Mr. Reeves' Account as Related to the SNS Posts When Mr. Reeves' posts and videos on SNS were discussed with him during the clinical interview, he acknowledged them with a smirk. He asked the evaluator how she had become aware of them. When he was told that, along with notification of his behaviors, his employer provided the information, Mr. Reeves leaned back with his arms crossed and asked what the evaluator thought about those posts and videos. Clarification was provided that the issue of importance in the present evaluation was his psychological state and decision-making process at the time he created and then posted these videos and pictures. At that point, he once again started looking around the room, gazing at the door, and stated he would not discuss the posts. He asserted he was only interested in ensuring the evaluator understood he had been discriminated against and the chain of command in the agency was "out to get him" because he was a whistleblower.

Suitability/Fitness Opinion and Recommendation

Based on the information outlined above, Mr. Reeves suffers from a pattern of pervasive and characterologically rooted issues and a history of depressive episodes which appeared to have become exacerbated into delusional symptomology during periods of stress. Mr. Reeves has also had a history of symptomology which have required medication management; however, other than the brief and inconsistent psychotherapy, no other modalities of psychological/therapeutic treatment had been utilized. During the evaluation, Mr. Reeves presented an inconsistent account of his use of psychotropic medications, previous treatment history, and experienced difficulties. Mr. Reeves presented with minimal insight into his behavior and the impact of his behavior including SNS posts and videos on others. He tended to blame others and engaged in rumination while attributing his behaviors to situations that he believed were brought on by the LE agency and other people's action towards him. He continuously minimized his role in the indicated situations. As noted above, he believed he was a hero because he brought forth the "corruption" within the LE agency. Of noteworthy concern was the fact that, despite being relieved of duty with pay and being away from the work environment, he had been psychiatrically hospitalized. Furthermore, based on the results of the objective testing, Mr. Reeves continued to report significant amount of distress related to work. Mr. Reeves' preoccupation with the discrimination along with the alleged harassment he believed he had endured and his hypervigilance for potential threats in the workplace may significantly impact him in performing his job functions as a peace officer.

As noted earlier, a safety sensitive position as defined by the CGC§1031 (f) requires that the individual "Be free of any physical, emotional, or mental conditions that might adversely affect the exercise of the powers of a peace officer." Based on the abovementioned behaviors and manifestation of symptomatology, Mr. Reeves was deemed as unable to meet the requirements of CGC§1031(f) due to his serious psychological and emotional impairment. Furthermore, considering POST psychological dimensions Mr. Reeves did not meet the following guidelines:

- **Social Competence:** ability to read people and an awareness of the impact of one's own words and behaviors on others; and being able to communicate with others in a tactful and respectful manner.
- **Teamwork**: working effectively with others to accomplish goals; and being able to establish and maintain effective working relationships with coworkers, supervisors, and clients.
- **Emotional Regulation/Stress Tolerance**: ability to maintain even-tempered composure and demeanor in highly charged emotional events and other stressful situations. This also includes being able to accept criticism of one's personal limitations and mistakes, and not become excessively defensive when challenged or criticized.
- **Decision Making/Judgment**: being able to make sound decisions and size up situations quickly to determine what to do and take appropriate action. This includes having common sense and using practical judgment while also prioritizing competing demands.
- **Adaptability/Flexibility:** adaptability and flexibility so that one may adjust to many different, sudden, and sometimes competing demands of the job.

Consequently, as a result of his hypervigilance for potential personal threats regarding discrimination and harassment on the job and based on the problematic nature of Mr. Reeves' exhibited behaviors and his preoccupation with the harassment and discrimination, it was opined that there is a higher risk for occurrence of a serious event that could result in harm to himself and/or others. Thus, Mr. Reeves was deemed as not fit to be a peace officer at the time of the evaluation.

How Did Social Media Impact This Case?

Mr. Reeves' posts and videos on the SNS were offered by the LE agency as providing further justifications for the request of the FFDE along with other documentation depicting the problematic behaviors Mr. Reeves had exhibited while on leave due to injury incurred at work. Due to their relevance to the essential functions of a peace officer, they were considered by this evaluator. In fact, there was a convergence of critical findings from the results of the administered psychological measures, review of treatment records and the in-depth clinical interview during the FFDE with the displayed behaviors and information, particularly videos, that were posted by Mr. Reeves on SNS. After diligently considering to the essential functions of a peace officer and POST psychological dimensions, the psychologist was unable to certify that Mr. Reeves could return to work and safely and reliably carry out the powers and privileges of a peace officer.

References

Allen, M. G., Hibler, N. S., & Miller, R. (2000). Fitness for duty evaluations of law enforcement officers in accordance with federal occupational health procedures. In D. Sheehan (Ed.), *Domestic violence by police officers*. Washington, DC: U.S. Department of Justice, Federal Bureau of Investigation.

Americans with Disabilities Act of 1990, Pub. L. No. 101–336, §2, 104 Stat. 328 (1991).

Beutler, L. E., Nussbaum, P. D., & Meredith, K. E. (1988). Changing personality patterns of police officers. *Police Psychology: Research and Practice, 19*, 503–507.

Brown v. Sandy City Appeal Board. (2014). *UT App*, 158.

California Government Code § 1031 (2005).

California Peace Officer Standards and Training Commission (POST) Regulation 1955.

Chambers, R., & Winter, J. (2017). Social Media and Selection: A brief history and practiacal recommendations. A "Hot Topics" white paper prepared by the Visibility Committee of the Society for Industrial and Organizational Psychology.

Cochrane, R., Tett, R. P., & Vandercreek, L. (2003). Psychological testing and the selection of police officers: A national survey. *Criminal Justice and Behavior, 30*, 511–537.

Corey, D. M. (2011). Principles of fitness-for-duty evaluations for police psychologists. In J. Kitaeff (Ed.), *Handbook of police psychology* (pp. 263–293). New York: Routledge Psychology Press.

Corey, D. M., & Borum, R. (2013). Forensic assessment for high-risk occupations. In R. K. Otto & I. B. Weiner (Eds.), *Forensic psychology* (Vol. 11, 2nd ed., pp. 246–270). Hoboken, NJ: Wiley, Inc..

Craig, R. J. (2005). *Personality-guided forensic psychology*. Washington, DC: American Psychological Association.

Cross-Tab, *Online Reputation in a Connected World,* January 2010., http://www.micorsoft.com/privacy/dpd/research.aspx. Accessed 7 Jan 2019.

Curran, S. F. (1998). Pre-employment psychological evaluation of law enforcement applicants. *The Police Chief, 65*, 88–93.

Curran v. Cousins, 509 F.3d 36 (1st Cir.2007).

Dantzker, M. L. (2005). *Understanding Today's police* (4th ed.). Monsey: Criminal Justice Press.

Dantzker, M. L. (2011). Psychological preemployment screening for police candidates: Seeking consistency if not standardization. *Professional Psychology: Research and Practice., 42*(3), 276–283.

Davis, R. D., & Rostow, C. D. (2008). *Matrix-predictive uniform law enforcement selection evaluation inventory*. North Tonawanda: Multi-Health Systems.

Decker, K. P. (2006). Introduction to fitness for duty evaluations in law enforcement personnel. In K. P. Decker (Ed.), *Fit, unfit or misfit: How to perform fitness for duty evaluations in law enforcement professionals* (pp. 3–31). Springfield: Charles C. Thomas.

California Fair Employment and Housing Act. Cal Code Regs. Tit.2, § 7285–7297.11 (2011).

Equal Employment Opportunity Commission. (2000). *EEOC enforcement guidance on disability-related inquiries and medical examinations of employees under the American with Disabilities Act: Compliance manual (Vol.w, sect. 902, no.915.002)*. Washington, DC: Author.

Equal Employment Opportunity Commission. (2002, October 29). *ADA technical assistance manual: January 1992*. (Publication EEOC-M-1A, Addendum).

Family Medical Leave Act, 29 U.S. C. § 2601 (1993).

Fischler, G. L., (2001). Psychological Fitness-For-Duty Examinations: Practical Considerations for Public Safety Departments. Reprinted with permission from Illinois Law Enforcement Executive Forum (Vol. 1, pp –77-92).

Fischler, G. L., McElroy, H. K., Miller, L., Saxe-Clifford, S., Stewart, C. O., & Zelig, M. (August 2011). The role of psychological fitness-for-duty evaluations in law enforcement. *The Police Chief, 78*, 72–78.

Haefner, R. (2009). More Employers Screening Candidates via Social Networking Sites. CareerBuilder June 10, 2009, http://www.careerbuilder.com/Article/CB-1337-Getting-Hired-More-Employers-Screening-Candidates-via-Social-Networking-Sites/?ArticleID=1337&cbRecursionCnt=I&cbsid=0b46ea4e1079427ea6ce9845d903d432-334081875-RP-4. Accessed 5 Jan 2019.

Hargrave, G. E., & Hiatt, D. (1989). Use of the California psychological inventory in law enforcement officer selection. *Journal of Personality Assessment, 53*, 267–277.

Hill v. Winona, 454NW 2d 659 (Minn.App. 1990).

International Association of Chiefs of Police, Police Psychological Services Section (2014). *Preemployment psychological evaluation guidelines.*

International Association of Chiefs of Police, Police Psychological Services Section. (2013). *Guidelines for psychological fitness-for-duty evaluations*. Arlington: Author.

Landers, R. N., & Schmidt, G. B. (2016). Social media in employee selection and recruitment: An overview. In R. N. Landers & G. B. Schmidt (Eds.), *Social media in employee selection and recruitment: Theory, practice and current challenges* (pp. 3–14). London: Springer.

Maplewood and Law Enf. Labor Serv., *108 LA (BNA) 572*. (Daly 1996).

Mayer, M. J., & Corey, D. M. (2016). Current issues in psychological fitness-for-duty evaluations for law enforcement officers: Legal and practice implications. In C. L.

McGreal v. Ostrov, 36 8F. 3d657 (7th Cir. 2004).

Merillat v. Michigan State University, 207 Mich.App. 241 (1994).

Mikkelson, K. (Summer 2010). Cybervetting and Monitoring Employees' Online Activities: Assessing the Legal Risks for Employers. *The Public Lawyer (Vol. 18)*, 2, 1–6.

Neylan, T. C., Metzler, T. J., Best, S. R., Weiss, D. S., Fagan, J. A., Liberman, A., Rogers, C., Vedantham, K., Brunet, A., Lipsey, T. L., & Marmar, C. R. (2002). Critical incident exposure and sleep quality in police officers. *Psychosomatic Medicine (March–April), 64*(2), 345–352.

O'Shea, K. A. (2012). Use of Social Media in Employment: Should I Fire? Should I Hire? http://www.cornellhrreview.org.

Occupational Safety and Health Act of 1970, 29 U.S.C. § 654, Pub.L. 91–596, 84 Stat. 1590, 91st Congress, S. 2193 (1970).

Patterson, G.T. (2001). The relationship between demographic variables and exposure to traumatic incidents among police officers. Australian Journal of Disaster & Trauma Studies. http://www.massey.ac.nz/~trauma/issues/2001-2/patterson2.htm.

Perrin, M. A., DiGrande, L., Wheeler, K., Thorpe, L., Farfel, M., & Brackbill, R. (2007). Differences in PTSD prevalence and associated risk factors among World Trade Center disaster rescue and recovery workers. *American Journal of Psychiatry, 164*(9), 1385–1394.

Reeves v. Town of Cottageville, #2:12-cv-02765, 2014 U.S. Dist. Lexis 120,619 (D.S.C).

Rose, A., Timm, H., Pogson, C., Gonzalez, J., Appel, E. & Kolb, N. (2010). Developing a Cybervetting Strategy for Law Enforcement (Special Report). Defense Personnel Security Research Center – US Department of Defense and IACP.

San Diego v. Roe, 543 US 77 (2004) n.d., http://www.oyez.org/cases/2009/2004/2004_03_1669.

Schlosser, L. & McAleer, G. P. (2018). Opioid Use Disorders Among Police and Public Safety Personnel: What Law Enforcement Leaders Need to Know. http://www.policechief magazine.org.

Segal, J. A. (2014). Social media use in hiring: Assessing the risks. *HR Magazine, 59*(9).

Society for Human Resource Management [SHRM]. (2015). Know Before You Hire: 2015 Employment Screening Trends. http://www.shrm.org/.

Stellman, J. M., Smith, R. P., Katz, C. L., Sharma, V., Charney, D. S., Herbert, R., Moline, J., Luft, B. J., Markowitz, S., Udasin, I., Harrison, D., Baron, S., Landrigan, P. J., Levin, S. M., & Southwick, S. (2008). Enduring mental health morbidity and social function impairment in the World Trade Center rescue, recovery, and cleanup workers: the psychological dimension of an environmental health disaster. *Environmental Health Perspectives, 116*, 1248–1253.

Tett, R. P., & Burnett, D. D. (2003). A personality trait based interactionist model of job performance. *Journal of Applied Psychology, 88*(3), 500.

Watts v. Alfred, 794 F.Supp.431 (D.D.C.1992).

White v. County of Los Angeles, No. B243471 (Cal.Ct. App. Apr. 15, 2014).

Chapter 8
Personal Injury and Disability

Lisa Drago Piechowski

Personal injury and disability evaluations are matters of civil litigation. Unlike criminal proceedings in which the government acts against an individual or entity accused of violating the law, civil litigation seeks to resolve legal disputes between parties. In personal injury cases, the "plaintiff" alleges that he has sustained damage due to the actions or inactions of another party (the "defendant") and is therefore entitled to monetary compensation for the damage incurred. In the case of forensic mental health assessments (FMHA), the claimed damage includes some aspect of psychological injury. This may take the form of the development or exacerbation of a mental health condition such as depression or anxiety, or the loss of cognitive capacity such as impaired concentration or decreased impulse control. In such cases, forensic mental health evaluators may be asked to examine the plaintiff and offer an opinion on the nature and extent of the psychological damage incurred by the plaintiff and the causal relationship (if any) between these injuries and the actions of the defendant. The following sections detail the standards and typical procedure associated with these evaluations, as well as the specific obligations of the FMHA evaluator.

8.1 Introduction to Personal Injury and Disability Evaluations

Personal injury is based in tort law, which is defined as a civil wrong. Torts can include both acts of commission and/or omission. For an act to be a tort, it must meet four criteria: (1) duty, (2) dereliction, (3) damage, and (4) causality. *Duty* refers to an obligation by the defendant to the plaintiff. *Dereliction* occurs when the defendant fails to fulfill a duty to the plaintiff. A tort action requires that, in addition

L. D. Piechowski (✉)
Independent Practice, Annapolis, MD, USA

A. B. Batastini, M. J. Vitacco (eds.), *Forensic Mental Health Evaluations in the Digital Age*, https://doi.org/10.1007/978-3-030-33908-1_8

to the dereliction of duty, some *damage* must have occurred. This can include monetary losses, physical injuries, or emotional distress. The final element of a tort is *causality*, which requires that the damage incurred by the plaintiff be directly related to the defendant's dereliction of duty. This concept is also known as *proximate cause*. The actions (or inactions) of the defendant must be a primary reason or a substantial factor in bringing about the harm.

As in personal injury cases, FMHA in disability cases also involves the assessment of mental injury. However, in disability, an individual (the "claimant") believes she is entitled to certain benefits, such as disability insurance, social security, or worker's compensation, due to a loss of work capacity resulting from an illness or injury. Each of these sources of benefits is controlled by a different set of laws, statutes, and regulations. To be eligible for benefits, the claimant must meet the specific definition of disability as determined by the policy or program under which benefits are sought. When questions arise as to the validity or severity of the claimant's reported condition or the extent to which the claimant's condition compromises her work functioning, a FMHA may be sought to clarify these issues.

8.1.1 The Role of the Forensic Mental Health Evaluator

In both personal injury and disability cases, a forensic mental health evaluator may be retained by either party. In the case of personal injury, the plaintiff may choose to have his or her own mental health examination to demonstrate the extent and validity of his or her injuries. In addition, the defendant has the right to have their own expert examine the plaintiff. Rule 35 of the Federal Rules of Civil Procedure (FCRP, 2018) provides that the defendant can force the plaintiff to undergo an examination when the plaintiff claims psychological injury as a basis for receiving damages. In such cases, the plaintiff is entitled to receive a written report describing the examiner's findings. This report must be detailed and disclose all the procedures used, the opinions reached, and the foundations for each opinion. In return, the plaintiff is required to provide the defendant any reports under the plaintiff's control addressing these same issues. Similarly, in disability cases, insurance policies include the right of the insurance company to have the claimant examined by an independent mental health professional to substantiate the claimant's condition and eligibility to receive benefits. The claimant may also choose to have an examination by his own expert to provide support for his claim or to challenge the findings of the independent evaluator.

A key concept in personal injury and disability cases is a change in functional capacity. That is, there must be a demonstrable decline in the examinee's functioning arising after the onset of the illness or injury. Further, this decline in functioning must be attributable to the illness or injury. This creates significant challenges for the forensic mental health evaluator who must not only assess the examinee's current functioning but must also establish her premorbid functional capacity and determine at what point in time her functioning began to change.

8.1.2 Assessing Mental Injury

The scope of the FMHA in personal injury or disability cases, is determined to a large extent by the referral source. Typically, the referring party will provide specific questions to be addressed in the evaluation. These may vary, but often the issues to be addressed include:

- Does the examinee have a valid mental health condition?
- Which specific symptoms does the examinee experience?
- How severe is the condition?
- How is the examinee's functioning compromised as a result of the condition?
- What factor(s) led to the decline in the examinee's functioning?
- What type of treatment is recommended?
- What is the prognosis for improvement or recovery?

From both ethical and legal standpoints, including the Ethical Principles of Psychologists and Code of Conduct (EPPCC; APA 2017), the Specialty Guidelines for Forensic Psychology (SGFP; APA 2013), and the Federal Rules of Evidence (FRE), examiners are required to base their opinions on sufficient and appropriate information and techniques. This means that examiners must collect comprehensive, relevant, and valid data; must interpret data appropriately; and must reach reasonable inferences based on the data collected. This is best achieved by collecting data from multiple reliable sources and attempting to corroborate data by comparing information across sources. As with many types of FMHAs, data sources in personal injury and disability cases often include the following:

- Records and documents
- Clinical interview
- Behavioral observations
- Psychological testing
- Collateral data

Each of these data sources has strengths and limitations. Records and documents can provide valuable information about the examinee's history and current functioning. They can be especially helpful in trying to understand the examinee's baseline functioning, particularly if such records include school transcripts, standardized test scores, or psychological evaluations performed prior to the claimed injury. Mental health treatment records can assist in understanding changes in the examinee's emotional functioning over time. Records can vary in usefulness, however, as any record is only as reliable as the person who created it. Inaccurate observations, typographical errors, omissions, and illegibility are some examples of possible threats to validity.

The clinical interview provides an opportunity to gather information from the examinee's perspective about her history, the events surrounding the alleged injury, and events subsequent to this. It can also provide information about specific symptoms and experiences that may be helpful in reaching diagnostic conclusions. Since most symptoms of mental health problems are subjective in nature, information obtained directly from the examinee can be extremely useful. However, the accuracy of this information can vary for a number of reasons, both unintended and intended. For example, the examinee's memory may be unreliable, or he may lack insight into his situation and psychological functioning. These sources of distortion are considered unintentional. However, distortion can be intentional on the part of the examinee, motivated by personal incentives including financial gain. Several authors have suggested that the accuracy of self-reported data is likely influenced by situational factors such as involvement in litigation or compensation seeking, such that in compensation situations, examinees were more likely to report superior premorbid functioning and poorer current functioning, and they were more likely to exaggerate the number and severity of their symptoms than examinees who were not seeking compensation (Lees-Haley et al. 1997; Williams et al. 1999; Greiffenstein et al. 2002).

The clinical interview, as well as the rest of the face-to-face examination, provides an opportunity for the examiner to collect data by directly observing the examinee's behavior. This allows the examiner to compare her own observations of the examinee's presentation with his self-reported complaints. The examinee's attention, concentration, memory, mood stability, judgment, comprehension, and interpersonal functioning can be informally assessed in this way. It is also important to note the internal consistency of the examinee's self-report, as well as the examinee's attitude toward the evaluation and the examiner over the course of an evaluation.

Psychological and neuropsychological testing is another source of potentially useful data about the examinee's emotional functioning, cognitive functioning, and response style. It is important to remember that testing can only assess an examinee's current functioning. No psychological or neuropsychological test can determine what an examinee's functioning was at some point in the past. Testing is useful in generating hypotheses about the examinee, but testing cannot directly answer the psycho-legal question. If testing is to be used, tests should be selected with care. Due consideration should be given to the context of the examination and to the characteristics of the examinee, including age, ethnicity, acculturation, educational level, and language fluency. Koch et al. (2006) cautioned that many tests commonly employed in clinical and forensic assessment may not have been evaluated scientifically in an ecologically valid manner for the population being assessed in a personal injury evaluation. Additionally, examiners should avoid tests that are uncommon or outdated. Tests should never be used for other than their intended purposes, and standard administration procedures should be followed.

Psychological testing in personal injury and disability cases typically includes some means of assessing the examinee's response style. This can include embedded validity scales in multi-scale inventories such as the Minnesota Multiphasic Personality Inventory-2 (MMPI-2; Butcher et al. 1989) MMPI-2-Restrucutred Form (MMPI-2-RF; Ben-Porath and Tellegen 2008/2011), and the Personality Assessment Inventory (PAI; Morey 1991), and stand-alone symptom validity or performance validity tests such as the Test of Memory Malingering (TOMM; Tombaugh 1996),

Validity Indicator Profile (VIP; Frederick 1997), and Structured Interview of Reported Symptoms-second Edition (SIRS-2; Rogers et al. 2010). Selection of the specific methods should be based on the nature of the examinee's claimed symptoms. Evaluating for possible malingered psychopathology calls for a different approach than when feigned cognitive symptoms are suspected. Rogers and Payne (2006) noted, "In the case of feigned mental disorders, the malingerer must create a believable set of symptoms, a likely onset and course of the disorder, and plausible effects on their day-to-day functioning." On the other hand, feigning a cognitive disorder requires "effortful failure"—that is, "While appearing invested in succeeding, [the examinee reports] incorrect responses on test items that measure cognitive abilities" (p. 650). Regardless of the methods employed, it is important to understand that tests cannot "prove" the examinee is malingering, but can provide data about whether the examinee engaged in poor effort or impression management.

Collateral data refers to data obtained from third-party sources. Collateral data can help to fill in gaps in the examinee's self-report, help the examiner obtain a better understanding of the examinee's prior functioning, and corroborate information obtained from the examinee during the interview and from psychological testing. There are many potential sources of collateral data. Selection of sources depends on the type of information the examiner is seeking, the examinee's situation, and the sources that are available in each specific case. Collateral data, like other forms of data, are vulnerable to distortion and misinterpretation. Heilbrun et al. (2003) identified factors that can limit the accuracy of information obtained from collateral sources. These include reluctance to participate in the evaluation, bias, lack of specific expertise, suggestibility, and memory loss.

8.2 The Use of Data from Social Networking Sites in Assessing Mental Injury

Data obtained from the Internet, including information from social networking sites (SNS), has been conceptualized as a form of collateral data (Pirelli et al. 2018; Pirelli et al. 2016). For the purpose of this discussion, SNS data is assumed to include words and images posted to sites such as Facebook, Instagram, Twitter, YouTube, LinkedIn, and dating websites, as well as blog postings, comments, and articles shared publicly online. Because evaluations in disability and personal injury cases always involve an assessment of how the examinee's functioning is now different than it was in the past, SNS data has the potential to address this issue by providing snapshots of the examinee's functioning at different points in time, including before and after the alleged injury or onset of illness.

In civil litigation, SNS data is often obtained by the opposing party through the process of discovery. In fact, this appears to be true for most FMHA in which SNS data is used (Coffey et al. 2018). Under the FRCP, parties may discover all "relevant" information so long as it is not "privileged" from discovery. Courts have generally not considered SNS data to be privileged (see Brown 2012). FRCP Rule 26(b)(1), as revised in 2015, states that parties may obtain discovery regarding non-privileged matters relevant to any party's claim or defense "and proportional to the needs of the case, considering the importance of the issues at stake in the action, the amount in controversy, the parties' relative access to relevant information, the parties' resources, the importance of the discovery in resolving the issues, and whether the burden or expense of the proposed discovery outweighs its likely benefit." (p. 40).

With few limits on the scope of discovery, litigants in civil cases frequently seek extensive access to SNS data during the discovery process (McPeak 2016). Defense attorneys in civil litigation often seek to admit a plaintiff's Facebook photographs to refute the plaintiff's claims of emotional injury or loss of enjoyment by comparing photos of the plaintiff posted before and after the claimed injury (Brown 2012). In *E.E.O.C. v. Simply Storage Mgmt., LLC (2010),* the court noted, "It is reasonable to expect severe emotional or mental injury to manifest itself in some [social media] content, and an examination of that content might reveal whether onset occurred, when, and the degree of distress. Further, information that evidences other stressors that could have produced the alleged emotional distress is also relevant." (434–436). Data from Facebook has been used in personal injury cases to contradict a plaintiff's claims of injury or damages and to reflect the plaintiff's emotional and mental state (McPeak 2013). For example, in *Romano v. Steelcase, Inc. (2010),* in which the plaintiff claimed that her injuries led to the loss of enjoyment in life, the defense presented material taken from her Facebook and MySpace pages that depicted the plaintiff engaged in an active lifestyle and "smiling happily."

The question of whether forensic evaluators should independently search for social media data is controversial. According to a 2018 study by Pirelli et al., professionals disagree as to whether it is appropriate for forensic practitioners to search the Internet for information about their examinees—6.9% believed that forensic evaluators are *required* to search the Internet about examinees, 5% believed forensic evaluators are *prohibited* from searching the internet about examinees, and 20.9% believed it is *advisable* for forensic evaluators to conduct such searches; others appeared unsure. Due to this lack of consensus and guidance from authoritative sources, forensic practitioners should proceed with caution when considering undertaking an independent search of the examinee's social media. This is especially true in cases where requests for discovery of such material have been denied by the Court.

When SNS is obtained, either through the discovery process or through the efforts of the forensic evaluator, one must consider how to incorporate such data into the forensic evaluation. As with other forms of collateral data, data from the Internet may be useful in providing information about the examinee's functioning over time and may help to corroborate (or disconfirm) aspects of the examinee's self-report. And, as with other forms of collateral data, SNS data are vulnerable to distortion and misinterpretation. It is important, therefore, to carefully assess and weigh these data and to determine its relevance to the psycho-legal questions presented in the evaluation. There are several aspects of SNS data to consider when using in forensic evaluations of personal injury or disability.

The first consideration is authenticity. This is especially relevant in personal injury or disability cases when the data comes from the opposing party and not from the examinee. Although it is beyond the expertise of most forensic evaluators to authenticate material posted online (see Chap. 1 of this volume), some basic information can be obtained to rule out obvious cases of misattribution or falsification. Material can also be authenticated by simply asking the examinee to identify it and verify that any images allegedly of the examinee are in fact the examinee and that the examinee is responsible for the material posted. If the examinee claims the data has been altered, edited, or distorted in some way, the evaluator can ask the examinee to produce the original, unaltered material. If screenshots or printouts are provided, the evaluator can ask for the original URL to attempt to independently locate the material online.

The next consideration is the context of the SNS data. The discovery process in civil litigation may yield vast amounts of information. The forensic evaluator, however, may only be provided with a small subset of this material. In terms of online data, several important pieces of information may not be disclosed, such as the date the material was posted, the circumstances in which photos or videos were taken, or other information posted around the same time that would place the material in context. Obtaining answers to these questions will give the forensic evaluator a better foundation for using these data to generate hypotheses about the examinee's psychological functioning.

The third consideration is representativeness. SNS data is, at best, a sampling of behavior in a virtual medium. It may or may not be an accurate depiction of the examinee's typical behavior. Postings on social media tend not to be a random sampling of the individual's life. Users of social media often prefer to post flattering pictures of themselves taken while engaged in interesting or pleasant activities. These images may not be typical of the individual's mood or activities. "Cherry picking" on the part of the attorney, that is selecting only the most advantageous pieces of data to share with the forensic evaluator, may further skew the evaluator's understanding of the material. For example, in a case involving the plaintiff's claimed depression, the defense might present the evaluator with five images from Facebook depicting the plaintiff smiling and laughing and omit 20 other images in which the plaintiff appears sad or worried. The examiner must be cognizant that social networking sites frequently do not paint a complete picture of the examinee.

The next question to consider is the relevance of the data to the psycho-legal issues raised in the evaluation. Does the data have the potential to help the forensic evaluator address issues related to the examinee's claimed emotional injury? Both the EPPCC and the SGFP discuss the importance of focusing on relevant data as the basis for evaluation. For example, this is discussed in the SGFP Guideline 10.01, "Forensic examiners seek to assist the trier of fact to understand evidence or determine a fact in issue, and they provide information that is most relevant to the psycho-legal issue." It is also addressed in the EPPCC in section 4.04 (a), "Psychologists include in written and oral reports and consultations, only information germane to the purpose for which the communication is made." It is up to the forensic evaluator to determine the relevance of the material to the evaluation and to decide what weight to give this material in forming opinions.

Finally, the evaluator should consider what kinds of inferences can be reasonably drawn from the material. As discussed above, images can be misleading. It is not necessarily possible to determine an individual's mood or state of mind from a photograph. Facial expressions, body posture, clothing, and location may provide useful information or may lead to unfounded assumptions. There should be some scientific basis for any conclusions drawn from data found on the Internet. Ideally, there would be studies that link some aspect of the social media data with some other outcome or condition. For example, is there a scientific basis to conclude that a man who posts derogatory jokes about women on Facebook is likely to sexually harass women in the workplace? Or is there support for a conclusion that a woman who posts photographs of herself with friends on vacation cannot be depressed? The evaluator should attempt to ensure that any conclusions drawn from social media data can be reasonably extrapolated from the material.

8.2.1 *Input from the Examinee*

One of the most useful ways to understand the meaning of social media data is to discuss the data with the examinee. This was emphasized by Pirelli et al. (2016) noting, "psychologists should provide examinees the opportunity to respond to all collateral with which they are provided, including data gathered using the Internet. Doing so would allow examinees to challenge the content of what was yielded, or explain its context, which is critical to considering the weight the examiner should provide it. Examiners who fail to discuss collateral data with examinees are likely to be challenged on cross-examination…" (p. 15). Surprisingly, 12% of surveyed professionals disagreed with this approach and 28% were unsure whether this was appropriate or not (Pirelli et al. 2018).

The discussion with the examinee can take place during or after the clinical interview. Sometimes the topic will be raised by the examinee who is aware that SNS data has been provided to the evaluator and wants an opportunity to explain the material. In other cases, the examinee may have no idea that this material has been obtained. As with any collateral data that seems to conflict with the examinee's self-report, it is useful to simply present the material and request the examinee's help in understanding how it comports with what the examinee has presented. For example, when an examinee reports that she has been so traumatized as a result of a car accident that she has been unable to travel more than 10 miles from her home, the evaluator can show her images from Instagram that seem to indicate that she has recently vacationed in the Caribbean, and ask her to help him understand what this means. When confronting the examinee with discordant data, the evaluator should do so in a respectful, inquisitive manner and avoid an accusatory approach.

Discussing SNS data with examinees has many potential benefits including helping to authenticate the data, determining the surrounding circumstances, and opening avenues for discussion that might not have otherwise arisen, thereby allowing the evaluator to obtain a great deal of useful information. Openly sharing this data with the examinee also speaks to fairness and impartiality. It communicates to the examinee that the evaluator remains openminded and is interested in and willing to consider the examinee's input. In addition, discussing this data with the examinee lessens the possibility that the evaluator will misinterpret the material or will leap to unwarranted conclusions.

8.2.2 *Ethical and Legal Considerations in the Use of Social Media Data*

A more detailed discussion of relevant ethical codes is presented in Chap. 1; however, several ethical issues must be considered when incorporating SNS data in a forensic evaluation of personal injury or disability. First is the issue of informed consent. Both the EPPCC and the SGFP address informed consent (EPPCC 3.10; SGFP 6, 6.03). As articulated in the SGFP, "Because substantial rights, liberties, and properties are often at risk in forensic matters, and because the methods and procedures of forensic practitioners are complex and may not be accurately anticipated by the recipients of forensic services, forensic practitioners strive to inform service recipients about the nature and parameters of the services to be provided." If the forensic evaluator will be utilizing social media data in the evaluation, the examinee should be made aware of this fact as part of the process of informed consent. This is also true in the case of court-ordered evaluations when the examinee is not required to give consent, but nonetheless, should be fully informed about the nature and purpose of the evaluation.

Forensic evaluators in personal injury and disability cases are expected to be transparent in describing the bases for their opinions. The inclusion of social media data in a forensic evaluation should be fully disclosed in written reports and sworn testimony. This is directly addressed in SGFP 11.03: "Forensic practitioners are encouraged to disclose all sources of information obtained in the course of their professional services, and to identify the source of each piece of information that was considered and relied upon in formulating a particular conclusion, opinion, or other professional product." (p. 17). And in SGFP 11.04, "…forensic practitioners strive to offer a complete statement of all relevant opinions that they formed within the scope of their work on the case, the basis and reasoning underlying the opinions, the salient data or other information that was considered in forming the opinions, and an indication of any additional evidence that may be used in support of the opinions to be offered." (p. 17). In both personal injury and disability reports, SNS and other internet data should be specifically listed in the sources of information.

Forensic evaluators should be prepared to discuss the rationale for including SNS or any Internet data in the evaluation and how inferences obtained from this material have a basis in scientific or professional knowledge. The EPPCC addresses this in

2.4, "Psychologists' work is based upon established scientific and professional knowledge of the discipline;" and in 9.01(a) "Psychologists base the opinions contained in their recommendations, reports, and diagnostic or evaluative statements, including forensic testimony, on information and techniques sufficient to substantiate their findings." As mentioned earlier in this chapter, evaluators should take care not to reach unsupported conclusions about the nature or extent of the examinee's alleged psychological damage on the basis of SNS.

In addition to these ethical considerations, forensic evaluators should be reasonably familiar with the legal contours of civil litigation as it relates to their role. As discussed above, the acquisition of material in civil litigation is governed by rules of discovery. Forensic evaluators, as expert witnesses are not always limited to material that has been deemed admissible as evidence. As stated in FRE 703, "An expert may base an opinion on facts or data in the case that the expert has been made aware of or personally observed. If experts in the particular field would reasonably rely on those kinds of facts or data in forming an opinion on the subject, they need not be admissible for the opinion to be admitted." However, the introduction of material not obtained through the discovery process can be extremely problematic. Before undertaking an independent search for social media data, the forensic evaluator should discuss the need for this with the retaining party to determine the most appropriate course of action. The best and simplest strategy is to direct any requests for additional material to the retaining party.

8.3 Recommendations for Use of Internet and SNS Data in Personal Injury and Disability Cases

Internet-based data, and in particular SNS data, when properly obtained and utilized, can serve as important collateral information in personal injury and disability evaluations. As an adjunct to other sources of data in a personal injury or disability evaluation, social media data can provide corroborating or disconfirming information about the examinee's condition and functional capacity over time. When SNS data is incorporated into a personal injury or disability evaluation, evaluators should explicitly disclose this fact to the examinee as part of the process of informed consent and should clearly identify this source of data in written reports and testimony. When working in the context of civil litigation, evaluators are encouraged to rely on material obtained through the discovery or investigative processes conducted by the parties. Conducting an independent internet search about an examinee can be highly problematic in the context of civil litigation.

When used in a FMHA, evaluators should be aware of the limitations of social media data. As with other forms of collateral data, data found on the Internet are vulnerable to distortion and misinterpretation. In determining the weight to give this data, the authenticity, context, representativeness, and relevance should be considered. Inferences and conclusions based on social media data should be done cautiously and in the context of the applicable psycho-legal issues.

Case Profile 1

Type of Evaluation

Personal Injury

Case Context

Roseanne Martin, a 41-year-old aide at a state high-security mental health facility, filed a law suit against her employer alleging that she was repeatedly sexually harassed by her supervisor over a three-year period. She claimed that as a result, she developed severe anxiety, was unable to leave her house, and was unable to sustain an intimate relationship with her significant other. This evaluation was requested by her attorney to determine the nature and extent of any emotional injury Ms. Martin suffered as a result of her employer's actions.

Sources of Information

1. Clinical interview
2. Mental status examination
3. Psychological testing:
   a. Minnesota Multiphasic Personality Inventory second Edition Restructured Form (MMPI-2-RF)
   b. Clinician-Administered PTSD Scale for DSM-5 (CAPS-5)
4. Mental health treatment records
5. Memoranda from employer
6. Screenshots of images from Ms. Martin's Facebook account

Relevant Background

Ms. Martin, a single mother of four children, had been employed as a mental health worker at a State Hospital for 17 years. This is a high-security facility where individuals who have been found not criminally responsible for violent crimes and who have been adjudicated to be a danger to themselves or others are housed. Ms. Martin worked the night shift which began at 11:00 PM and ended at 7:00 AM. Ms. Martin reported that she enjoyed her job. She preferred working at night because she found it quieter and it allowed her to spend time with her children, who range in age from

13 to 21. Ms. Martin, who has never been married, reported she has always been the sole source of financial support for her family. She was proud of the fact that she had always been able to provide for her children. She had one long-term romantic relationship lasting 12 years. This relationship ended about two years ago.

Ms. Martin reported that about 3.5 years ago, a new supervisor, Gordon Everett was assigned to her unit. According to Ms. Martin, Mr. Everett began making suggestive remarks to her indicating he wished to have a sexual relationship with her. On one occasion he called her into his office, locked the door, and told Ms. Martin it was "just a matter of time until I get you into bed." She said she was shocked by this and was "speechless." She told him that she would not sleep with him. When she attempted to leave, Mr. Everett stood between her and the door and told her she could not leave until she kissed him. Ms. Martin reported she felt terrified and was afraid to resist. Ms. Martin then went back to her unit. She said she barely made it through her shift. She did not tell anyone about this incident. She hoped he would leave her alone since she did not encourage him.

However, according to Ms. Martin, Mr. Everett continued to press her for sexual favors. She attempted to avoid him whenever possible. Eventually, Mr. Everett became more insistent. He told her that if she did not start being more "friendly" to him, that she would be sorry and made reference to how one of the patients had recently attacked and seriously injured another staff member. Mr. Everett allegedly told Ms. Martin, "It would be a shame if something like that happened to a nice-looking woman like you."

Ms. Martin then reported Mr. Everett's behavior to the human resources department. Although they promised to investigate the allegations, Ms. Martin said that nothing changed. A few weeks later, Ms. Martin said that one of the patients on the unit told her that he had heard that other patients had been approached by someone on staff who offered them $50 to "mess her (Ms. Martin) up." The following week, Ms. Martin said that she was in a supply room looking for towels when Mr. Everett came into the room behind her and shut the door. She said that he verbally berated her for "snitching" on him. He then told her he "knew what [she] really wanted." He pushed her against the shelves, forcibly kissed her on the mouth, and groped her breasts. He told her there was "more to come," and warned her to cooperate or start watching her back.

Ms. Martin left work after her shift and put in for sick leave. She has not returned to work since. She reported she has experienced significant distress, including trouble eating, sleeping, and concentrating; as well as anxiety, panic attacks, and fatigue. She has become increasingly withdrawn and spends most of her time alone in her room. She lost interest in sex and this contributed to the breakdown of her relationship with her significant other. They eventually broke up after more than 12 years together.

Ms. Martin sought mental health treatment from a psychiatrist and a counselor. Despite this, she reported she has had little improvement in her symptoms. She continues to be socially isolated, anxious, fearful, and unable to sleep. She reported suddenly becoming overwhelmed with fear and panic in the grocery store and having to run out of the store, leaving her groceries behind. She said she sometimes has to pull over to the side of the road while driving due to her heart racing and having difficulty catching her breath. She finds herself being irritable and cranky with her children. She is jumpy at home and startles easily. She has lost interest in social activities that she formerly enjoyed. She has not returned to work.

Behavioral Observations and Mental Status

Ms. Martin was accompanied to the evaluation by her adult daughter who remained in the waiting room during the evaluation. Ms. Martin was appropriately dressed in clean, casual attire, with an acceptable level of grooming. She described her mood as "miserable." She appeared to be quite sad. Her eyes were downcast. Her overt emotional expression was generally flat, although she became tearful when discussing her interactions with Mr. Everett. She moved slowly and appeared tired. She was responsive to all questions and produced coherent, although at times, very lengthy responses. There were no obvious problems with memory or concentration. She appeared to be of roughly average intelligence. She cooperated with all examination procedures.

Summary of Test Results

The MMPI-2-RF was used to obtain additional information about Ms. Martin's psychological and emotional functioning. The MMPI-2-RF is a 338-item self-report instrument used to assess psychopathology and personality. This test also contains scales to assess under- or over-reporting of symptoms and other ways of responding that compromise validity.

Ms. Martin produced a valid profile. She appeared to understand the content of the questions and responded in a consistent fashion. She reported more symptoms than was typical in the normative sample, but this appeared to reflect a high level of distress rather than an attempt to exaggerate her symptoms. She appeared to be responding frankly to the test items and did not attempt to present herself in an unrealistically positive light.

Ms. Martin's responses suggest she may be experiencing a high level of anxiety, marked by fear, worry, irritability, and a sense of dread. The degree of anxiety she is experiencing appears to be interfering with her daily activities. In addition to subjective feelings of worry and dread, her anxiety appears to manifest as somatic symptoms including gastrointestinal distress, headaches, tingling and numbness in her limbs, and an overall sense of weakness and exhaustion. She expresses great difficulty trusting other people and reports feeling that others may be intentionally trying to harm her.

The CAPS is a 30-item structured interview that corresponds to the DSM-5 criteria for diagnosing PTSD. In addition to assessing the twenty DSM-5 PTSD symptoms, questions target the onset and duration of symptoms, subjective distress, the impact of symptoms on social and occupational functioning, overall response validity, overall PTSD severity, and specifications for the dissociative subtype (depersonalization and derealization).

A diagnosis of PTSD requires that all criteria A through G are met. Ms. Martin's responses to the CAPS indicate that the nature of the trauma she described meets Criterion A; she reported four intrusive symptoms, including intrusive memories, distressing dreams, and psychological and physiological reactions related to the trauma (Criterion B); one avoidance symptom—i.e., avoidance of memories associated with the trauma (Criterion C); five cognitive and mood symptoms including exaggerated negative beliefs or expectations, distorted cognitions leading to blame, a persistent negative emotional state, diminished interest or participation in activities, and attachment or estrangement from others (Criterion D); four arousal and reactivity symptoms including irritability, hypervigilance, exaggerated startle response, problems with concentration, and sleep disturbance (Criterion E); the duration of her symptoms has been for more than two years with no delayed onset (Criterion F); and she has experienced subjective distress as well as impairment in her social and occupational functioning (Criterion G).

Diagnostic Conclusions

There is considerable consistency among Ms. Martin's self-report, the records of her mental health treatment, her performance on psychological testing, and her observed behavior during this examination—all suggesting that Ms. Martin is experiencing an extremely high degree of psychological distress. She is anxious, panicked, hypervigilant, depressed, and withdrawn. She has extremely disrupted sleep resulting in an exacerbation of her subjective distress, as well as physical fatigue and poor concentration.

Diagnostically, Ms. Martin's symptoms best fit a diagnosis of PTSD. As indicated on the CAPS, she meets every diagnostic criterion and endorsed 14 out of a possible 20 symptoms. Ms. Martin's daily functioning has been significantly compromised as a result of the stress she has experienced. She has felt unable to function at work. She is irritable with her children. She is avoiding social interaction and broke up with her long-time significant other. She struggles to complete relatively common activities, such as driving and grocery shopping, as a result of her symptoms.

Summary of Data Relevant to Psycho-Legal Question

Mental Health Treatment Records Records from Ms. Martin's psychiatrist and counselor indicate she has been in treatment for 2.5 years. During her initial psychiatric evaluation, she complained of "persistent feelings of depression and anxiety that interfere with her ability to function and interact with others." She reported that she had sought help from human resources in dealing with "multiple frequent episodes of sexual harassment…Prior to her complaint and conflicts on the job, the patient enjoyed her place of employment and looked forward to going to work," but Ms. Martin now "fear[s] for [her] safety and her job." Ms. Martin's symptoms included depressed mood, tearfulness, irritability, fatigue, decreased concentration, loss of interest, and social isolation. She reported severe sleep disturbance and was taking up to six Benadryl capsules to sleep. The psychiatrist prescribed Vyvanse, Xanax, Trazodone, and Neurontin. Subsequently, Neurontin and Trazodone were discontinued and Klonopin and Seroquel were added.

Ms. Martin also met with a therapist on a weekly basis. Notes from these sessions indicate Ms. Martin was often agitated and fearful. She reported feeling paralyzed mentally and physically. She complained of poor sleep and loss of interest in activities including socializing and having sexual relations with her significant other.

Memoranda from Employer A memorandum from Ms. Martin's employer confirmed that Ms. Martin had lodged a complaint against her supervisor alleging that he had engaged in a pattern of sexual improprieties, unwanted physical contact, physical restraint, and threats of physical harm. Another memorandum described an interview with Mr. Everett about these allegations. According to this memorandum, Mr. Everett acknowledged some "flirtatious behavior" may have transpired. He identified Ms. Martin as the instigator of this contact and reported that she had become angry with him when he told her he was married and was not willing to become involved with her. The memorandum indicated that Mr. Everett should be formally chastised for engaging in flirtatious behavior with one of his subordinates.

Facebook Images During the deposition of the evaluator, the defense counsel presented the evaluator with three pages of images allegedly obtained from Ms. Martin's Facebook account. These images depicted Ms. Martin wearing a tight-fitting, low cut, short dress and high heels. The defense counsel asked the examiner how she could assert that Ms. Martin had lost interest in sex given that these "provocative" photos were posted on her Facebook account. The examiner responded that without more information and context, that she could not form any opinion about these images and their relationship, if any, to Ms. Martin's interest in sex.

Ms. Martin's Account of the Facebook Images After the deposition, the examiner spoke to Ms. Martin's lawyer and asked him if she could meet with Ms. Martin to discuss these images with her. At this meeting, Ms. Martin identified the images as being of her and acknowledged the images were posted to her Facebook account. She clarified that she had posted the photos approximately three years ago. At that time, her relationship with her significant other was starting to deteriorate due to her anxiety and to her waning interest in having sexual relations. She reported that she was "pushing" herself to try harder with him because she loved him and did not want to lose the relationship. She stated, "I would try to get dressed up like this because he loved it and I thought it would make me feel better about myself. And it did, for a little while, but I just couldn't keep it up and I couldn't follow through." She reported that the photos in question were taken at a New Year's Eve party. She indicated that there were several other photos posted to Facebook that were taken that same night of her with her significant other and with other guests at the party which she showed the examiner. The other female guests were dressed in a similar fashion.

Clinical Forensic Opinion

There were no indications that Ms. Martin experienced symptoms of PTSD prior to the alleged events in her workplace. Prior to these events, she was a well-functioning single parent who was able to care for her family both emotionally and financially. Ms. Martin had no history of mental health treatment prior to the alleged events. She had no history of substance abuse. The onset of Ms. Martin's symptoms and the decrease in her functional capacity appear to be directly related to the events in her workplace. The evaluation of Ms. Martin and review of her medical records did not identify any other life circumstances or potential causative factors unrelated to the alleged sexual harassment and retaliation that could explain the decline in Ms. Martin's mental health and functional capacity.

Recommendations

No specific recommendations were offered as part of this evaluation.

How Did Social Media Impact This Case?

After the discussion with Ms. Martin, the examiner determined that the Facebook postings did not change her opinion regarding Ms. Martin's loss of interest in sex as a result of the alleged sexual harassment at her workplace. The reasons for this are as follows. First, the context of the images had not been disclosed by the defense attorney. Placed in the context of a New Year's Eve party, Ms. Martin's attire was not unusual. Second, the photos had been posted three years prior to the evaluation. At that time, the alleged sexual harassment had just begun, and Ms. Martin was still able to function at work. Finally, there is no evidence that a person's attire is dispositive of their interest in sex. It cannot be inferred from Ms. Martin's clothing that she did or did not have decreased interest in engaging in sexual relations with her significant other.

Case Profile 2

Type of Evaluation

Disability

Case Context

Jason Anderson, a 24-year-old bank employee, claimed to be totally disabled from his job after a motor vehicle accident in which he sustained minor physical injuries. According to Mr. Anderson, as a result of this accident he became unable to work due to anxiety about driving, poor concentration, and an inability to work with numbers. The disability insurance company requested an independent evaluation of Mr. Anderson's work capacity.

Sources of Information

1. Clinical interview
2. Mental status examination
3. Psychological testing:
   a. Minnesota Multiphasic Personality Inventory, second Edition (MMPI-2)
   b. Validity Indicator Profile, verbal subtest (VIP)
   c. Wechsler Adult Intelligence Scale, fourth Edition (WAIS-IV)
4. Academic records
5. Performance evaluations
6. Emergency medical service records
7. City Hospital records
8. Mental health treatment records
9. Print out of Mr. Anderson's Twitter postings

Relevant Background

Mr. Anderson, a single 24-year-old man, had been employed by a local bank as a teller for nine months. He has lived with his father continuously since his parents divorced when Mr. Anderson was 13 years old. He has a high school diploma and completed one year at a community college majoring in general studies. He was previously employed as a cashier at a supermarket. He reported he took the job at the bank with the hopes of eventually becoming a financial analyst. He stated that he had planned to finish college and then obtain an MBA via online classes while continuing to work at the bank.

Mr. Anderson reported that he was involved in a motor vehicle accident when he was driving home from work. He was struck from behind while stopped at a traffic light. He opined that he must have "blacked out" for a minute. He woke up, touched his face and realized he was bleeding. The airbags had deployed. Paramedics arrived. They told him he had been in an accident. He reported he could not remember his name, phone number, whether there had been anyone else in his car, or where he was coming from. He was taken to the emergency department of City Hospital by ambulance. He was examined and given a CT scan which was read as normal. He had facial lacerations which were treated and some bruising on his chest from the airbag. He was given medication for pain and was told to follow up with his primary care physician. He was discharged from the emergency department after approximately three hours when his father arrived to pick him up.

Mr. Anderson reported he stayed in bed for the rest of the day and just slept. The following day he reported he felt stiff and sore. He had his father call the bank to explain what had happened and to tell them he needed to take some sick time. After about one week, his lacerations had healed and he reported his pain had significantly decreased, but he still "wasn't myself." He did not feel able to return to work and took short-term disability.

Over the next several months, Mr. Anderson reported he felt very emotional and anxious. He also noticed he was having trouble remembering numbers and would invert digits. He said he was having difficulty concentrating, was working more slowly, and having trouble completing tasks. He was very uncomfortable driving or even riding in a car. He reported he had very limited social interactions. "My father is my only friend." He reported he sought treatment from Dr. Rivera, the psychiatrist his father had been seeing. Based on Mr. Anderson's description of the accident and his difficulties, Dr. Rivera diagnosed Mr. Anderson with a traumatic brain injury. No neuropsychological testing was done. Mr. Anderson then applied for long term disability.

Mr. Anderson reported he will never be able to return to his job at the bank and will be unable to complete his education or become a financial analyst as he had planned. "The biggest thing is my inability to deal with numbers. How can I work in a bank and analyze investments if I can't work with numbers? I just can't focus for long periods of time and the idea of driving to work gives me a panic attack. I just can't do it anymore."

Behavioral Observations and Mental Status

Mr. Anderson arrived early for the evaluation. He was unaccompanied and reported he had driven himself to the office which he stated was 20 min from his home. Mr. Anderson was appropriately attired in casual clothing consisting of a sweatshirt and jeans. He displayed adequate grooming. He was responsive to all questions and was cooperative throughout the evaluation, although he expressed anger and resentment about having to participate in the evaluation. He described his mood as "annoyed." His overt display of emotions was variable and appropriate to the content of the discussion. He maintained intermittent eye contact. His responses to questions were logical and cogent, although he reported having difficulty recalling some dates and names. For example, he reported he could not recall the month in which the accident had occurred. Mr. Anderson appeared to be of average intelligence. He displayed no difficulty in maintaining his concentration during the 5.5-hour evaluation and took only one brief break after about 3.5 hours.

Summary of Test Results

Validity Indicator Profile—Verbal Subtest (VIP) The VIP Verbal subtest was utilized to assess effort and motivation. Mr. Anderson produced an invalid/inconsistent profile. Although he generallyv responded correctly to easier items, he became less engaged with the task and did not make a consistent effort as the items became more difficult.

Wechsler Adult Intelligence Scale, 4th Edition (WAIS-IV) The WAIS-IV is an individually administered assessment of cognitive abilities designed for adults ages 16–69. The subtests on the WAIS-IV are used to calculate a Full Scale IQ (FSIQ) and four composite scores, each of which assesses a different aspect of cognitive functioning: Verbal Comprehension Index (VCI) which assesses verbal reasoning, Perceptual Reasoning Index (PRI) which assesses nonverbal reasoning, Working Memory Index (WMI) which assesses immediate memory, and Processing Speed Index (PSI) which assesses the speed of cognitive processing.

Mr. Anderson's full scale IQ was at the lower end of the average range (25th percentile). Likewise, all four index scores were in the low average or average ranges. There were no significant differences among these scores. Consistent with his performance on the VIP, Mr. Anderson tended to give up quickly on more difficult tasks. He responded "I don't know" to a number of items and even with encouragement, he was not willing to guess at an answer.

Minnesota Multiphasic Personality Inventory, 2nd Edition (MMPI-2) The MMPI-2 was used to obtain additional information about Mr. Anderson's psychological and emotional functioning. The MMPI-2 is a 567-item self-report instrument used to assess psychopathology and personality. This test also contains scales to assess under- or over-reporting of symptoms and other ways of responding that compromise validity.

Mr. Anderson completed this test in approximately one hour, which is at the low end of the typical completion time of 60 to 90 min. However, he responded to the test questions in an inconsistent and contradictory manner, yielding a profile of questionable validity. Other validity indicators suggest that there was some tendency to present himself in a negative light. This suggests that the following test results may not be reliable indicators of Mr. Anderson's actual functioning.

If taken at face value, Mr. Anderson's responses suggested he was experiencing mild to moderate emotional distress characterized by a sad mood, worrying, a lack of enjoyment in life, and hostility and anger towards others. However, given the variability of his responses, this interpretation may be inaccurate.

Diagnostic Conclusions

Due to Mr. Anderson's inconsistent effort during this evaluation and evidence from other sources that contradicted aspects of his self-report, firm diagnostic conclusions could not be reached.

Summary of Data Relevant to Psycho-Legal Question

Academic Records Mr. Anderson's high school transcript indicated he graduated with a final grade point average of 2.8. Notably, he failed one semester of Algebra and finished this class with a grade of C-. His final grade in Geometry was D. He did not take Algebra II.

Mr. Anderson's community college transcript indicated he failed the math placement test and was enrolled in a pre-college algebra course in his first semester. He earned a grade of C in this class. In his first semester he also took an introductory sociology course in which he earned a grade of B- and a music appreciation class in which he earned a grade of C+. In his second semester, Mr. Anderson enrolled in a college algebra course. He dropped this class at the midterm with a failing grade. He did successfully complete courses in English composition (B-) and an introductory course in world history (C).

Work Performance Evaluations During his nine months of employment at the bank, Mr. Anderson received two performance evaluations—one after three months of employment and another after six months of employment. Both evaluations rated Mr. Anderson in the average range. Strengths were listed as "friendly" and "liked by customers." Areas needing further development included "complete tasks on time," "pay attention to details," and "motivation."

Emergency Medical Service Records The first contact with Mr. Anderson was at 5:59 PM, approximately five minutes after the accident. Records indicated he provided his name, date of birth, and a list of medications and allergies. He reported that his chest hurt. He was described as alert and oriented with a normal neurological status. He told emergency responders that he was unsure if he had lost consciousness. His Glasgow Coma Score was 15 (Note: this is the highest possible score, indicating he was completely conscious).

City Hospital Records Mr. Anderson was admitted to the emergency department at 6:39 PM on the date of the accident having been brought in by emergency medical services. His injuries were listed as blunt force trauma and lacerations. There was a question of loss of consciousness as Mr. Anderson reported that he did not remember the accident. He was experiencing moderate pain in his chest, neck, and head. He was alert and oriented. At 7:02 PM he was observed talking to his mother on the phone. A CT scan was performed. The results were "normal." No mass, fractures, intracranial hemorrhage or hydrocephalus was found. A CT scan of the cervical spine was normal. The abdomen was "largely unremarkable." His lacerations were sutured. He was given pain medication. He verbalized understanding of the discharge instructions. He was discharged to his home at 9:43 PM.

Mental Health Treatment Records Mr. Anderson was seen by Dr. Rivera for an initial evaluation having been referred by another patient (his father). Mr. Anderson reported he had been in an accident six months earlier. He reported he had lost consciousness for "six or seven hours" after the accident and had been kept in the hospital overnight. Dr. Rivera indicated that he did not believe Mr. Anderson met the diagnostic criteria for PTSD and suspected he might have sustained a head injury. Dr. Rivera told Mr. Anderson and his father, "I'm not an expert in head injury, but that was my take." Dr. Rivera noted a provisional diagnosis of 293.83 (mood disorder secondary to a general medical condition).

Twitter Postings A print out of Mr. Anderson's Twitter postings (tweets) was provided. This consisted of 1258 tweets posted by Mr. Anderson beginning a month before he was hired by the Bank and ending three weeks before this evaluation. Most (i.e. over 900) of these tweets referred to playing blackjack at a casino in a neighboring state and were marked with a hashtag naming this casino. Some included photos of Mr. Anderson holding chips or cash. The content of these tweets typically referred to his success and winnings or losses at blackjack. There were several references to him participating in blackjack tournaments. The frequency and content of these tweets did not change over time—that is he was posting just as often after the accident as he had before the accident. Based on these tweets, it appeared that Mr. Anderson was visiting this casino, located about 60 miles from his home, about three times each week.

Mr. Anderson's Account of Twitter Postings Mr. Anderson acknowledged that he visited this casino regularly to play blackjack. He reported he has been doing so for years. These visits typically take place at night. He usually arrives around 9:00 PM and stays until around 3:00 AM. His father often goes with him, but he does go alone if his father is unable to accompany him. He stated that driving there is difficult, but "I'm trying to push myself to get better." When asked how he is able to play blackjack, given his reported inability to work with numbers, Mr. Anderson replied, "I've been doing it so long, it's muscle memory." He denied that playing blackjack (even in tournaments) requires facility with numbers or concentration.

Clinical Forensic Opinion

Disability is conceptualized as an interaction between personal capabilities and situational demands. When situational demands exceed the individual's capabilities, a disability exists. Therefore, disability analysis involves defining the relevant contextual demands as well as determining the individual's capabilities. Disability also implies a change in functional capacity—that is, the individual's capabilities have decreased as a result of an illness or injury. The examinee's current functional capacity is compared to his functional capacity prior to the injury. The questions to address are: (1) what could the examinee do before the injury that he can no longer do; and (2) are these changes significant enough to prevent him from working as a bank teller?

According to Mr. Anderson, prior to the accident, he was functioning very well and was on his way to achieving his goal of becoming a financial analyst. He claimed that as a result of the accident he is no longer able to work as a bank teller because he is unable to work with numbers, has decreased concentration, and has difficulty driving. However, the findings of this evaluation do not support these claims. A review of Mr. Anderson's academic records indicates that he never had strong numeric skills. He struggled with high school math, failed the placement test at the community college, and had to withdraw from the only college-level math class he took due to failing grades. In addition, his continuing to play blackjack at a casino argues against an inability to work with numbers, sustain concentration, and to drive long distances.

It is beyond the scope of this evaluation to determine if Mr. Anderson did sustain a brain injury in the motor vehicle accident. However, the existing evidence argues against this possibility. The only medical professional to support that diagnosis was Dr. Rivera, who did not have access to medical records or neuropsychological testing, admitted he lacked expertise in brain injury, and based his diagnosis on Mr. Anderson's inaccurate self-report in which he claimed to have been unconscious for six or seven hours and had been kept in the hospital overnight. Records from emergency medical services and from the hospital contradict these assertions. Additionally, intellectual testing, despite Mr. Anderson's variable effort, yielded scores that were likely consistent with his premorbid intellectual functioning.

In short, there was no convincing evidence that Mr. Anderson's functional capacity has declined in any significant way following the motor vehicle accident. He remains as capable as he ever was of working as a bank teller.

Recommendations

No specific recommendations were offered as part of this evaluation.

How Did Social Media Impact This Case?

Mr. Anderson's Twitter postings provided information about his daily activities that he had not previously disclosed in the examination. When confronted with his tweets, Mr. Anderson acknowledged their authenticity and confirmed the context. He admitted that he traveled to a casino 60 miles from his home several times a week in order to play blackjack for up to six hours.

This information did have direct relevance to the forensic issue in this case in that it provided evidence that Mr. Anderson was routinely engaging in activities that were inconsistent with his claimed impairments. The fact that he continued to play blackjack in tournaments contradicted his claim of being unable to work with numbers or to sustain concentration. His ability to drive to the casino, located 60 miles from his home, undermined his report of being unable to drive to work. Mr. Anderson's tweets also corroborated the information obtained from other sources of data, including the psychological testing, that suggested inconsistent effort and possible exaggeration of symptoms, and his academic and work records that argued against a decline in his functional capacity.

References

American Psychological Association (2013). Specialty guidelines for forensic psychology. American Psychologist, 68(1), 7–19. doi:http://dx.doi.org/https://doi.org/10.1037/a0029889.

American Psychological Association. (2017). Ethical principles of psychologists and code of conduct. Retrieved from http://apa.org/ethics/code/index.aspx

Ben-Porath, Y. S., & Tellegen, A. (2008/2011). *MMPI-2-RF (Minnesota multiphasic personality Inventory-2-restructured form): Manual for administration, scoring, and interpretation.* Minneapolis: University of Minnesota Press.

Brown, K. R. (2012). The risks of taking Facebook at face value: Why the psychology of social networking should influence the evidentiary relevance of Facebook photographs. *Vanderbilt Journal of Entertainment and Technology Law., 14*(2), 357–393.

Butcher, J. N., Dahlstrom, W. G., Graham, J. R., Tellegen, A., & Kaemmer, B. (1989). *The Minnesota multiphasic personality Inventory-2 (MMPI-2): Manual for administration and scoring*. Minneapolis: University of Minnesota Press.

Coffey, C. A., Batastini, A. B., & Vitacco, M. J. (2018). Clues from the digital world: A survey of clinicians' reliance on social media as collateral data in forensic evaluations. *Professional Psychology: Research and Practice, 49*(5-6), 345–354. https://doi.org/10.1037/pro0000206.

E.E.O.C. v. Simply Storage Mgmt., LLC, 270 F.R.D. 430, 432 (S.D. Ind. 2010).

Federal Rules of Civil Procedure (2018). Washington, DC.: U.S. Government Publishing Office.

Frederick, R. I. (1997). *Validity Indicator Profile manual*. Minnetonka, MN: NCS Assessments.

Greiffenstein, M. F., Baker, W. J., & Johnson-Greene, D. (2002). Actual versus self-reported scholastic achievement of litigating postconcussion and severe closed head injury claimants. *Psychological Assessment., 14*(2), 202–208.

Heilbrun, K., Warren, J., & Picarello, K. (2003). Third party information in forensic assessment. In I. B. Weiner (series Ed.) & a. M. Goldstein (Vol. Ed.), *Handbook of psychology: Vol. 11. Forensic psychology* (pp. 69–86). Hoboken: Wiley.

Koch, W. J., Douglas, K. S., Nicholls, T. L., & O'Neill, M. L. (2006). *Psychological injuries: Forensic assessment, treatment, and law*. New York: Oxford.

Lees-Haley, P. R., Williams, C. W., Zasler, N. D., Marguilies, S., English, L. T., & Stevens, K. B. (1997). Response bias in plaintiffs' histories. *Brain Injury, 11*(11), 791–800.
McPeak, A. A. (2013). The Facebook digital footprint: Paving fair and consistent pathways to civil discovery of social media data. *Wake Forest Law Review, 48*, 56.
McPeak, A. (2016). Social data discovery and proportional privacy. Cleveland State Law Review, 65, 17.
Morey, L. C. (1991). Personality Assessment Inventory professional manual. Odessa, FL: Psychological Assessment Resources.
Pirelli, G., Hartigan, S., & Zapf, P. A. (2018). Using the internet for collateral information in forensic mental health evaluations. *Behavioral Sciences & the Law, 36*(2), 157–169. https://doi.org/10.1002/bsl.2334.
Pirelli, G., Otto, R. K., & Estoup, A. (2016). Using internet and social media data as collateral sources of information in forensic evaluations. *Professional Psychology: Research and Practice, 47*(1), 12–17. https://doi.org/10.1037/pro0000061.
Rogers, R., & Payne, J. (2006). Damages and rewards: Assessment of malingered disorders in compensation cases. In *Behavioral sciences and the law, 24* (pp. 645–658).
Rogers, R., Sewell, K. W., & Gillard, N. D. (2010). *Structured Interview of Reported Symptoms, 2nd edition (SIRS-2)*. Odessa, FL: Psychological Assessment Resources.
Romano v. Steelcase, Inc. 907 N.Y.S.2d 650, 653–54 (N.Y. Sup. Ct.) (2010).
Tombaugh, T. M. (1996). Test of Memory Malingering manual. North Tonawanda, NY: Multi-Health Systems, Inc.
Williams, C. W., Lees-Haley, P. R., & Djanogly, S. E. (1999). Clinical scrutiny of litigants' self- reports. *Professional Psychology: Research and Practice, 30*(4), 361–367.

Chapter 9
General Recommendations for Integrating Internet-Based Data in Forensic Mental Health Assessments and What We Still Need to Know

Ashley B. Batastini, Michael J. Vitacco, and Ashley R. Bozeman

As detailed in Chap. 1 of this volume, a growing proportion of youth and adults use social networking sites (SNS) on a regular basis to share their thoughts, feelings, and behaviors, often to global audiences. This increased reliance on the Internet can have a wide range of intended and unintended consequences for users; often these are desirable (e.g., social equity, financial gain) but, many times they are not (e.g., lack of privacy, negative social comparison). With such normative use of social platforms and the Internet in general, it is no surprise that information gathered from online sources have become a focus of discussion among professional communities including legal and psychological. Through the use of de-identified, real-world case examples, this book highlighted the frequency with which evaluators encounter Internet-based data, particularly social media, in forensic mental health assessment (FMHA) and the impact they can have on their conclusions. While the areas of focus were limited to seven common categories of psycho-legal issues, we hope the information and insights provided can be transferable to other types of forensic cases that were not explicitly described. This final chapter will synthesize themes from the previous chapters, offer more specific practice recommendations for integrating online data into forensic clinical opinions, and propose directions for continued research to better understand the prevalence of its use and the influence virtual evidence may have on clinical and legal decision-making.

A. B. Batastini (✉) · A. R. Bozeman
University of Southern Mississippi, MS, Hattiesburg, USA
e-mail: ashley.batastini@usm.edu; ashley.bozeman@usm.edu

M. J. Vitacco
Augusta University, Augusta, GA, USA
e-mail: mvitacco@augusta.edu

A. B. Batastini, M. J. Vitacco (eds.), *Forensic Mental Health Evaluations in the Digital Age*, https://doi.org/10.1007/978-3-030-33908-1_9

9.1 A Source Like Any Other

While many forensic practitioners are skeptical of data from the Internet, and especially from social media profiles where posted information can be cherry-picked, distorted, or manipulated (see Coffey et al. 2018), the cases presented throughout this book suggest that such data can be quite useful, even central to answering the psycho-legal question. As we have acknowledged elsewhere, Internet and SNS data are not entirely infallible and caution must be exercised when viewing and determining the relevance of these data in FMHA. However, in some ways, data derived from the Internet can offer a clearer (or at least alternative) window from which to view our examinees. SNS data, the primary online source used in most of the case profiles, helped evaluators tailor interview questions, disconfirm or corroborate statements made by examinees, piece together a timeline of events, gain insight into the tone, content, and severity of one's reported behaviors, as well as understand others' immediate responses to these actions.

Yet, no author described using Internet-based data in isolation as This, of course, would be against best practices and inconsistent with our professional codes of conduct. Rather, the overarching message across chapters was to approach Internet data in much the same way as any other collateral source, with an awareness of its merits and flaws. Just as any data source used in FMHA can prove useful, they can also be confounded by impression management, personal biases, half-truths, a misunderstanding of context, and a myriad of other variables. It is our job as evaluators to use the tools at our disposal and our clinical judgment to determine how valid or credible a data source likely is and, subsequently, how much weight we should place on it when drawing conclusions. In other words, Internet data may be a horse of a slightly different color, but it is still a horse.

Without explicit guidelines for how to integrate Internet data into FMHA, authors relied primarily on existing standards outlined in the Ethic Principles of Psychologists and Code of Conduct (EPPCC; APA 2017) and the Specialty Guidelines for Forensic Psychology (SGFP; APA 2013). And, the data they reviewed was typically included with discovery. Several authors explicitly discouraged independent searches by evaluators, especially for information that is not already in the public domain. Certainly, existing guidelines are useful, but Internet data can present with nuanced challenges and dilemmas that are not fully clarified at present. Though all guidelines, to some extent, are vague for the purposes of flexibility in making case-by-case determinations (psychologists have a tendency to take on an "it depends" perspective), it nonetheless seems useful to begin a dialogue about best practices for navigating Internet data specifically. Next, we offer some practice recommendations and considerations, with the understanding that their applicability will likely "depend" on the situation at hand and that some practitioners may find reason to disagree. Again, these suggestions are intended to move our profession to the next phase of discussion and convergence on a set of standardized guidelines.

9.2 Practice Recommendations

When forensic evaluators rely, as they should, on collateral information, to support their opinions in forensic reports, they must deal with a host of ethical factors and clinical challenges. As the authors of previous chapters pointed out, more general guidance on this can be found in the EPPCC (APA 2017) and the SGFP (APA 2013). When using SNS data, those universal challenges are amplified by the uniqueness of these data and the fact that much, if not all, of the data has already been made available for public consumption. Postings to any social media platform, like Facebook or Instagram allow for the behaviors, thoughts, and feelings of someone become accessible with little effort. Often accessibility of information from SNS is available to strangers. As has been outlined in the eight previous chapters, information from SNS can be highly relevant and pertinent to psycho-legal questions. Yet, the information obtained from SNS can be quite overwhelming. With the ability to access so much personal information of defendants or litigants so easily, we must also be cautious to not overstep our mandate to complete the evaluation.

In addition to guidance on accessibility, there are several other factors that must be considered when deciding to incorporate SNS data as collateral information into a forensic evaluation. As the first to explore more definitive guidelines, Pirelli et al. (2016) suggest categorizing practices related to the use of social media information in FMHA as required, permitted, or prohibited. We agree this is a useful mechanism by which to sort out practices that should ethically be avoided versus practices that may be allowable under certain circumstances, thereby leaving flexibility for the "it depends" scenario. With this scaffolding of handling collateral data in mind, we will foray into rules and regulations regarding the use of SNS as collateral data in forensic evaluations.

9.2.1 Use and Access

What information is usable? In today's digital world, it is becoming more likely that information obtained from SNS sites will be routinely included within discovery information given to forensic examiners from attorneys as part of source case material. In these situations, the decision to integrate relevant material is more straightforward. Forensic examiners encounter more challenging situations when they independently discover or seek SNS material. Our reading of both the SGFP (2013) and the EPPCC (2016) would not prohibit the evaluator from independently looking for collateral data from SNS. Publicly available data are fair game for consideration. However, Guideline 8.03 of the SGFP (2013) states: "Forensic practitioners strive to access information or records from collateral sources with the consent of the relevant attorney or the relevant party…" (p. 14). This would suggest that access to online data through independent Internet searches would need to be discussed with or at least disclosed to the so-called "client" of the forensic service.

Although there are no prohibitions against unilaterally reviewing SNS data, some data more problematic than others. For example, we agree with Heilburn et al. (2020, Chap. 4) that forensic evaluators not search for information from the "dark web" or "darknet" as part of their evaluation. The dark web is encrypted online content that, if searching independently, evaluators may find themselves engaging in illegal activity. Moreover, as discussed by Gottfried et al. (2020, Chap. 5), certain data (e.g., naked pictures of children) available through the Internet may also be illegal to be in possession of. Forensic evaluators must be aware of statutory requirements when handling any collateral data. Similarly, we suggest evaluators avoid searching the deep web for information on evaluees. The deep web contains information that does not appear in web searches such as personal email and online banking accounts. While the content found on these sites is unlikely to be illegal in and of itself, "hacking" into such accounts is highly unadvisable for obvious reasons.

In sum, we propose that evaluators are required to consider relevant SNS data provided in discovery, permitted to conduct searches on publicly accessible data relevant to the referral question, and prohibited from hacking private accounts and independently accessing illegal content. Relevance and legality are key considerations when deciding what and how to access SNS data. A more detailed discussion on relevance is next.

9.2.2 Relevance

Similar to all collateral data, the forensic evaluator is tasked with determining the relevance of material reviewed. The evaluator must separate the "wheat from the chaff" when determining what information from SNS is relevant. Again, this can become especially muddied when evaluators take to "Googling" for themselves. Evaluators must be cognizant of the potential of being exposed to mountains of irrelevant material that can cause bias by contaminating views of the evaluee. As an illustrative example, an evaluator may discover through a review of SNS data that the evaluee holds diametrically different social or political beliefs. Or, perhaps you discover that your examinee is "friends" with a mutual acquaintance or also follows your favorite celebrity chef on Instragram. Although an examiner may deny extraneous information led to bias, it is impossible to know for sure, as bias is frequently subtle (Edmond et al. 2015). In colloquial terms, one may not be able to unring the bell once exposed to information. Later in this chapter, we further discuss the impact of bias in the context of SNS and call for more research on its undue influence in FMHA. However, similar issues of bias must be navigated regardless. For example, an examinee may provide an off the cuff or jarring remark during interviews or a stack of medical records may contain information peripheral to the psycho-legal question at hand. Thus, while bias is not unique to SNS, it is compounded by the extensiveness of information available and the different ways in which information is shared (e.g., visual, text).

One way to counteract a potential for bias is to work in tandem with another professional by having one person review the information to decide its relevance and the another to apply the material to the specific case. Although that may be time (and money) intensive, it provides a safety mechanism to avoid having the forensic evaluator be unduly influenced by irrelevant source material. Another strategy is to rely on the court to provide such information (e.g., via screenshots). Even if SNS is not already provided in discovery, evaluators could request this information through the court or retaining party. Such a request might be prompted by an examinee or other third-party source who notes the existence of potentially useful data on social media. This places the burden of relevance elsewhere and may minimize access to biasing or.

9.2.3 Weight of Evidence

Forensic evaluators are perpetually assigned with determining not only the relevancy of collateral data, but also how much weight to place on those data when formulating forensic opinions. SNS data is again no different in this regard. At times, the information obtained from SNS may border on dispositive regarding the relevant psycho-legal issue. Take for instance the case example discussed in the Chap. 2 in which the pretrial defendant acknowledged via a SNS instant message that his behavior was against the law and he needed to vacate the area to avoid apprehension. This post strongly suggested an awareness of the wrongfulness of his criminal behavior. However, most SNS data are not so clear cut. This is complicated by the fact that forensic evaluators view data from SNS as inherently less trustworthy (Batastini et al. 2019) compared with data obtained from a traditional medical record. If used as a source of information, examiners should be aware of potential bias that may result simply because of the medium through which the data were made available. As evidenced throughout this book, it would be unwise, and arguably unethical, to discard SNS data solely because of its source, as the evaluator may inadvertently discard relevant and—in many cases—central information that could majorly impact the outcome of the FMHA. Determining the weight of SNS evidence is a dilemma that is perhaps best navigated by taking the "source like any other" approach. That is, evaluators should employ whatever decision-making processes they routinely use when determining evidence weight regardless of whether it comes from the Internet or not.

9.2.4 Involving the Examinee

We do not advocate acquiring permission from the defendant or litigant before relying on social media as collateral data in forensic evaluations. Informing evaluees about the assessment process in general, including that the evaluator will be consulting collateral information, is an ethical courtesy afforded by the SGFP (APA 2013). Yet, we do not allow evaluees to dictate what can and cannot be weighed into the forensic opinion. However, it may be useful to allow the examinee to respond to specific questions developed as the result of SNS data (see Pirelli et al. 2016). As described by Vitacco et al. (2020, Chap. 2) pretrial defendants are often asked for their version of events in forensic evaluations. The same should hold true for data from SNS where the examinee may be able to provide appropriate context and description of the SNS data. An examinee may be able to clarify information about a picture or statement relevant to the relevant forensic question. Consider the hypothetical situation in a disability evaluation (see Piechowski 2020; Chap. 8) where an image posted to Instagram depicts the plaintiff engaging in behavior that he claimed during the interview he was unable to currently perform as a result of a work-related injury. The evaluee, when questioned on the existence of the picture, may indicate the picture was taken prior to the injury (though it may have been posted after) or provide a viable explanation surrounding the circumstances of the picture that gives new insight into the material.

9.2.5 *Report-Writing*

This final section addresses the integration of SNS findings into forensic reports. At its most basic level, this begins by listing the material in the sources of information section of the report. As recommended by both the SGFP (2013) and the EPPCC (2016), all material that was reviewed should be listed, even if it did not provide useful information. All relevant parties should be made aware that the material was reviewed as part of the forensic examination. And, if relied on, the report must also specify the nature of the material and the degree to which it was relied on in generating the forensic opinion should be carefully delineated in the report and, if relevant, subsequent testimony. A clear description of the material and how it was used provides ample opportunities for ferreting out information on both direct and cross-examination. In writing and testifying on any report, the old adage from math class comes to mind regarding the importance of 'showing your work' to receive full credit. The same holds true for forensic report writing where principles of transparence and relevancy are critical (DeMier 2013; Melton et al. 2018). By doing this, the forensic evaluator can explain how they used the information in a cogent manner that relates to the psycho-legal question. In this regard, evaluators should seek to answer the following questions in their reports and related testimony:

1. How was the Internet data obtained (e.g., discovery, independent search)?
2. What type of site(s) was the data posted to or downloaded from?
3. Who likely authored the post, blog, etc.? And are there any suspected issues with authenticity?
4. What specific content was relied on when deriving the forensic opinion?
5. How was Internet data weighted against other data sources?

6. To what extent was the Internet data consistent with or contradictory to other information? And, how were discrepancies reconciled?
7. Was there any evidence to suggest the data were doctored or otherwise manipulated?
8. Was the examinee or other relevant third-parties provided an opportunity to explain the data? If so, how did they respond (content and noteworthy behavioral observations)? And if not, why?

9.3 Suggested Areas for Future Research

Existing research involving online information in FMHA is currently limited. In fact, in their 2016 publication of preliminary recommendations for incorporating social media into FMHA, Pirelli et al. noted, "There is no published literature addressing the use of Internet data in forensic psychological evaluations" (p. 16). Since then, some attention has been paid to this topic (see Burke 2019; Coffey et al. 2018; Pirelli et al. 2018) and it seems likely this will only increase. Drawing largely on what Pirelli and colleagues proposed in 2016 as well as existing literature in other areas, we offer several ideas of for future research.

9.3.1 Prevalence in FMHA and Professional Consensus

We agree with Pirelli et al. (2016) that obtaining information on current and acceptable practices among the professional community is an important first step. Most of the existing research on the Internet and social media in FMHA has focused on surveying practitioners' use and attitudes toward use. A recent survey (unpublished dissertation; Burke 2019) of 70 practitioners revealed that about 69% conducted their own Internet searches on evaluees (mostly using Google and Facebook), even though most (70%) reported concerns over admissibility of such evidence in court and the authenticity of online information. Pirelli et al. (2018), on the other hand, reported only 39% of forensic evaluators conducted an Internet search on their examinee; 26% of their respondents were opposed to independent Internet searches. In Coffey et al. (2018), nearly 83% of forensic evaluators consulted an evaluee's SNS profile at least once, with over half (53%) receiving it in discovery material. Similar to Burke (2019), Coffey et al. (2018) also showed some concern over admissibility and authenticity; however, those who used SNS in FMHA had significantly less concerns over its use and most reported no challenges to their use of SNS in court. These findings suggest that many hesitations expressed by evaluators may be mitigated by experience. Additional surveys are needed to determine the extent to which attorneys and triers of fact also consider online data acceptable in forensic mental health practice and on what potential grounds online data could be damaging to an expert's credibility via cross-examination.

Pirelli et al. (2016) advocate for research on consensus regarding practice guidelines. Several recommendations (most of which appear in this chapter) have now been put forth. Yet, there are certainly areas of potential disagreement. As previously noted, inflexible rules regarding the use of collateral information generally do not hold well in forensic mental health practice given myriad unforeseen circumstances. However, an established set of guidelines is not beyond the scope of our profession and very few forensic clinicians agree there is sufficient guidance to date (less than 10%; see Pirelli et al. 2018). But, how well do professionals agree with these recommendations and where do they belong? Using the five recommendations proposed in their 2016 article (see also Chap. 1), Pirelli et al. (2018) surveyed forensic clinicians on their agreement and received 62% to 90% agreement; the highest of which was for considering SNS on a case-by-case basis and weighing probative value against potential prejudicial effects (90%) followed by being explicit about the use of such data in reports and testimony (86%). Additional research is needed to determine professional consensus, including those who are on the receiving end of FMHA, regarding the more detailed out set of recommendations above and whether the SGFP should be expanded to include special considerations for online data. Again, we must include attorneys and the Court in these discussions, and determine where and to what extent psychological ethics codes fit with or contradict legal precedent.

Beyond self-reported surveys of professionals' use and opinions, a systematic assessment of FMHA reports that incorporate Internet data as collateral and a case law review would offer useful information to guide professional conduct and structure standards of practice. For example, researchers might elect to code reports for the specific referral question, jurisdiction of the order, type of Internet data used, where the data came from (i.e., discovery or personal search), other related procedures used by the evaluator (e.g., was it explicitly discussed as part of notification and consent?), number of other data sources consulted, basic demographics of the evaluee (e.g., gender, age, index offense type, presence of psychiatric history), the frequency with which Internet-data is mentioned throughout the report, whether Internet data was discussed as a basis for the forensic opinion or conclusion, and the final determination or recommendation(s) made by the evaluator. Comprehensive case law reviews would help uncover common themes regarding the circumstances in which Internet data is challenged in court or upheld as a valid factor in determining legal outcomes.

9.3.2 *Impact on Decision-Making*

Although Internet-based data, when admissible and relevant, should be treated much the same as other collateral sources, the way in which information is presented online is often inherently different than other information found in discovery or unveiled during a clinical interview. Consider, for example, the reaction you may have to an examinee explaining the collection of semi-automatic weapons he stores in his basement versus the reaction you may have to seeing the same examinee in a Facebook post displaying those weapons posed in military attire with a proud smirk on his face and Nazi symbols in the background. Would the image speak louder than his words? Might this imagery impact your impression of this person, thereby biasing the conclusions you make about his functioning as it relates to the psycho-legal question at hand? While forensic evaluators are encouraged to be conscientious of personal bias, as our role is to serve as an objective party, there is a body of evidence suggesting we are not immune (Murrie et al. 2013; Neal and Grisso 2014). Triers of fact may also fall victim to biases. For example, several studies suggest that graphic, gruesome, or emotionally charged evidence leads to higher conviction rates and higher levels of anger toward the offender (Bandes and Salerno 2014; Bright and Goodman-Delahunty 2006; Matuso and Itoh 2015). Research can help us understand the ways in which we are biased and inform strategies to mitigate it. Currently, few studies (other than the authors' own efforts discussed below) have explored whether differential decisions are made when experts and/or triers of fact are faced with Internet data compared to other data sources. However, there is some research in other professional areas that may provide some direction for studying the relationship between online information and perception in forensic contexts.

Research on SNS usage in healthcare contexts, for example, has evaluated the effects of social media on stigma related to certain health conditions. In their study on obesity stigma, Lim and An (2018) found that more frequent social media exposure to body image content (i.e., images promoting physical appearance or weight loss) led to higher levels of obesity stigma (Lim and An 2018). Including visuals when disseminating health information also appears to have an impact on whether the information is shared, retweeted, or interacted with in some manner (e.g., liking, reacting to, etc.; Linquist and Ramirez 2019). Based on the increased activity in response to online data, healthcare systems are increasingly integrating virtual treatment approaches and health-related social media into patient care (e.g., educational materials, SNS-housed support groups; Keller et al. 2017; Cate et al. 2019). Based on this evidence, it is possible that social media and other online information—particularly posts with visual content—could likewise be attended to or relied on more heavily in forensic or legal decision-making (in one direction or the other) than would be warranted or appropriate.

In addition to the impact of SNS in general healthcare, SNS data has become a topic of investigation in the field of psychology specifically. In Chap. 1 of this book we summarized research on the association between social media use and psychological well-being, behavioral outcomes, and personality factors. However, there are far fewer studies looking at how social media exposure can impact the therapeutic relationship or clinical decision-making. In one such study (Kolmes and Taube 2014), 56% of mental health professionals who searched for or otherwise encountered information about their clients reported their knowledge of clients' SNS activity had no effect on treatment and 40% of these mental health professionals described positive effects of client SNS data on treatment (e.g., resolving crises, uncovering information about suicidal intent, incarceration status, and other information the client may be struggling to divulge or intentionally withholding). Additionally, 72% of mental health professionals who did have such knowledge reported no loss of objectivity toward the client as a result of being exposed to SNS information and 90% reported no change in his or her ability to maintain a professional relationship with the client and provide adequate therapeutic services. However, this data was based solely on the clinicians' assessment of their own behavior, which is likely biased in and of itself (again, research shows that even professionals are not the best at recognizing our own biases; Walfish et al. 2012). Experimental manipulations are needed to draw firmer conclusions about the likely impact of SNS exposure on client-therapist relationships, diagnostic decisions, treatment planning, and client success.

This type of research can be extended to forensic mental health evaluators as well. While no surveys have yet to explicitly ask forensic clinicians about whether social media exposure impacts their objectivity, respondents in Coffey et al. (2018) who had used SNS felt it could potentially increase the validity of a FMHA, particularly cases requiring assessment of retrospective behavior or mental status. As briefly discussed in Chap. 1, the first known experimental design to test the relationship between SNS exposure and bias was conducted by Batastini et al. (2019) in which the authors manipulated the data modality (Twitter post, medical record, forensic report excerpt) and content (suggestive of a mental illness or not) in the context of a criminal responsibility evaluation using separate samples of forensic experts and laypersons. The key finding from this between-subjects study was that both groups viewed the Twitter post as significantly less credible despite containing the same information from the same source (i.e., the defendant's self-report). Further, experts reported they would give the Twitter comment significantly less weight when rendering their opinions than the other two data modalities.

Another in-progress study by this same group of researchers essentially replicates this experimental paradigm, but in the context of parental fitness evaluations. As highlighted in Chap. 6, as well as the Coffey et al. (2018) survey, SNS data is used with some frequency in these contexts. This study manipulates the parental party (mother vs. father) and data modality (Instagram post vs. emergency room medical record). In addition to perceived credibility, expert participants will be asked to rate how likely they would be to opine the parent is fit so we can better determine the impact of the information on actual decisions. Similar studies could be conducted for other types of psycho-legal questions and may even compare different SNS outlets to each other; for example, Twitter (a text-oriented site) to Instagram (a visual-oriented site). Studies should also examine moderator variables such as variations of SNS posts (e.g., emotionally charged vs. neutral, pictured with others vs. alone, engaged in age-appropriate vs. inappropriate behavior) may change perceptions or decision-making.

As before, we recommend including legal professionals (i.e., defense and prosecuting attorneys, judges) and jury-eligible laypersons in studies on perceptions and decision-making whenever possible, as they may share or contradict these biases. For example, social media posts may differentially impact attorney recommendations or motions (e.g., raising the issue of mental competency, pursuing prosecution), sentencing or diversion decisions, not guilty by reason of insanity acquittals, juvenile transfers to adult court, and civil commitment of sexual predators among other outcomes. We look forward to additional work exploring the many ways SNS and Internet-based data can impact the practice of forensic psychology.

9.4 Final Remarks

As demonstrated throughout this text, Internet-based data, and most frequently those obtained from social media, are not only useful but often pivotal to the accurate formulation of psycho-legal opinions. Discrediting or disregarding Internet data without considering its relevance is simply bad practice that could lend courts and other stakeholders (e.g., employers, insurance companies) to base high-stakes decisions on an incomplete work product. Despite the need for continued research, we hope the guidelines provided within this chapter and the insights gleaned across this book will encourage forensic mental health evaluators to view Internet data more openly and improve their competence regarding the appropriate use of these data in their assessments.

References

American Psychological Association (2013). Specialty guidelines for forensic psychologists. American Psychologist, 68(1) 7–19. https://doi.org/10.1037/a0029889.

American Psychological Association (2017). Ethical Principles of Psychologists and Code of Conduct. Retrieved from https://www.apa.org/ethics/code/.

Bandes, S. A., & Salerno, J. M. (2014). Emotion, proof, and prejudice: The cognitive science of gruesome photos and victim impact statements. *Arizona State Law Journal, 46*(3), 1003–1056.

Batastini, A. B., Vitacco, M. J., Jones, A. C. T., Davis, R. M. (2019). *Perceived credibility of social media data as a collateral source in criminal responsibility assessment using an experimental design*. Manuscript in prep.

Bright, D. A., & Goodman-Delahunty, J. (2006). Gruesome evidence and emotion: Anger, blame, and jury decision-making. *Law and Human Behavior, 30*(2), 183–202.

Burke, M. (2019). *Perceptions and uses of internet-based data in forensic mental health assessment: A survey of forensic psychologists.* (Unpublished dissertation). Dissertation Abstracts International: Section B: The Sciences and Engineering. ProQuest Information & Learning.

Cate, C. T. D., Schnurr, K., Stinson, J., & McPherson, A. C. (2019). Connected for health: Examining the use of a health-related social media platform for children with chronic medical conditions. *Child: Care, Health and Development, 45*(4), 585–591.

Coffey, C. A., Batastini, A. B., & Vitacco, M. J. (2018). Clues from the digital world: A survey of clinicians' reliance on social media as collateral data in forensic evaluations. *Professional Psychology: Research and Practice, 49*(5–6), 345–354. doi: 10.1037/pro0000206

DeMier, R. L. (2013). Forensic report writing. In R. K. Otto & I. B. Weiner (Eds.), *Handbook of psychology: Forensic psychology* (pp. 75–98). Hoboken: John Wiley & Sons Inc..

Edmond, G., Tangen, J. M., Searston, R. A., & Dror, I. E. (2015). Contextual bias and cross-contamination in the forensic sciences: The corrosive implications for investigations, plea bargains, trials and appeals. *Law, Probability and Risk, 14*(1), 1–25. https://doi.org/10.1093/lpr/mgu018.

Keller, M. S., Park, H. J., Cunningham, M. E., Fouladian, J. E., Chen, M., & Spiegel, B. M. R. (2017). Public perceptions regarding use of virtual reality in health care: A social media content analysis using Facebook. *Journal of Medical Internet Research, 19*(12), e419.
Kolmes, K., & Taube, D. O. (2014). Seeking and finding our clients on the internet: Boundary considerations in cyberspace. *Professional Psychology: Research and Practice, 45*(1), 3–10.
Lim, Y., & An, S. (2018). Effects of attributions and social media exposure on obesity stigma among Korean adolescents. *Social Behavior & Personality: An International Journal, 46*(12), 2049–2061.
Linquist, L. A., & Ramirez, Z. V. (2019). Visual abstracts to disseminate geriatrics research through social media. *Journal of the American Geriatrics Society, 67*(6), 1128–1131.
Melton, G. B., Petrila, J., Poythress, N. G., Slobogin, C., Otto, R. K., Mossman, D., & Condie, L. O. (2018). *Psychological evaluations for the courts: A handbook for mental health professionals and lawyers* (4th ed.). New York: Guilford Press.
Matsuo, K., & Itoh, Y. (2015). Effects of emotional testimony and gruesome photographs on mock jurors' decisions and negative emotions. *Psychiatry, Psychology and Law, 23*, 1–17. https://doi.org/10.1080/13218719.2015.1032954.
Murrie, D. C., Boccaccini, M. T., Guarnera, L. A., & Rufino, K. A. (2013). Are forensic experts biased by the side that retained them? *Psychological Science, 24*(10), 1889–1897.
Neal, T. M. S., & Grisso, T. (2014). The cognitive underpinnings of bias in forensic mental health evaluations. *Psychology, Public Policy, and Law, 20*(2), 200–211.
Pirelli, G., Hartigan, S., & Zapf, P. A. (2018). Using the internet for collateral information in forensic mental health evaluations. *Behavioral Sciences & the Law, 36*, 157–169. https://doi.org/10.1002/bsl.2334.
Pirelli, G., Otto, R. K., & Estoup, A. (2016). Using internet and social media data as collateral sources of information in forensic evaluations. *Professional Psychology: Research and Practice, 47*(1), 12–17.
Walfish, S., McAlister, B., O'Donnell, P., & Lambert, M. J. (2012). An investigation of self-assessment bias in mental health providers. *Psychological Reports, 110*(2), 639–644.

Index

A. B. Batastini, M. J. Vitacco (eds.), *Forensic Mental Health Evaluations in the Digital Age*, https://doi.org/10.1007/978-3-030-33908-1

FSC
www.fsc.org
MIX
Papier aus verantwortungsvollen Quellen
Paper from responsible sources
FSC® C105338

If you have any concerns about our products,
you can contact us on
ProductSafety@springernature.com

In case Publisher is established outside the EU,
the EU authorized representative is:
Springer Nature Customer Service Center GmbH
Europaplatz 3, 69115 Heidelberg, Germany

Printed by Libri Plureos GmbH
in Hamburg, Germany